CAMBRIDGE
Global English

Teacher's Resource

4

Nicola Mabbott,
Claire Medwell and Jane Boylan

CAMBRIDGE
UNIVERSITY PRESS

CAMBRIDGE
UNIVERSITY PRESS

University Printing House, Cambridge CB2 8BS, United Kingdom

One Liberty Plaza, 20th Floor, New York, NY 10006, USA

477 Williamstown Road, Port Melbourne, VIC 3207, Australia

4843/24, 2nd Floor, Ansari Road, Daryaganj, Delhi – 110002, India

79 Anson Road, #06–04/06, Singapore 079906

Cambridge University Press is part of the University of Cambridge.

It furthers the University's mission by disseminating knowledge in the pursuit of
education, learning and research at the highest international levels of excellence.

Information on this title: www.cambridge.org

First published 2014

20 19 18 17 16 15 14 13 12 11 10 9 8

Printed in Great Britain by CPI Group (UK) Ltd., Croydon CR0 4YY

A catalogue record for this publication is available from the British Library

ISBN 978-1-107-69074-5 Teacher's Resource

Additional resources for this publication at www.cambridge.org/

Cambridge University Press has no responsibility for the persistence or accuracy
of URLs for external or third-party internet websites referred to in this publication,
and does not guarantee that any content on such websites is, or will remain,
accurate or appropriate. Information regarding prices, travel timetables, and other
factual information given in this work is correct at the time of first printing but
Cambridge University Press does not guarantee the accuracy of such information
thereafter.

Contents

Map of the Learner's Book

Listening / Speaking	School subjects	Pronunciation / Word study	Critical thinking / Values

Strategy: Prediction
Talk about families and activities
Ask about relationships
	Geography: Kenya,
	   Patagonia
		Present simple 3rd person *s*
		Capital letters
			Values: Being kind and helpful
			Venn diagrams
			Comparing and contrasting lives
			   of children

Strategy: Prediction Table completion Listen to: *The Seekers* Comprehension questions Talk about people	Art: Drawing	Word stress Punctuation in speech	Values: Being brave Identifying different types of stories Forming opinions about stories Classifying characters

The Earth's landscape
Complete an animal fact file
Multiple choice
Listen for specific information
	Geography: Landscapes
	   Norway
	Science: Planets, animal
	   fact files
		Rhyming words	Expressing opinions about poetry
			Comparing natural landscapes
			Identifying planets in solar system
			Understanding a story described in
			   poetic form

Descriptions of homes
Match conversations
Descriptions of strange buildings
Talk about where they'd like to live
Check facts
Listen to *The Hobbit*
	Ecology
	Geography: Peru, famous
	   landmarks in many
	   countries
		Intonation: Question tags	Values: Being a responsible person
			Organising information
			Identifying materials
			Expressing opinions about unusual
			   types of houses
			Expressing preferences

Different ways of travelling to school Note completion Tourist office Listen for specific information Directions	Geography: Map interpretation Space travel	*-ed* endings	Value: Taking advice Understanding road safety issues

Jamie Oliver school lunches
   (comprehension)
Organise a party
Talk about what people around the
   world eat
	Geography: Food in other
	   countries
	Science: How food is made
		Connected speech	Values: Being generous
			Distinguishing between healthy and
			   unhealthy meals
			Classifying food types
			Understanding basic food preparation

A weather report Australian endangered animals Talk about maps Follow the topic	Geography: Australia, climate Maths: High numbers Science: Animals	Pronounciation of numbers	Values: Not being jealous Comparing countries Giving factual examples Giving explanations about endangered animals Understanding traditional stories
Descriptions of people A description of a thief Follow instructions Talk about traditional dances	Geography: New Zealand, Spain Arts: Dance, sports History/Art: Da Vinci	Homophones Speech marks	
What you enjoy doing in the holidays Interviews Talk about school Survey	Arts and crafts Maths: Make a bar chart	Pronunciation in questions Exclamation marks	Values: Being sympathetic Interpreting advertisements Making predictions about trips Surveying and classifying information

Welcome to *Cambridge Global English Stage 4*

Cambridge Global English is an eight-level English course for young learners from the beginning of primary school to the end of junior secondary (roughly ages 6–13). The course has been designed to fulfil the requirements of *Cambridge Primary English as a Second Language Curriculum Framework*. These internationally recognised standards provide a sequential framework for thorough coverage of basic English concepts and skills.

The materials reflect the following principles:

- *An international focus.* Specifically developed for young learners throughout the world, the themes, situations and literature covered by *Cambridge Global English* strive to reflect this diversity and help learners learn about each other's lives through the medium of English. This fosters respect and interest in other cultures and leads to awareness of global citizenship.
- *An enquiry-based language-rich approach to learning.* *Cambridge Global English* engages children as active, creative thinkers. As learners participate in a wide variety of curriculum-based activities, they simultaneously acquire content knowledge, develop critical thinking skills through tasks that encourage a personal response and practise English language and literacy. The materials incorporate a 'learn to learn' approach, helping children acquire skills and strategies that will help them approach new learning situations with confidence and success.
- *English for educational success.* To meet the challenges of the future, children need to develop facility with both conversational and more formal English. From the earliest level, *Cambridge Global English* addresses both these competencies. *Cambridge Global English* presents authentic listening and reading texts, writing tasks and culminating unit projects similar to those students might encounter in a first language school situation. Emphasis is placed on developing the listening, speaking, reading, and writing skills students will need to be successful in using authentic English-language classroom materials. At Stage 4, basic learning strategies and tips for study skills are introduced and practised. This lays the foundations for the use of effective study skills for future use.
- *Rich vocabulary development.* Building a large and robust vocabulary is a cornerstone to success in both conversational and academic English. *Cambridge Global English* exposes learners to a wide range of vocabulary. Many opportunities for revising these words and using them in personalised, meaningful ways are woven into the activities and lesson plans.

- *Individualised learning.* We approach learning in an individual way by both acknowledging the individual nature of the knowledge and background of each child and encouraging their specific input. We also provide for differentiated learning in the classroom by offering a range of activities of varying difficulty and extra challenges. Unit by unit support for this is provided in the unit notes in this book.
- *Integrated assessment.* Throughout the course, teachers informally assess their students' understanding of language and concepts. The Teacher's Resource provides suggestions for extending or re-teaching language skills based on learners' demonstrated proficiency. At the end of each unit, learners apply the skills and knowledge they have acquired as they work in groups to create and present a project of their choice. This provides teachers with an excellent performance assessment opportunity. An end-of-unit quiz in the Activity Book provides another evaluation measure: a quick progress check on learners' understanding of key ESL and early literacy skills.

Cambridge Global English can be used as a stand-alone ESL curriculum or it can be used as part of an innovative suite of materials created by Cambridge University Press for young learners at international primary schools:

- *Cambridge Primary Science*
- *Cambridge Primary Mathematics*
- *Cambridge Primary English (L1)*
- *Cambridge Global English.*

We encourage you to learn more about these complementary courses through the Cambridge University Press website: education.cambridge.org

We very much hope that you and your students will enjoy using these materials as much as we enjoyed developing them for you.

The *Cambridge Global English* team

How to use *Cambridge Global English*

A Components

Cambridge Global English offers the following components:

- The **Learner's Book** provides the core input of the course. It consists of nine thematic units of study. Each unit contains six lessons developed around a unifying theme that is also linked to a main question at the beginning of the unit. The materials feature skills-building tasks, including listening, reading, writing, speaking, as well as language focus, catering for the needs of learners studying in a primary context. In addition, we have included a strong vocabulary-building element. We also specifically explore ways of introducing basic learning skills and strategies, so that the children become aware of the act of learning and how it works through such features as:
  - Overt objectives at the beginning of each unit
  - Language and Writing tips
  - Listening and Reading strategies
  - Language detective
  - Reflect on your learning
  - Look what I can do!

  We try to aim our materials at the whole child with all the experiences that they bring to the classroom. We encourage the learners to see the moral and social values that exist in many of our texts and find opportunities for reflecting on these. We feel that the learner needs to be exposed to many different forms of text topics and styles in order to develop the skills of assessing, interpreting and responding appropriately. This means that the learners will see factual texts, imaginary text, dialogues, poetry, etc. on a range of different topics at the appropriate level.
- The **Audio CDs** include all the listening material needed for the Learner's Book and Activity Book. The listening material supports the Learner's Book with listening, pronunciation and phonics activities, as well as songs and read-along stories. We recommend that learners use the Audio CDs at home to practise the songs and stories and to show their parents what they know.
- The **Activity Book** provides additional practice activities, deepening learners' understanding of the language skills and content material introduced in the Learner's Book.

- The **Teacher's Resource** provides valuable guidance and support for using *Cambridge Global English* in your classroom. We understand that within each class there are children of different ability, particularly when children come from different pre-primary backgrounds. We think it is very important to support differentiated work in the classroom and we try to do this through suggestions in the unit notes, with additional differentiation 'challenge' activities in the Activity Book. In addition, the production required in the project work can be graded in terms of ability.
  At the end of this book, we provide photocopiable activities for additional work. These are referred to in the unit notes. We also provide a selection of lesson-by-lesson spelling words which you can photocopy, cut out and give to the children to learn.

B Learner's Book structure

Cambridge Global English consists of nine thematic units of study roughly set out to cover three units per term in most systems. The Stage 4 Learner's Book is organised as follows:

- **Main units:** Nine thematic units provide a year's curriculum.
- **Revision pages:** Every two units we provide two revision pages to revise and consolidate learning.

C Unit structure

Each unit is divided up into six lessons. The length of lessons will vary from school to school, so we have not prescribed a strict time limit for each lesson. The lessons are organised as follows:

- **Lesson 1 Opening:** This lesson introduces the main topic, and the Big question which you will find in the unit notes of this book. We also set out the unit objectives for the teacher to share with the learners. This overt teaching of objectives is part of the 'learning to learn' strategy. The main lesson begins with a 'Talk about it' activity in which the children are expected to react to information, ideas or visuals. There is a contextualised listening or speaking text which leads to exploitation of vocabulary and grammar. A free-speaking activity usually ends the lesson.

- **Lessons 2–4 Skills:** In these lessons we explore the topic in various ways using a variety of short listening and reading texts which do include cross-curricular topics. The lessons focus on the mechanics of reading, including phonics, spelling or pronunciation and use of English and integrate the four skills. Guided writing activities are included in these lessons.
- **Lesson 5 Literacy:** This literacy lesson involves reading authentic extracts, stories, poems and factual texts of longer length. It allows the learner to explore a variety of text types with the class and develop comprehension and writing skills through related activities. The literacy lessons can include some word focus and strategies for approaching new text types and usually include value-related activities.
- **Lesson 6 Choose a project:** This is the consolidation and production section of the unit in which the learners produce language related to some element in the unit. This lesson begins with the learners taking an active role in choosing a project, carrying it out and presenting it to the class. Then they reflect on their learning and do a short self-assessment activity: *Look what I can do!*

D Activity Book

Each lesson in the Learner's Book is supported by two Activity Book pages which reinforce and extend the material introduced in the Learner's Book. It also provides opportunities for personalisation and creative work, as well as challenge activities to support differentiated classroom situations. In these activities, more confident learners can do additional work at a higher level. The last lesson of each unit offers additional assessment/self-assessment opportunities.

E Customising your lessons

We provide support for planning each lesson in the unit pages of this book. We also clearly set out the teaching objectives. Please bear in mind the following:

- These are ideas and guidelines only and you should adapt them to your situation and the needs of your learners. Do not be afraid to change things and bring in additional elements.
- Monitor your learners. If they need additional support for some elements, tailor the material to their needs.
- Bring as much 'real' material into the classroom as possible in order to create more interest for the lessons.
- Be creative in developing extension activities and role plays. We give some suggestions; however, there is much more that can be done.

- Encourage learning/teaching/showing between classes, even of different age groups.
- Don't forget to draw on parent support where possible – please see our home–school link suggestions.

When using the book, the following guidelines might be useful:

Before using the Learner's Book

- Use warm-up activities (songs, TPR, vocabulary games, alphabet chant, etc.).
- Pre-teach and practise key language that learners will encounter in the Learner's Book and Audio CDs. (Try to make learning experiences concrete, interactive, motivating.)

While using the Learner's Book

- Keep learners engaged in an active way.
- Use the illustrations as a conversation starter – ask learners to name everything they see; play *I Spy,* etc.
- Vary the group dynamics in the lesson: move from whole group response to individual response to pairwork, etc.
- Provide opportunities for learners to ask questions, as well as to answer them.
- Encourage learners to act out the language in the lessons.
- Encourage learners to use language structures and vocabulary to talk about their own ideas, opinions and experiences.
- In class discussions, write the learners' ideas on class charts. You can refer back to these charts in later lessons.
- Adjust your reading and writing expectations and instructions to suit the literacy level of your learners.

Using the Activity Book and further suggestions

- Use the Activity Book pages related to the Learner's Book pages.
- Depending on the ability of the learners, use the 'Additional support and practice' activities and/or 'Extend and challenge' activities suggested in the Teacher's Resource at the end of every lesson.
- Do a 'Wrap up' activity or game at the end of every lesson.

We would strongly recommend that you supplement this core material with the following:

- An extended reading programme to provide the children with lots of practice of different types of books leading to reading independence. It is recommended that you regularly set aside time for the children to read books of their choice in class and that they are encouraged to read at home.

- Exposure to additional audiovisual material such as television programmes, songs, film excerpts – so that the learners begin to feel confident in their ability to decode and understand a range of resources.
- Supplementary handwriting and phonics material to help build on those skills at this crucial time.

F Setting up the primary classroom

We know that there is not always a lot of flexibility in this, but, if possible, it would be useful to set up the classroom in this way:

- Have some open space where learners can do role plays, etc.
- Have a flexible seating arrangement, so that you can mix up the groups and pairs, and the learners become flexible about working in different ways.
- Make sure that you have display areas where you and the learners can bring in pictures and items linked to the themes you're working on. Also display examples of good work and creative work. Make small cards and display important words for the learners to remember.
- Change displays regularly to keep the learners interested and engaged.

G Assessment

We recommend that you take the time and opportunity to observe and monitor the progress and development of your learners. We provide many opportunities for informal assessment through the projects, as well as self-assessment *(Look what I can do!)* in the main units of the Learner's Book. The Activity Book contains revision material at the end of each unit.

At the beginning of the year, create individual portfolio folders to keep work that shows how the children have been meeting the curriculum objectives. Use the portfolio to look over with the learners and create a feeling of achievement and pride in what they have achieved. Keep this portfolio for parent–teacher meetings and send it home to show the parents/carers either at the end of each term or the end of the year. You might want to include a letter to parents/carers outlining what learners have achieved.

If you would like further learner assessment opportunities, a table of how the Cambridge English Language Assessment exams for primary stages fits in with the *Cambridge Global English* levels is set out below.

Cambridge English Language Assessment exam for primary stages

Stage	Assessment	CEFR level
6	Cambridge English: Key (KET) for Schools	A2
5		
4	Cambridge English: Flyers (YLE Flyers)	
3		
2	Cambridge English: Movers (YLE Movers)	A1
1	Cambridge English: Starters (YLE Starters)	

H Home–school relationship

Support and encouragement at home is extremely important at this age. Encourage parents either face to face or via letter/email to become as involved as possible in their child's learning process by asking them what they have learned after every lesson, allowing children to 'teach' them what they have learned, taking an interest in what they bring home or want to perform for them and supporting any work the learners might try to do at home. We make suggestions for creating home–school links in the unit notes of this book.

I Icons

The following icons have been used to clearly signpost areas of special interest or as shorthand for specific instructions:

Audio and track number reference. These appear in the Learner's Book, the Activity Book and the Teacher's Resource.

Speaking opportunity / activity recommended for pairwork. These appear in the Learner's Book, the Activity Book and Teacher's Resource.

Cross-curricular maths and science topics. These appear in the Learner's Book, the Activity Book and the Teacher's Resource.

Direct links and references to the Activity Book. These appear in the Learner's Book and the Teacher's Resource.

Activity to be written in the learner's notebook. These appear in the Learner's Book and the Activity Book.

Activity to be done out of the book, in a more active classroom setting. These appear in the Teacher's Resource.

Framework correlations

Learning objectives from the Cambridge Primary English as a Second Language Curriculum Framework:
Stage 4 correlated with Cambridge Global English, Stage 4

Below you will find a table setting out specifically where to find coverage of the framework objectives for Stage 4.

Cambridge Primary English as a Second Language Framework: Stage 4	CGE Unit 1	CGE Unit 2	CGE Unit 3	CGE Unit 4	CGE Unit 5	CGE Unit 6	CGE Unit 7	CGE Unit 8	CGE Unit 9
Reading									
R1 Recognise, identify and sound (with some support) a range of language at text level		✓	✓		✓				✓
R2 Read and follow (with limited support) familiar instructions for classroom activities						✓			
R3 Read (with some support) an increasing range of short fiction and non-fiction texts with confidence		✓	✓	✓			✓	✓	✓
R4 Understand the main points of an increasing range of short, simple texts on general and curricular topics by using contextual clues	✓		✓	✓	✓	✓		✓	✓
R5 Understand (with little or no support) specific information and detail in short, simple texts	✓		✓	✓	✓	✓	✓	✓	
R6 Recognise the difference between fact and opinion		✓	✓	✓	✓				

Cambridge Primary English as a Second Language Curriculum Framework: Stage 4	CGE Unit 1	CGE Unit 2	CGE Unit 3	CGE Unit 4	CGE Unit 5	CGE Unit 6	CGE Unit 7	CGE Unit 8	CGE Unit 9
R7 Recognise the attitude or opinion of the writer in short, simple texts on an increasing range of general and curricular topics		✓	✓						
R8 Use (with support) a familiar paper and digital reference to check meaning and extend understanding	✓	✓	✓		✓	✓	✓	✓	✓
Writing									
W1 Plan, write, edit and proofread work at text level with support and a limited range of general and curricular topics	✓	✓	✓	✓					
W2 Write (with support) a sequence of short sentences in a paragraph on a limited range of general and curricular topics	✓	✓	✓						✓
W3 Write (with support) factual and imaginative descriptions at text level which describe people, places and objects	✓	✓		✓				✓	

Cambridge Primary English as a Second Language Curriculum Framework: Stage 4	CGE Unit 1	CGE Unit 2	CGE Unit 3	CGE Unit 4	CGE Unit 5	CGE Unit 6	CGE Unit 7	CGE Unit 8	CGE Unit 9
W4 Use joined-up writing in a range of written work across the curriculum with some speed and fluency		✓	✓						
W5 Link (with some support) sentences into a coherent paragraph using a variety of basic connectors on a limited range of general and curricular topics			✓			✓		✓	
W6 Use (with some support) appropriate layout at text level for a limited range of written genres on familiar, general and curricular topics	✓	✓	✓	✓	✓		✓		
W7 Spell most high-frequency words accurately for a limited range of general and curricular topics when writing independently			✓			✓			
W8 Punctuate written work at text level on a limited range of general and curricular topics with some accuracy when writing independently		✓							✓

Cambridge Primary English as a Second Language Curriculum Framework: Stage 4	CGE Unit 1	CGE Unit 2	CGE Unit 3	CGE Unit 4	CGE Unit 5	CGE Unit 6	CGE Unit 7	CGE Unit 8	CGE Unit 9
Use of English									
UE1 Use a growing range of common noun phrases describing times and location, on a limited range of general and curricular topics			✓						
UE2 Use quantifiers *many, much, a lot of, a few* on a limited range of general and curricular topics						✓			✓
UE3 Use a growing range of adjectives and comparative and superlative adjectives (both regular and irregular) on a limited range of general and curricular topics	✓				✓		✓	✓	✓
UE4 Use determiners including *any, no, each, every* on a limited range of general and curricular topics						✓			

Cambridge Primary English as a Second Language Curriculum Framework: Stage 4	CGE Unit 1	CGE Unit 2	CGE Unit 3	CGE Unit 4	CGE Unit 5	CGE Unit 6	CGE Unit 7	CGE Unit 8	CGE Unit 9
UE5 Use questions, including question tags to seek agreement and clarify on a limited range of general and curricular topics	✓								
UE6 Use basic quantitative pronouns *some, any, something, nothing, anything* on a limited range of general and curricular topics	✓								
UE7 Use simple perfect forms of common verbs to express what has happened (indefinite time)		✓		✓		✓	✓		✓
UE8 Use future forms *be going to* to talk about already decided plans on a limited range of general and curricular topics					✓				✓
UE9 Use simple present forms to describe routines, habits and states on a limited range of general and curricular topics	✓		✓					✓	

Cambridge Primary English as a Second Language Curriculum Framework: Stage 4	CGE Unit 1	CGE Unit 2	CGE Unit 3	CGE Unit 4	CGE Unit 5	CGE Unit 6	CGE Unit 7	CGE Unit 8	CGE Unit 9
UE10 Use past continuous forms for background actions on a limited range of general and curricular topics		✓	✓						
UE11 Use common impersonal structure *it, there,* on a growing range of general and curricular topics: with *be made of; be, look, sound, feel, taste, smell like*				✓		✓			
UE12 Use adverbs of definite time on a limited range of general and curricular topics				✓					
UE13 Use *might, may, could,* to express possibility on a limited range of general and curricular topics				✓				✓	
UE14 Use prepositions of direction *to, into, out of, from, towards* on a limited range of general and curricular topics					✓			✓	

Cambridge Primary English as a Second Language Curriculum Framework: Stage 4	CGE Unit 1	CGE Unit 2	CGE Unit 3	CGE Unit 4	CGE Unit 5	CGE Unit 6	CGE Unit 7	CGE Unit 8	CGE Unit 9
UE15 Use common verbs followed by infinitive verb/ verb +ing patterns. Use infinitive of purpose on a limited range of general and curricular topics	✓		✓		✓				
UE16 Use con-junctions *so, if, when, where, before, after* to link parts of sentences on a limited range of general and curricular topics			✓				✓		
UE17 Use defining relative clauses with *which, who, that* and *where* on a limited range of general and curricular topics		✓							
UE18 Use if clauses (zero conditional)					✓				
Listening									
L1 Understand a sequence of supported classroom instructions			✓					✓	✓

Cambridge Primary English as a Second Language Curriculum Framework: Stage 4	CGE Unit 1	CGE Unit 2	CGE Unit 3	CGE Unit 4	CGE Unit 5	CGE Unit 6	CGE Unit 7	CGE Unit 8	CGE Unit 9
L2 Understand an increasing range of unsupported basic questions which ask for personal information									✓
L3 Understand an increasing range of unsupported basic questions on general and curricular topics								✓	
L4 Understand the main points of supported extended talk on a range of general and curricular topics	✓					✓			
L5 Understand most specific information and the detail of a short, supported talk on a wide range of familiar topics	✓			✓	✓	✓	✓	✓	
L6 Deduce meaning from context in a short, supported talk on an increasing range of general and curricular topics				✓	✓	✓			
L7 Recognise the opinion of the speaker in a basic, supported talk on an increasing range of general and curricular topics		✓							

Cambridge Primary English as a Second Language Curriculum Framework: Stage 4	CGE Unit 1	CGE Unit 2	CGE Unit 3	CGE Unit 4	CGE Unit 5	CGE Unit 6	CGE Unit 7	CGE Unit 8	CGE Unit 9
L8 Understand supported narratives, including an extended talk on an increasing range of general and curricular topics		✓	✓					✓	
L9 Identify rhymes and repetition		✓							
Speaking									
S1 Provide basic information about themselves and others at sentence level on an increasing range of topics	✓		✓	✓	✓	✓		✓	✓
S2 Ask questions to find out general information on an increasing range of general and curricular topics	✓		✓	✓	✓				
S3 Give an opinion at sentence level on an increasing range of general and curricular topics		✓	✓	✓	✓		✓	✓	
S4 Respond with limited flexibility at sentence level to unexpected comments on an increasing range of general and curricular topics									✓

Cambridge Primary English as a Second Language Curriculum Framework: Stage 4	CGE Unit 1	CGE Unit 2	CGE Unit 3	CGE Unit 4	CGE Unit 5	CGE Unit 6	CGE Unit 7	CGE Unit 8	CGE Unit 9
S5 Organise a talk at sentence level using connectors on an increasing range of general and curricular topics	✓		✓	✓		✓	✓	✓	✓
S6 Communicate meaning clearly at sentence level during pair, group and whole class exchanges			✓	✓	✓	✓		✓	✓
S7 Keep interaction going in basic exchanges on a growing range of general and curricular topics	✓					✓			✓
S8 Relate basic stories and events on a range of general and curricular topics		✓							

4 CEFR guidelines

The Cambridge Primary English as a Second Language curriculum framework is based on the Council of Europe's common European Framework of Reference for Languages (CEFR). For more information about the CEFR framework, please visit their website. The framework correlation to the *Cambridge Global English* stages (or levels) is set out in the table below. However, the material in the course may move more fluidly between levels since it has been written for an ESL context where it is difficult to have rigid conceptions about language level.

CEFR levels for CIE stages

Cambridge Global English Stage						
	1	2	3	4	5	6
Reading CEFR level	Working towards A1	Low A1	High A1	Low A2	Mid A2	High A2
Writing CEFR level	Working towards A1	Low A1	High A1	Low A2	Mid A2	High A2
Use of English CEFR level	Low A1	High A1	Low A2	Mid A2	High A2	Low B1
Listening CEFR level	Low A1	High A1	Low A2	Mid A2	High A2	Low B1
Speaking CEFR level	Low A1	High A1	Low A2	Mid A2	High A2	Low B1

1 Family circles

Big question Why are families special?

Unit overview

In this unit learners will:

- compare and contrast family lives
- learn about children's lives and routines in different countries
- talk about and describe sports: *I play, I go, I do*
- identify third person endings: /s/ *plays*, /z/ *goes*, /iz/ *catches*
- write a letter using correct punctuation
- read and listen to a piece of literature
- read a poem about someone's favourite things.

Learners will explore the concept of families and what makes them special through looking at different types of families and reflecting on their own family. They can compare and contrast their family life with that of another. They will build communication and literacy skills as they interview partners about the sports they do, read about a young sporting hero, what life is like for learners in Kenya, and read a letter from a 10-year-old girl in Argentina.

At the end of the unit, learners will apply and personalise what they have learned by writing about their daily routine, what they like doing and what they are good at in a letter to a penfriend. Finally, they will talk about their families and read a traditional Indian story.

Language focus

Simple present tense, third person endings

Verb + infinitive + ing

Sports: *play, go, do*

Punctuation: *capital letters*

Adjectives: *both, too, whereas*

Vocabulary topics: families, daily routines, chores, phrasal verbs (relationships)

Self-assessment

- I can compare and contrast family lives.
- I can compare and contrast the lives of different children.
- I can talk about and describe sports and activities.
- I can write a letter using correct punctuation.
- I can read and understand a literary text.
- I can write a project related to the unit.

Teaching tip

Reading strategies and high-level vocabulary

Throughout the course, learners will encounter texts which contain difficult words and structures for their level. They will practise different reading strategies to deal with such texts. Make sure learners understand the aim of each reading exercise, as often the questions test skills like scanning, skimming and looking for specific information. For example, they may only need to find enough information to match headings to the paragraphs or find specific information to check if statements are true or false.

Remember to be sensitive to family situations and, if necessary, devise strategies so that learners in difficult situations do not feel uncomfortable.

Lesson 1: Family circles

Learner's Book pages: 6–7

Activity Book pages: 4–5

Lesson objectives

Listening: Listen and match family members to the activities they do.

Speaking: Ask about family relationships, talk about similarities and differences.

Critical thinking: Think about where families are from and the differences within families; assess advantages and disadvantages of large and small families.

Language focus: Present simple, third person endings.

Vocabulary: *family, grandma, grandpa, cousin, dad, mum, aunt, uncle, me;* phrasal verbs: *get on well, tells me off, take after, grow up, looks after;* connecting words: *whereas, both, too*

Materials: Optional for **Activity 4**, bring in photos to illustrate the following phrasal verbs: a child who looks similar to (*takes after*) their parent, an adult *looking after* children, children playing happily (*getting on well*), etc.

Learner's Book

Warm up

* Ask learners: *Have you got a grandma?* If the learner says *yes,* then ask: *What's her name?*
* Ask questions about other family members:

  > Teacher: *Have you got a grandma?* (or *grandpa, cousin, (an) aunt, (an) uncle*)?
  > Learner: *Yes, I have.*
  > Teacher: *What's her/his name?*
  > Learner: *It's ... .*

* You could ask learners to raise their hands if they know the age of their grandfather/grandmother, then ask: *How old is he/she?*

1 💬 Talk about it

* Tell the class they are going to talk about what people in their families do. Elicit some suggestions before focusing attention on the quotes. Read the second quote and then nominate learners and ask the questions: *Does your mum help you with your homework? Is she really good at Maths?*
* Use the other quotes to carry out an informal class survey. In order to involve as many learners as possible, tell learners to raise their hands when their mothers/fathers do the same.
* **Critical thinking:** Build on this by speaking about the other activities that family members do.

Answers
Learners' own answers.

2 💬 Talk

* If necessary, introduce and explain any new vocabulary. It might be worth highlighting variations in family terms: *Grandmother, Grandma, Granny,* etc. Also, if it comes up, explain that you use an initial capital letter with family names (e.g. *Mum*) if you are using it as a proper name. If you are referring to a person in a more generic way (e.g. *John's mum*), you don't need a capital at the beginning.
* If it will help, nominate learners and sketch their family trees on the board.
* Help learners make predictions from the content of their listening. Ask: *What do you think she/he likes doing?*

Answers
Learners' own answers.

[AB] **For further practice, see Activity 1 in the Activity Book.**

3 Listen

* Tell learners they are going to check their predictions from the previous activity. Check their understanding of the words in the box. Pre-teach the words if necessary.
* After you have listened to the text, check understanding by asking learners which activities each family member from the photos does.

Audioscript: Track 2

Interviewer: In today's episode of 'Global children' we're going to speak to Chao-xing from China.

Interviewer: Hi Chao-xing! Tell us about your family and where you are from.

Chao-xing: Hello, I'm from Shanghai, the largest city in China. I live with my family: my mum, my dad, my grandpa and my grandma in a small apartment.

Interviewer: Do you all get on well together?

Chao-xing: Yes we do. We do lots of things together although sometimes my mum tells me off for not tidying my room.

Interviewer: What time do you go to school?

Chao-xing: I go to school at 7.30 a.m. and I finish at 5.00 p.m.

Interview: What do you do in the evenings?

Chao-xing: After school I go to my extra-curricular violin class. I take after my dad because he plays the violin too. I'm not as good as he is, but I play quite well. When I grow up, I'd like to be a violin teacher.

Interviewer: Do you enjoy living with your grandma and grandpa?

Chao-xing: Yes, I love it! Grandma looks after me when I get home from school because my parents are working. She prepares my dinner and then she goes to practise Tai Chi in the local park. Grandpa and I both like playing chess. He taught me how to play a few years ago and now we play most evenings together when I've finished my homework. Mum loves doing exercise whereas I prefer to play my violin. She often goes to the community square to do outdoor fitness and dance classes.

Interviewer: Well, thank you Chao-xing for telling us about your family and your daily life. It's been very interesting talking to you.

Answers
Dad, violin; Grandma, Tai Chi; Grandpa, chess; Mum, fitness and dance.

---

4 Read

- Elicit the meaning of the highlighted words. If possible, show the class photos of children to demonstrate the expressions. If you have difficulty finding photos, use other strategies. Learners could mime. For *get on well,* point to two class members who are good friends. Alternatively, listen again to relevant parts of the audioscript and encourage learners to guess meanings from context.

Answers
Learners' own answers.

---

5 Word study

- Look back at the expressions from **Activity 4** and make sure learners understand these are phrasal verbs. Check they understand that a phrasal verb is made up of at least two words, i.e. a verb and preposition(s), etc.
- Direct the learners' attention to the first phrasal verb and the list of definitions. Ask: *Which is the correct definition?*
- Repeat the procedure with the other phrasal verbs, checking all learners have understood. If there are any difficulties, return to the examples and encourage learners to use context to help them with meaning.

Answers
1 get on with
2 tell (someone) off
3 take after
4 look after
5 grow up

 For further practice, see Activities 2 in the Activity Book.

6 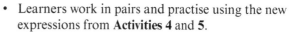 Talk

- Learners work in pairs and practise using the new expressions from **Activities 4** and **5**.
- Ask learners: *Who tells you off in your family and why?*
- Make sure learners understand they need to remember their partner's answers for later.
- Learners work in pairs asking and answering questions about each other's families.
- Circulate and monitor, offering help with pronunciation and the vocabulary they need to answer the questions.

Answers
Learners' own answers.

---

7 Talk

- Look at the sentences, particularly the words in bold. Explain the meaning and use of *too, both* and *whereas*.
- Ask for learners to give you example sentences about families using these words. Write them on the board.
- Learners work in pairs, exchanging information about people in their families and what they like to do. They make at least three sentences using *too, both* and *whereas*.
- They tell their sentences to the class.

 For further practice, see Activities 3 and 4 in the Activity Book.

Wrap up

- To finish off, ask learners to report back to the class about what they have found out about their partners' families.

Activity Book

1 Vocabulary

- Learners find seven names for family members in the grid.

Answers
across: grandma, dad, mum, cousin, grandpa
down: aunt, uncle

---

2 Word study

- Learners practise using the phrasal verbs from **Activity 5** in the Learner's Book by matching sentence halves.

Answers
1 c 2 a 3 e 4 b 5 d

---

3 Use of English

- Learners look at the activities the family like to do in the cartoon pictures and complete the sentences to compare and contrast.

> **Answers**
> 1 both like making cakes
> 2 dad does too
> 3 (various answers possible)
> 4 play the violin
> 5 Grandpa does too
> 6 (learners' own answer)

4 Challenge

- Learners personalise their knowledge of *too, both* and *whereas* by writing about the similarities and differences in their families. They are then asked to draw their family tree.

> **Answers**
> Learners' own answers.

Differentiated instruction

Additional support and practice

- Offer extra opportunities to practise the phrasal verbs in **Activity 4** in the Learner's Book. They may seem difficult to learners of English, but they are extremely common in everyday speech. To consolidate, learners could write a series of sentences containing these verbs for homework and/or perform mini roleplays about their families containing phrasal verbs. As always, be sensitive about difficult family situations. You could make a running list of phrasal verbs on the wall for a month, continually adding to it.
- Review learners' work on all the activities in order to determine areas of strength and areas where extra practice is needed. Use this information to customise your teaching as you proceed through the unit.

Extend and challenge

- For extra practice of names of family members, learners can ask: *Have you got a grandma?, grandpa?*, etc. Add extra words, e.g. *niece, nephew, younger brother.*
- Each learner could then choose one of their partner's family members to ask questions and write about.
- **Home–school link:** Learners interview their families to find out more about the family members then report back to the class.

Lesson 2: Global children

Learner's Book pages: 8–9
Activity Book pages: 6–7

Lesson objectives

Reading: Scan a text to find specific information.

Speaking: Compare school life with that of a child in Kenya.

Critical thinking: Awareness of what school is like in different countries; the differences in life for young people in different parts of the world.

Language focus: Adverbs of frequency.

Vocabulary: *school, average class, compulsory (have to), free of charge, shared, lack of books, secondary school, pupils, chores, working the land, cooking, fetching water, Science, English, settlement*

Materials: Pictures of children in different schools throughout the world and pictures of places in Kenya.

Learner's Book

⇨ Warm up

- Learners will read some facts about school in Kenya and responsibilities that children have there. Please note that this article about Kenya is designed to teach respect and a positive attitude towards situations where children are faced with special challenges brought on by poverty – not to pity them in any way. This can be part of a general discussion in the classroom.
- To generate interest in schools in different countries, show pictures of children at school around the world and ask: *Are there a lot of children in your class? How many?*
- To generate interest in the topic of the reading, ask learners *Yes, I do /No, I don't* questions like: *Do you have to come to school? Do you have to cook/help your parents/fetch water/work the land?*

1 🗪 Talk about it

- Ask the class if they know anything about schools in different countries. Show pictures of children in different schools throughout the world. Ask: *How are the schools in the pictures different?*
- Tell learners they are going to read about education in Kenya. Ask if anyone knows how it is different from their country. Help them by pointing to the pictures and asking about what they can see. Ask questions like: *Is your class bigger or smaller?* (They may not know comparative forms, but they should understand from the context.)

- Pre-teach difficult words and expressions, for example: *average class, compulsory (have to), free of charge, shared, lack of books, secondary school, working the land, cooking, fetching water.* See the **Teaching tip** on page 21 about reading strategies and high-level vocabulary.

> **Answers**
> Learners' own answers.

2 Read

- Generate interest by pointing at the picture of Jeremiah and asking: *What's his name? How old do you think he is? Where do you think he's from?* etc.
- Tell the class they are going to read a text and look for specific information about Jeremiah.
- Make sure they have read the questions and they understand it's not necessary to understand every single word, because when we *scan* a text, we look only for the information we are interested in. Not knowing the difficult expressions in the text (e.g. *engineer, a proper house, the tap*) will not prevent learners from answering the five questions.
- While learners write the answers, circulate and check they are only looking for the information they need and not trying to understand every single word.
- **Critical thinking:** Ask for comments about the differences. If there are problems, read the text together and elicit responses by pausing after each fact and asking them a question, for example: *Is education compulsory in (learners' country)?*

> **Answers**
> 1 Nairobi in Kenya
> 2 his sister, aunt, grandma and his cousin
> 3 He has to fetch clean drinking water from a nearby village.
> 4 Science and English
> 5 His favourite sport is football.

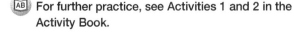 For further practice, see Activities 1 and 2 in the Activity Book.

3 Read

- Write three headings on the board. *My daily routine. Jeremiah's daily routine. Me and Jeremiah (same).*
- Ask the class to find the activities in the text. Write them in the correct column.
- **Critical thinking:** Direct attention to the Venn diagram and check learners understand how to complete it. Then ask them to work alone to draw their own.
- Ask a learner to tell the class one thing from each part of his/her diagram.
- Circulate and monitor while learners tell their partners about the things they do which are different from and the same as Jeremiah. Draw conclusions as a class.

> **Answers**
> Learners' own answers.

Language detective

- Write the frequency adverbs *usually* and *always* on the board. Focus on the **Language detective** box and then ask learners to look for other examples in the text.
- Demonstrate the difference in meaning. Write examples which are relevant to learners on the board, for example: *I ___ come to school, I ___ do my homework, I ___ listen to my teacher, I ___ brush my teeth.* Ask *concept-check questions* to make sure learners understand that if they use *usually* it means *sometimes they <u>don't</u>* do an action.
- Ask learners for examples about their routines and to explain the difference in meaning. Ask about the position of *usually* and *always* in sentences (*present simple* – between subject and verb; *present continuous* – between auxiliary and main verb).

For further practice, see Activity 3 in the Activity Book.

4 Over to you

- Write *I usually ... . I always ... . I don't ... .* on the board and work together to come up with a list of chores.
- Tell learners to write a list of ways in which they help around the house. Circulate and monitor.
- When they have done this, ask learners questions, for example:
  Teacher: *What do you do to help?*
  Learner: *I always/usually wash the dishes.*

> **Answers**
> Learners' own answers.

Wrap up

- Create a poster *'What we do to help around the house'.* Learners write sentences on strips of paper, for example: *I always wash up (child's name).* Use large letters. Stick them on a large sheet of paper or on the board.

Activity Book

1 Read

- Open the Activity Book at page 6. Look at the information required for the language passport. Learners read the text and find the information.

> **Answers**
> **Name:** Masami
> **Age:** 12
> **Favourite subject:** Music
> **Brothers/sisters:** one sister, one brother
> **Favourite food:** udon noodles
> **City/town:** Furukawa
> **Future job/profession:** pianist
> **School subjects:** Japanese, Maths, Science, Social Studies, Music, Crafts, PE, traditional Japanese arts

2 Vocabulary

- Learners circle the household chores they do and look up new words in their dictionaries.

> **Answers**
> Learners' own answers.

3 Use of English

- Learners use the rule from the **Language detective** box to re-order sentences containing *adverbs of frequency*.

> **Answers**
> 1 Masami usually feeds the animals.
> 2 Mum always makes the beds.
> 3 I often tidy my bedroom.
> 4 My brother never cleans his bike.
> 5 Dad usually washes the car at the weekend.

4 Write

- Learners write sentences about what chores they do in the home.

> **Answers**
> Learners' own answers.

Differentiated instruction

Additional support and practice

- Test whether learners are developing awareness of different education systems and help them use the new expressions to talk about how school in their country is different from Kenya. Write prompts with the new expressions on strips of paper – *class size, is their education free of charge?*, etc. and use these as the basis for a class quiz.
- If your class needs extra practice with the use of the frequency adverbs, for homework ask learners to write sentences containing *usually* and *always* about their routines.

Extend and challenge

- Learners have started to learn the strategy of reading a text for specific information without needing to understand the difficult expressions contained in it. To start to develop this useful reading strategy, learners could read other texts (e.g. on the Internet) to find specific information about schools in another country. Elicit a list of things learners would like to know. Tell them to find them out and use the information to write a paragraph. The emphasis should be on developing the reading skill mentioned.
- To give higher-level learners an extra challenge, ask them to make a comparison between their school day and school in the past. They will need to find this information from older people, books or the Internet. They should use the words *too, both* and *whereas* from **Lesson 1**.

Lesson 3: Sporting talent!

Learner's Book pages: 10–11
Activity Book pages: 8–9

Lesson objectives

Speaking: Talk about the sports we play.

Reading: Match headings to paragraphs of a text about a sporting hero.

Language focus: Present simple third person singular; pronunciation; *play, go* or *do*

Vocabulary: *sports, baseball, bungee jumping, football, diving, judo, rhythmic gymnastics, rollerblading, skateboarding, swimming, (table) tennis, trampolining, water-skiing, wakeboarding, to catch, to win a gold/bronze medal*

Materials: Pictures of Olympic sports and sports people to generate interest in the reading tasks.

Learner's Book

☞ Warm up

- To generate interest in the topic of sports, learners come to the front and mime a sport and the class guess its name. Build up a list of sports on the board under the columns *play, do* and *go*. Leave for future reference.
- Point to one of the sports on the board (e.g. *go swimming*) and ask the first learner: *Do you like going swimming?* Have the class clap and chant:

  Class: *Do you like going swimming?*
  Teacher: (Say a learner's name.)
  Learner: *Yes, I do./No, I don't.* (Keep asking until learner gives a positive reply.)
  Teacher: (Write *usually* and *always* from previous lesson on the board.)
   When do you go swimming?
  Learner: *I usually/always go on Saturdays.*

- Repeat with other learners and other sports from the list.

1 🗨 Talk about it

- Discuss the questions as a class, before allowing the learners time to ask and answer questions with a partner.

> **Answers**
> Learners' own answers.

2 🗨 Talk

- Nominate two teams of learners to have a competition to see who scores the most points. Point at each picture and ask the pairs alternately: *What are they doing?* Give two points for each correct answer.

> **Answers**
> a football   e skateboarding
> b swimming   f diving
> c rhythmic gymnastics g tennis
> d baseball   h judo

3 Read

- Generate interest in the text by showing pictures of Olympic sports and sports people. Talk about Olympic athletes from the learners' country. Ask what they can see in the pictures. Then look at the picture of Tom Daley. Ask questions like: *What do you think he does? Do you think he won the Olympics? Where do you think he's from?*
- Check they understand the difference between *win* (*gold*) and *win bronze* (i.e. to come third).
- Tell the class to read the headings and explain they all come from a text about Tom Daley. Ask them to read the text and match each heading to a paragraph. Make sure learners understand the aim of this exercise is to find only enough information to match the headings to the paragraphs. They will have more time to read later for greater understanding.
- Give class feedback.

> **Answers**
> 1 d 2 a 3 b 4 c

4 Read

- Allow the learners to read the text in more detail. Discuss the text with them.
- **Critical thinking:** Reflect on the role of families for young athletes. How can they help them?
- Tell the class to read the statements about Tom Daley. Check they understand that some are false.
- Tell the class to read the text again, to find out if the information 1–5 is true or false.
- Learners complete the exercise individually.

> **Answers**
> 1 true
> 2 true
> 3 false (He started diving when he was 12.)
> 4 true
> 5 false (His dad died a year before the Olympics.)

Language detective

- Point to the *play* column on the board. Ask learners if they can see a similarity between the sports. (They are all sports which need a ball.)
- Repeat for the *go* and *do* columns. (*go:* they are sports which end in *-ing; do:* for all other sports)
- Show learners the **Language detective** box and tell them to use it for future reference.
- Ask learners for some other examples using *play, go* and *do.*

5 ✏️ Use of English

- Cover up the lists of sports on the board.
- Tell the class they are going to look back at **Activity 2** and say if the sports go with *play, go* or *do.*
- Do the first three together, and if learners are struggling, remind them of the rule in the **Language detective** box.

- Let them finish the activity individually before giving class feedback. Add any sports they didn't think of in the **Warm up** to the lists on the board.
- Leave the lists of sports on the board for **Activity 7.**

> **Answers**
>
> | play | go | do |
> |------|------|------|
> | football | skateboarding | rhythmic gymnastics |
> | baseball | diving | judo |
> | tennis | swimming | |

[AB] **For further practice, see the Language detective box and Activity 1 in the Activity Book.**

6 ✏️ Pronunciation

- Discuss the third person singular ending for various present simple verbs.
- Tell the class they are going to listen to the pronunciation of third person singular verb forms.
- Before listening, nominate two learners and have a game to see who can predict more verb endings.
- Pause the audio after each verb to check learners have time to think and write.
- Learners can copy the table from **Activity 2** in the Activity Book (page 9) to complete this exercise.

> **Audioscript:** Track 3
> plays
> goes
> catches
> jumps
> dances
> does
> watches
> speaks
> works
> studies
> fetches

> **Answers**
>
> | /s/ | /z/ | /iz/ |
> |------|------|------|
> | jumps | plays | catches |
> | speaks | goes | dances |
> | works | does | watches |
> | | studies | fetches |

7 💬 Talk

- Tell learners to write down the names of four sports they would like to try.
- Write: *Have you tried … ?* then nominate two learners to ask and answer questions about their sports.

  Learner 1: *Have you tried playing football?*
  Learner 2: *Yes (I have)/No (I haven't).*

- Nominate more learners and repeat the procedure.

- For higher-level learners, in the case of a negative answer add the questions *Would you like to try playing football?* then *Why?/Why not?* Build up a list of adjectives that could be used for the answer to the last question. (*It's fun, fast, exciting, boring, etc.*)

  Learner 1: *Would you like to try playing football?*
  Learner 2: *Yes (I would)/No (I wouldn't), it's ... .*

- Refer the learners to the activity. Demonstrate by nominating learners and asking them the questions.
- Allow them a few minutes to tell their partners while you circulate helping with new vocabulary.

Answers
Learners' own answers.

🖙 Wrap up

- Higher-level learners write a sequence of sentences about *A sport I'd like to try* on a piece of paper. Answer the questions *Why? Where? Who with?* Lower-level learners write about *A sport I like doing.*
- Mix the pieces of paper up and ask learners to guess who wrote about which sport.

Activity Book

1 Vocabulary

- Open the Activity Book at page 8. Learners consolidate their knowledge of sports activities by writing the correct verb and sport under each picture.

Answers

1 go water-skiing	7 go skateboarding
2 play football	8 go rollerblading
3 do rhythmic gymnastics	9 do judo
4 play tennis	10 go diving
5 play table tennis	11 go paddle surfing
6 go swimming	12 play baseball

Language detective

- Learners look at the **Language detective** box to revise the rule about when to use *play, do* and *go* with sports activities.

2 📝 Pronunciation 58 [CD2 Track 31]

- Learners practise the pronunciation of the third person singular -*s* ending by listening to examples and writing the verbs in the correct column.

Audioscript: Track 58

does

watches

makes

goes

finishes

wins

starts

plays

Answers

/s/	/z/	/iz/
starts	plays	watches
wins	goes	finishes
makes	does	

3 📝 Read

- Learners read about the two famous sports people and say whether the sentences are true or false.

Answers
1 false (He was born in Argentina.)
2 true
3 false (She was born in April 1987.)
4 true
5 false (She won a silver medal in the 2012 Olympics.)

Differentiated instruction

Additional support and practice

- Ask learners *how often* they do the sports in the list. Pre-teach *every week, every now and again.* Ask the class to chant *Do you play football?*, etc. (using the correct verb – *play, do* or *go*). In the case of a *yes* answer, the class should chant *How often?*
- 💬 Have a competition in teams to see which team can remember the most sports with *play.* Repeat the procedure with the verbs *go* and *do.* Use the learners' performance to see if extra revision is necessary before going on to **Lesson 4**.

Extend and challenge

- Ask learners to write a series of sentences about their favourite sports person. They should answer the following questions: *Which sport? Where is he/she from? What are his/her greatest moments?*
- For homework, tell learners to find out about a new sport which they would like to try. They could find information on the Internet, at the library or from someone they know. Tell them to find out about clothing, equipment, where you can do it and (if applicable) rules and players.

Lesson 4: Penfriends

Learner's Book pages: 12–13
Activity Book pages: 10–11

Lesson objectives

Listening: Listen to sentences and write the correct verb form.

Speaking: Talk about writing letters.

Reading: Match headings to the paragraphs in a letter.

Writing: Write about family, daily routines and free time activities in a letter to a penfriend; punctuation: use capital letters.

Critical thinking: How daily routines are different in different countries.

Language focus: *like / love / enjoy* + verb + *ing* vs *hope / learn / want* + infinitive

Vocabulary: Recycle from previous lessons in the unit: families, daily routines, chores, sports and free time activities

Materials: A letter (if possible with a foreign stamp on it), a world map, some adhesive and some labels **Photocopiable activity 1**.

Learner's Book

⮑ Warm up

- To generate interest in the topic of penfriends, show learners the world map and ask if they know the names of any countries.
- Ask learners ways of communicating with friends who live a long way away: *letter, email, text, Skype,* etc.
- Find out if anyone keeps in contact with a friend like this. Ask: *Have you got a penfriend?* and *Where from?* in the case of a positive answer.
- If a learner has a penfriend, write the learner's name on an adhesive label and ask if anyone in the class can indicate where the country is before attaching it to the relevant part of the world map.
- Repeat for other learners with penfriends and establish who has the friend who lives the furthest away. If the learners don't have penfriends, they can talk about people they know in different places.

1 🗨 Talk about it

- Tell learners to read the four questions and give them a few moments to think about their answers.
- Check understanding by asking learners the questions, before allowing time for them to ask and answer the questions in pairs.

> **Answers**
> Learners' own answers.

2 Read

- Point to the girl in the picture and ask: *What's her name?* Then ask: *Where is she from?* and encourage learners to guess.
- Tell the class that Camila wrote the letter and they are going to read it and find out where she lives and what she likes doing. Tell them they will have time to read the letter again later.
- Allow time to read before inviting learners' responses and giving feedback. If learners are not familiar with the region, show Argentina/Patagonia on the world map.

> **Answers**
> She lives in Patagonia in Argentina. She likes cooking, trekking and tennis.

3 Read

- Now tell the class to read the headings and discuss what the function of the headings could be. Explain they are going to read the letter again and match each heading to a paragraph.
- Allow time to read the letter again before giving feedback on answers.

> **Answers**
> **1** b **2** c **3** a

Language detective

- Write *love / like / enjoy / prefer* on one side of the board and *hope / want / learn* on the other.
- Ask learners if they know the difference between the verbs in the two columns. If they don't know, tell them to read Camila's letter again and identify any sentences with these verbs in. (They won't find *learn, hope* or *enjoy.*) Encourage them to make observations on the form of the verbs these verbs precede.
- Show learners the **Language detective** box and elicit more examples about learners and their families.

4 ✍ Listen ▸4

- Tell the class they are going to listen to some sentences and write the verbs in the correct column.
- Play the recording, pausing to allow learners time to write.

> **Audioscript:** Track 4
> **1** I enjoy fishing with my brother and my dad.
> **2** 'I hope to participate in future Olympics,' said Tom Daley.
> **3** I'm learning to cook with my mum.
> **4** I love cooking!
> **5** I want to be a violin teacher when I grow up.

> **Answers**
>
> | verbs + to + infinitive | verbs + *ing* |
> | --- | --- |
> | hope | enjoy |
> | learn | love |
> | want | |

5 ✍ Use of English

- Write activities from the previous lesson on the board (e.g. *play tennis, go swimming, do judo*).
- Nominate learners and ask questions using the verbs from the **Language detective** box, for example: *What does your mum like doing? What do you want to do after class? What do you hope to do at the weekend?*

- Write full sentence replies on the board, for example: *My mum likes playing tennis.* This provides a framework for the activity.
- Learners write at least one sentence for each verb *love / like / enjoy / prefer / hope / want / learn.*
- Allow time for this while you circulate and offer help where necessary.
- After class feedback on any typical mistakes, learners should tell partners what they have written.

> **Answers**
> Learners' own answers.

 For further practice, see Activity 1, the Language detective box and Activity 2 in the Activity Book.

Writing tip

- Tell learners to read the text again and look for all the words that begin with capital letters.
- Ask learners why the capital letters are used and show learners the **Writing tip**.

 For further practice, see Activities 3 and 4 in the Activity Book.

6 Write

- **Portfolio opportunity:** Tell learners they are going to write a reply to Camila, giving information about themselves and their families.
- There are four steps for writing the letter, so this is an ideal homework activity. However, if learners need extra support, use Camila's letter to help them and discuss some ideas about the kinds of things they could write.

> **Answers**
> Learners' own answers.

Wrap up

- Mix up the letters and read them to class. Ask learners to guess who wrote which letter.

Activity Book

1 Read

- Open the Activity Book at page 10. Learners become more familiar with the verb patterns from the **Language detective** box. They are then asked to insert the sample phrases into a letter.

> **Answers**
> 1 We all enjoy swimming
> 2 They don't like swimming
> 3 they love running
> 4 My sister is learning to paint
> 5 I want to hear

Language detective

- Learners look at the **Language detective** box to revise the use of the *ing* form after *like* and *love* and the infinitive after *want* and *hope.*

2 Read

- Learners practise the use of the *ing* form after *like* and *love* and the infinitive after *want* and *hope* by answering questions about Faye and her family.

> **Answers**
> 1 She enjoys swimming in the lake.
> 2 They love running to catch sticks.
> 3 She's learning to paint.
> 4 She loves gardening.
> 5 She wants to hear about where you live and the activities you like doing.

3 Punctuation

- Learners use capital letters to punctuate the sentences.

> **Answers**
> 1 I live in Canada with my family.
> 2 My name's Faye and my brother's name's Ben.
> 3 I enjoy swimming in the lake with my family.
> 4 My sister goes to painting class on Tuesdays and Thursdays.

4 Challenge

- Learners read the information about Fei Yen and use it to write her letter to a penfriend.

> **Answers**
> Learners' own answers.

Differentiated instruction

Additional support and practice

- In **Lesson 3**, the language focus was on the pronunciation of the third person singular present simple ending. To revise this, ask questions about Camila which prompt third person singular replies, for example: *Does she live in a house or flat? What time does she get up? How does she get to school?*
- Learners use the words *too, but* and *whereas* from **Lesson 1** and compare themselves with Camila, for example: *Camila likes cooking, whereas I don't./We both like cooking.*

Extend and challenge

- **Photocopiable activity 1:** *Sports Snakes and Ladders.* A fun way to practise sports which combines vocabulary from **Lesson 3** and *ing* vs infinitive from **Lesson 4**.

Lesson 5: *How the Moon was kind to her mother*

Learner's Book pages: 14–17
Activity Book pages: 12–13

Lesson objectives

Listening and reading: Read and listen to a traditional story from India.

Speaking: Talk about ways of being kind.

Study skill: Match words to meanings.

Values: Being kind and helpful.

Critical thinking: Understand what makes a traditional story.

Vocabulary: Adjectives: *rustled, spread, greedy, selfish, thoughtless, thoughtful, pale, slender, blazing, unpleasant, calm, flowing;* Verbs: *(hide)* → *hid, share, reach, bring* → *brought, tossed her head, wrapped, speak* → *spoke, burn, will be blessed;* Nouns: *supper, the Star, the Moon, the Thunder and Lightning, gown, rays, heat, pleasure*

Materials: Pictures showing scenery and people in India to help generate interest in the story (if necessary). **Photocopiable activity 2.**

Learner's Book

👉 Warm up

- Revise family vocabulary and different ways of helping your family from previous lessons. Have a competition between groups of learners to see who can come up with the most words and expressions.

1 💬 Talk about it

- Tell learners to read the two questions and give them a few moments to think about their answers.
- Demonstrate the activity by nominating learners to answer the questions.
- Allow learners time to ask and answer the questions with a partner.
- Nominate pairs, and see how many ways of being kind they can come up with within a set time limit.

Answers
Learners' own answers.

2 Read and listen 5

- Tell learners they are going to read a traditional Indian story.
- **Critical thinking:** Tell the class to look at the title of the story and the characters and discuss what kind of story it could be and how realistic they think it will be. Talk about traditional stories. What makes

a traditional story different from other stories? Ask the class to think about this as they read the story. Suggestions might include: *a lot of people know the story; it's often told, not written down; it's usually not a true story; it usually teaches you something.* The sorts of things traditional stories teach can be discussed when you reach **Activity 6**.

- **Reading strategy:** Remind learners that it is not necessary to understand everything as they will have time to read the story again later. When there are lots of high-level words in a reading text, learners can use clues like illustrations, titles and context to help them.
- Play Track 5 on the audio CD as the learners read. At the end, remind learners of the question.

Audioscript: Track 5
See Learner's Book pages 14–17.

Answers
She shared her supper with her.

3 Read

- Now tell the class to read the first part of the story again and match the family names to the correct picture.
- Be prepared to help if necessary before giving feedback on answers.

Answers
mother – the Star, sister – the Sun, aunt – the Lightning, sister – the Wind, uncle – the Thunder, sister – the Moon

4 Read

- Learners read questions 1–7 on pages 15–17. Tell them they are going to read the rest of story again to find the answers.
- Allow time to do this individually while you circulate and monitor. If learners struggle, encourage them to think where they might find the answers or point to the section of text where the answer is located.

Answers
1 Thunder and Lightning
2 ice creams, cakes and fruit
3 in her long, white fingers
4 They were greedy and selfish and they didn't give her any of their supper.
5 The Sun will burn everything and people will need to cover their heads when she appears. The Wind, blowing in the heat from the Sun, will be very unpleasant. No-one will love them any more.
6 She will be cool and calm and beautiful. People will love her.
7 Learners' own answers.

📖 For further practice, see Activity 1 in the Activity Book.

5 Word study

- Point out the words in blue in the text. Tell the class that the words 1–5 are the meanings of the words in blue and they are going to match these meanings with the blue words. Encourage learners to use the context and other clues like the pictures to help them understand these new words.
- Allow time for this while you circulate and offer help where necessary before offering class feedback.

> **Answers**
> **1** gown **2** pleasant **3** supper **4** slender **5** unpleasant

6 Values

- Ask the class the values they have learnt from the text.
- Discuss ways learners show these values, for example: being kind, thoughtful, sharing and thinking of others in their own lives.
- **Critical thinking:** Focus attention on situations 1–4. Allow time in pairs to think of ways of being kind and helpful in the situations.

> **Answers**
> Learners' own answers.

[AB] **For further practice, see Activities 2, 3 and 4 in the Activity Book.**

Wrap up

- Ask for volunteers to tell the story again. They will probably need some support from the teacher.
- **Home–school link:** Suggest that the learners read or tell this story to their family in English when they go home.

Activity Book

1 Read

- Open the Activity Book at page 12. Learners read the story again and test their understanding by putting the sentences in order.

> **Answers**
> **1** g **2** a **3** d **4** h **5** c **6** f **7** j **8** b **9** e **10** i

2 Vocabulary

- Learners practise using *un-* prefixes to make opposites of words. They use the words with and without the prefixes to complete sentences.

> **Answers**
> **1** kind/unkind   **2** helpful/unhelpful
> **3** unpleasant/pleasant   **4** happy/unhappy

3 Word study

- Learners match sentence halves to complete the similes. The second half of each sentence begins with *like* or *as*.

> **Answers**
> **1** b **2** c **3** f **4** a **5** d **6** e

4 Challenge

- Learners invent their own similes. If necessary, ask concept-check questions to check learners know *as* is a conjunction and *like* is a preposition used if someone looks similar or does something in a similar way.

> **Answers**
> Learners' own answers.

Differentiated instruction
Additional support and practice

- Ask learners to work in pairs to try and retell the story.
- **Photocopiable activity 2:** Reorder the version of the story.

Extend and challenge

- Ask learners the names of some traditional stories and to explain what they are about.
- Learners tell a traditional story from their country.

Lesson 6: Choose a project

Learner's Book pages: 18–19
Activity Book pages: 14–15

Lesson objectives

Speaking: Family members – use adjectives to say what they are like and describe what they like doing.

Writing: A special person – describe what they are like and say why they are special.

Language focus: Unit 1 Review

Materials: Tell learners to bring in pictures of their family; a hat/container for a game in the **Warm up**.

Learner's Book

Warm up

- Give learners ideas for step 1 in **1 A special person in my family** and revise the names of family members by having a competition to see who can think of the most family members within a time limit. Repeat the procedure for adjectives that could describe the family members. Avoid gender stereotyping.

- Tell learners they will play a game. Give each learner two pieces of paper. Learners write *My* and the name of a family member, e.g. *brother,* on each piece of paper. Tell them not to let other learners see.
- On one piece of paper, learners write an adjective to describe the family member, for example: *My brother is kind.* On the other, they write an activity the family member enjoys – *My brother enjoys / likes baseball.*
- Fold the papers in half and put them in a hat. Mix them up and ask learners to pull a piece of paper out of the hat and read it to the class. The class should guess who wrote it.

Choose a project

- Introduce and describe each project. Ask the learners to decide which one they would like to do. In this unit, both projects are probably best done by individuals.

1 A special person in my family

- Steps 1–2: Focus attention on the three word clouds and tell learners to think of a special person in their family. Ask them to draw their own word clouds and write words about the family member.
- Nominate learners to tell the class what they have written.
- Step 3: Learners use these ideas to write three short paragraphs describing what this person is like and why they are special. While learners are writing, circulate and monitor, offering help and suggestions about paragraph structure and giving them ideas if necessary.

2 Compare and contrast the lives of two people in the unit

- Step 1: Ask learners if they can remember the names of the people they have read about in **Unit 1**. (Learner's Book: *Jeremiah, Tom Daley, Camila;* Activity Book: *Masami, Lionel Messi, Maria Sharapova, Fei Yen.*)
- Tell them to choose two of these people to compare and contrast.
- Step 2: Focus on the questions and tell learners to make a list of all the information they will need.
- Elicit examples of sentences with *whereas, both* and *too,* before allowing learners time to write about the lives of the two people they have chosen. Offer help and suggestions about paragraph structure, giving ideas if necessary.

⮕ Wrap up

- Ask volunteers to present what they have written to the class.
- **Portfolio opportunity:** If possible, leave the learners' projects on display for a short while. Then consider filing the projects, photos or scans of the work in learners' portfolios. Write the date on the work.

Reflect on your learning

- Reintroduce the Big question from **Lesson 1**: *Why are families special?* Discuss learners' responses to the question now and compare them with their comments at the beginning of the unit. Has much changed?
- There are different approaches to the revision activities. If your class is very spontaneous, you could use these steps for oral practice. However, most classes will benefit from being given time to think and write down their answers, which could then be used as future revision notes.
- You might like learners to work in class individually or in groups or pairs. Alternatively, you could set these tasks for homework/self-study.

> Answers
> Learners' own answers.

Look what I can do!

- **Aim:** To check learners can do all the things from **Unit 1**.
- Again, there are various different approaches to these revision exercises. You could nominate learners, or ask for volunteers to show the class evidence that they can do one of the things on the list. You could turn it into a competition to make it more fun for the learners.
- You might like learners to work in pairs or in groups and show their partner(s) evidence from their notebooks while you circulate and monitor.

> Answers
> Learners' own answers.

Activity Book

Unit 1 Revision

- Open the Activity Book at page 14. This activity tests what learners remember from **Unit 1**. If there is anything learners do not remember, tell them to go back to the relevant lesson and revise.

> Answers
> 1 b   2 c   3 b   4 b   5 c   6 c
> 7 b   8 b   9 b   10 c   11 b   12 c

My global progress

- Learners answer the questions about the unit. This provides useful feedback for the teacher.

> Answers
> Learners' own answers.

> ### Differentiated instruction
>
> 🗩 Divide the class into teams and nominate learners from each team to show the relevant part of their notebooks. Award them points for the content of what they show. The team with the most points at the end is the winner.

2 Stories

Unit overview

In this unit learners will:
- talk about reading habits
- describe personal qualities
- design and describe a superhero character
- plan a short story
- understand a short story
- write and talk about past events
- talk about brave actions.

Learners will practise reading and listening skills by exploring two different kinds of stories before creating their own piece of writing. They will read or listen to a short adventure story, *The Seekers,* and a story about a boy who won a judo tournament. To help learners build their creative writing skills, they will learn adjectives for describing personal qualities and talk about what people can do. They will learn to make their own superhero, to write a story plan, use sequencing words and learn how to report what characters say. Finally, learners will use their newly acquired knowledge to produce either their own comic strip or their own ending to *The Seekers*.

In addition, learners will build communication skills by interviewing partners about what they like reading and their favourite characters. They talk about what they are good at doing and are able to show other people what they can do. The photocopiable activities give learners the opportunity to practise asking, answering and reporting back to the class using the past simple as well as a quiz to practise relative clauses.

Language focus
Past continuous

Defining relative clauses with *who, that, where*

Simple perfect forms

Vocabulary topics: character qualities, adjectives (*good, naughty, evil*), action verbs

Self-assessment
- I can talk about things I like reading.
- I can use different words to describe personal qualities.
- I can draw and describe a superhero.
- I can plan a story and understand what the different parts are.
- I can write a short story.
- I can understand a short story.
- I can write and talk about things that happened in the past.
- I can pronounce some adjectives with three or more syllables.
- I can talk about brave actions.

Teaching tip

Listening and reading strategies

Make sure learners realise that when listening for specific words or information, they should just listen out for these, and that it is not necessary to understand (or even hear) every word.

Make sure learners understand the importance of making predictions. If necessary, before listening to an audio, make a point of asking for predictions, writing the predictions on the board and comparing them with the audio after listening.

There are often clues that can help the listener or reader make predictions about what happens next. For example, stories, comics, newspapers and magazines usually have pictures that can help learners to imagine what is going to happen.

Review the learners' work, noting areas where learners demonstrate strength and areas where they need additional instruction and practice. Use this information to customise your teaching as you continue to **Unit 3**.

Lesson 1: Stories

Learner's Book pages: 20–21

Activity Book pages: 16–17

Lesson objectives

Speaking: Talk about books and story preferences.

Reading: Look for similarities, read for specific details.

Critical thinking: Develop choices and opinions about what we read.

Language focus: *keen on, read about, be into, like/enjoy* + verb + *ing.*

Vocabulary: likes and dislikes

Materials: Some authentic English reading material to help generate interest in the topic of reading, for example learners could bring in their favourite book or comic to show the class.

Learner's Book

👉 Warm up

- Show the reading material to the class and point to the pictures in the book. Discuss words for the different things people read.
- Point to the word *book* and ask a learner: *Do you like reading books?*
- Ask other learners about books and other reading material, for example newspapers, magazines, comics.

1 🗨 Talk about it

- If learners have brought their favourite book with them, tell them to show their book to the class. Write a list of books that learners have enjoyed on the board. Compare them and draw out learners' reasons for choosing them. With a high-level class ask: *Have you read …?*
- **Critical thinking:** Introduce the big question: *What makes a good story?* Discuss this with the learners. Write down their ideas and save them for the end of the unit.
- Focus attention on the two questions and if necessary pre-teach *for fun.* Ask learners the questions.

> **Answers**
> Learners' own answers.

2 Read

- Generate interest in the text by telling the class they are going to read what four learners say about reading to see if they like reading the same things.
- **Critical thinking:** Learners reflect on the opinions of the readers and contrast them to their own.

> **Answers**
> comics, stories, cartoons, factual books, encyclopaedia, fictional stories, websites, historical stories, futuristic stories

3 ✍ Read

- Focus attention on the table and tell learners to copy the table into their notebooks.

- **Critical thinking:** Tell the class they are going to read the text again to find out the specific details in order to transfer them to the table. Ask them to analyse how the information is organised in the table.
- Learners complete the activity individually. If they struggle because of the new words, remind them that they don't need to understand every word to find the information requested.

> **Answers**
>
> | What you can read | Why? |
> | --- | --- |
> | Comics | Read about adventures. Read about characters that do amazing things. Look at cartoons. |
> | Factual books | Learn about Science. Find out how things work. |
> | Websites | Make up your own stories. Find out new things. Do online quizzes. |
> | Story books | Imagine different places. |

4 Word study

- Focus on the sentences and tell learners to find them in the text (in **Activity 2**, on page 20) and fill in the missing words.

> **Answers**
> 1 love   2 enjoy   3 into   4 about   5 into   6 on

📖 **For further practice, see Activities 1, 2 and 3 in the Activity Book.**

5 🗨 Talk

- Tell learners that they are going to practise using the new expressions from **Activity 4**.
- Nominate learners and ask the first learner: *Are you into comics?*
- Ask other learners this and other questions from the exercise, while the class clap and chant:
  Class: *Are you into comics?*
  Teacher: (Say another learner's name.)
  Learner: *Yes, I am./No, I'm not.*
- Tell learners they are going to practise telling their partners about themselves using these expressions.
- Nominate learners to demonstrate the activity.
- Make sure learners understand they need to remember their partner's answers for the next activity.
- Allow learners five minutes to practise in pairs.

> **Answers**
> Learners' own answers.

📖 **For further practice, see Activity 4 in the Activity Book.**

👉 Wrap up

- To finish off, nominate learners to tell the class about what they have found out about their partners, for example: *Helga is into comics, but she isn't keen on reading encyclopaedias.*

Activity Book

1 Vocabulary

- Focus on **Activity 1** on page 16. Learners read the information in the speech bubbles and match them with the boxed items.

Answers		
1 comic	**2** encyclopaedia	**3** futuristic stories
4 cartoons	**5** websites	**6** historical stories

2 Read

- Learners revise the different expressions for expressing likes and dislikes from **Lesson 1** by underlining phrases that describe what Sophie likes and dislikes.

> Answers
> **likes:** really enjoy, love looking at, really into, like reading, enjoy reading
> **dislikes:** not very keen on, not into

3 Vocabulary

- Learners personalise their new knowledge by completing the expressions for expressing likes and dislikes and writing something that is true for them.

> Answers
> Learners' own answers.

4 Challenge

- **Home–school link:** Learners talk to a friend or family member about their reading habits and then write a paragraph about it.

> Answers
> Learners' own answers.

Differentiated instruction

Additional support and practice

- Offer extra opportunities to practise the expressions from the **Word study** as they are extremely common in everyday speech. Play: *Who wrote that?* Learners make up similar sentences about themselves and write them on a slip of paper. Mix them up and read random sentences and ask the class to guess who wrote them.
- Learners could practise further by talking about what family members like reading.

Extend and challenge

- If your class is interested in reading, take them to the school library and encourage them to take out an easy reader or comic in English.
- Alternatively, you could ask them to find a review of a new children's book in English which looks exciting. Ask them to bring these to the lesson to generate interest among other learners.

Lesson 2: The PowerPals

Learner's Book pages: 22–23

Activity Book pages: 18–19

Lesson objectives

Listening: Make predictions and listen for details.

Speaking: Talk about favourite story characters, pronunciation: syllable stress.

Writing: Write a paragraph about a story character using adjectives and relative pronouns.

Critical thinking: What makes a character? Describe characters and talk about what they can do.

Language focus: Relative pronouns: *who* (people), *where* (places), *that* (things).

Vocabulary: Adjectives for describing personal qualities: *agile, athletic, fearless, intelligent, powerful, muscular, wicked*

Materials: Pictures of popular cartoon/story characters to generate interest in the topic, **Photocopiable activity 3**.

Learner's Book

Warm up

- Generate interest in: *What makes a character?* Show pictures of famous characters from stories and cartoons and ask the class their names. Elicit adjectives to describe them and write a list on the board.
- Ask learners: *Who's your favourite story character?* Then ask: *What's he/she like?* to elicit use of adjectives from the list (or other adjectives).

1 Talk about it

- **Critical thinking:** Focus attention on the first two questions. Nominate learners and ask them the questions.
- Point to each character in the Learner's Book and ask the last two questions. Use this opportunity to demonstrate *agile, intelligent, powerful* and *athletic* ahead of the **Word study**.

> Answers
> Learners' own answers.

2 Word study

- Tell learners they are going to listen to some information about the PowerPals. To help them understand, there are some new words they need to learn.
- Focus attention on the list of adjectives and ask the class if there are any adjectives that anyone remembers from the previous activity.
- Ask learners to complete the activity.

> Answers
> **1** c **2** e **3** d **4** a **5** f **6** b

Listening strategy

- Look back at the **Teaching Tip** on page 34 about listening and reading strategies.
- Ask learners why they think it will be easier to understand a text if they make some predictions about what they will hear before they listen.

3 Listen 6

- Tell learners that now they are going to listen and check their predictions about the characters' special powers.

Audioscript: Track 6

Speaker 1: Ever wondered about those quiet kids at the back of the class with their noses in their books? Could there be more than meets the eye? In this amazing adventure story, watch four geeky friends transform themselves into epic superheroes when they discover a secret potion during a class science experiment ... and save their city from a terrifying attack by wicked alien invaders! For Leila, Mike, Abdul and Cassie, life suddenly got a whole lot more exciting!

Watch four ordinary kids find extraordinary powers to become the PowerPals. And in the face of a deadly ground invasion and terrifying cyber-attack, it is not a moment too soon!

Leila suddenly finds she can leap and jump her way from building to building with athletic and agile moves that leave the bad guys standing and gawping. Very handy when you have a whole army of villains on your tail!

Mike finds powerful muscles that were certainly never there before! As the alien invaders jump, he is suddenly strong enough to catch them mid-air with his bare hands ... and save his friends from a terrifying attack!

Abdul used to be scared of almost everything. Then suddenly the fear disappeared and he became ... fearless! When his friends are captured, he shows just how brave he can be and breaks into the place where the villains are hiding to rescue his friends from danger.

And Cassie is the girl who really saves the day! She becomes super-intelligent and works out the code that breaks the cyber-attack – just in time to save the city.

Answers
Learners' own answers.

4 Listen 6

- Tell the learners they are going to listen to the audio again and this time they have a different task. Focus on the table in **Activity 4** and tell them to copy it into their notebooks.
- Explain they are going to listen for more details about the PowerPals and then play the recording.
- Repeat, pausing the audio if necessary.

Answers

Character	Adjectives	Why? What can he/she do?
Leila	agile, athletic	She can jump from building to building.
Mike	powerful	He can catch alien invaders with his bare hands.
Abdul	fearless	He breaks into a place where villains are hiding.
Cassie	super-intelligent	She works out a code that breaks the cyber-attack.

5 AB Pronunciation 7

- Tell learners they are going to focus on four. Explain that they need to listen very carefully to see how many parts they can hear in each word. Ask if anyone knows the name for parts of words (*syllables*).

Audioscript: Track 7
beautiful

athletic

intelligent

powerful

Answers
beautiful 3 syllables, athletic 3 syllables, intelligent 4 syllables, powerful 3 syllables.

Language detective

- Write the relative pronouns *who, where* and *that* on the board. Listen to the audio Track 6 from **Activity 4** (page 23) again and tell learners to shout *Stop!* when they hear these words.
- Focus on the first of the three sentences in the **Language detective** box. Ask learners why *where* is used (it refers to a place). Ask about *who* and *that* (*who* refers to a person and *that* to a thing).
- See **Additional support and practice** for more activities about relative pronouns.

6 Use of English

- Point to the description of the superhero and tell learners they are going to complete the gaps using the relative pronouns from the **Language detective** box.
- Check they remember the criteria for choosing the correct relative pronoun.
- Read the first sentence and ask which pronoun we use with people. Repeat for the other gaps.

Answers
who, that, who, where.

AB For further practice, see Activities 1 and 2 in the Activity Book.

7 Write

- Step 1: Allow learners a few moments to write down a story or comic character they like. As a class, put together a list of famous story or comic characters and adjectives to describe them.
- Step 2: Tell learners to choose one character and write a description about him/her using these and other adjectives as well as relative pronouns. Circulate and offer help with new words.
- Learners give the description to another pair. Make sure they haven't written the name of the character.
- Encourage the other pair to guess who the character is.

Answers
Learners' own answers – Portfolio opportunity.

 For further practice, see Activities 3 to 7 in the Activity Book.

Wrap up

- Nominate learners and ask them to tell the class about their partner's character.

Activity Book

1 Use of English

- Learners revise the use the relative pronouns *who, where* and *that* by choosing the correct pronouns in a description of a superhero.

Answers
1 who **2** that **3** where **4** who **5** who **6** that

2 Use of English

- Further practice of the use of relative pronouns by using *who, where* and *that* to complete sentences.

Answers
1 where **2** that **3** who **4** that **5** where **6** who

3 Vocabulary

- Learners revise new vocabulary by finding synonyms in the text.

Answers
1 powerful **2** fearless **3** wicked **4** intelligent

4 Synonyms

- Learners revise new vocabulary by finding synonyms for adjectives with help from their dictionaries.

Answers
Potential answers could include: **2** big **3** scared **4** weird **5** amazing.

5 Pronunciation 59 [CD2 Track 32]

- Learners practise word stress by listening to the audio recording, repeating and analysing how many syllables there are in the words.

Audioscript: Track 59

a amazing

b fearless

c mysterious

d afraid

Answers
a 3; on the second syllable   **b** 2; on the first syllable
c 4; on the second syllable   **d** 2; on the second syllable

6 Listen 59 [CD2 Track 32]

- Learners listen again to Track 59 and match the adjectives with the stress pattern.

Answers
1 afraid   **2** fearless   **3** amazing   **4** mysterious

7 Challenge

- Learners apply and personalise their new knowledge by drawing and then writing a description of their superhero. They use the questions to help them structure their description.

Answers
Learners' own answers – Portfolio opportunity.

Differentiated instruction

Additional support and practice

- **Photocopiable activity 3: *Relative clauses quiz cards*** help learners practise using the relative pronouns.

- For more practice with relative pronouns, play *Guess where! who! what!* Write examples on the board, for example: *School – a place where we learn. Pen –something that we use to write. Doctor – it's who you see when you're ill.* Help learners write more sentences on pieces of paper with information about places they know, using *where*; with people they know using *who*; and with objects using *that*. Shuffle the sentences and read them out at random, for example: *a place where we learn – guess where!* to elicit the response *school.*

Extend and challenge

- Give each learner the name of a famous character (real or fictional) and tell them to find some information about this character (e.g. from books and the Internet).
- Watch a cartoon that learners enjoy in English and discuss the characteristics of the main characters.

Lesson 3: Make a superhero

Learner's Book pages: 24–25

Activity Book pages: 20–21

Lesson objectives

Speaking: Talk about what we are good at and what we can show other people to do.

Reading: Read instructions for how to draw a cartoon superhero character.

Critical thinking: What makes a superhero? What does a superhero look like? What does he/she wear and what does he/she hold?

Language focus: Giving instructions.

Vocabulary: Describing superheroes: *wearing a mask, wearing armbands, wearing a cape, wearing a belt, the expression on his/her face, body*; how to draw: *stick people, press hard, erase/rub out*

Materials: Pictures of popular cartoon/story characters from **Lesson 2**, preferably showing above expressions to describe superheroes. Learners could bring in pictures of their personal favourites.

Learner's Book

☞ Warm up

- Practise the expression *good at* + noun/verb + *ing.* Write *I'm good at ...* on the board. Ask for volunteers and ask the question: *What are you good at?* Write the correct answers in two columns on the board under the headings: *I'm good at* + noun and *I'm good at* verb + *ing.*
- Then ask the class to clap and chant:
    Class: *What are you good at?*
    Teacher: (Say a learner's name.)
    Learner: *I'm good at football/playing football.*
    Teacher: *Can you show me?*
    Learner: *Yes, I can./No, I can't.*

1 ☺ Talk about it

- Ask learners the two questions before allowing them a minute to practise asking and answering in pairs.
- Ask volunteers about their partners: *What is ... good at? Has he/she ever shown anyone else how to do anything?*

> **Answers**
> Learners' own answers.

2 Read

- Tell learners they are going to draw their own superhero using the instructions in **Activity 2.** Ask them to scan the text and look only for the information required, i.e. the first and last things you draw when drawing a superhero.
- For advice about vocabulary, see **Additional support and practice.**

> **Answers**
> Draw the superhero's head. Add some colour.

Language detective

- Tell learners to read the text again and look for all the words that are used for giving instructions.
- Focus on these verbs and the verbs in the **Language detective** box. Ask learners why there is no subject to these verbs.
- Tell them to draw a head for their superhero.
- See **Extend and challenge** for more practice on giving instructions in other situations.

3 Over to you

- Step 1: Allow learners time to follow the instructions and finish drawing their superhero. Circulate, offering help where necessary and checking learners don't show the drawings to their partners.
- Step 2: Tell learners they are going to draw their partner's superhero without seeing the picture.
- Show learners the **Language detective** box and the example and remind them how to give instructions, i.e. using the base form of the verb and no subject.
- Nominate two learners to demonstrate the activity to the class. One learner gives instructions and the other draws the superhero on the board.
- Allow learners time to do the exercise in pairs.
- Step 3: Ask for volunteers to compare their picture with their partner's. See second suggestion from **Additional support and practice.**

> **Answers**
> Learners' own answers – Portfolio opportunity.

> **AB** For further practice, see the Language detective box and Activities 1 to 4 in the Activity Book.

☞ Wrap up

- Learners write a paragraph describing their superhero and put the pictures and the paragraphs up on the wall.
- **Home–school link:** Learners can also take home their superhero and ask their families to help them name him/her. Then they can bring their superhero back and tell the class the name.

> **Answers**
> Learners' own answers.

Activity Book

Language detective

- Learners look at the **Language detective** box and revise the rule for using the imperative form for giving instructions.

1 Use of English

- Focus on **Activity 1** on page 20. Learners match sentences to pictures. This activity pre-teaches expressions for the next exercise.

2 Use of English

- Practise using the positive or negative imperatives using the expressions from the previous activity.

Answers
1 Don't speak English in class.
2 Don't play football in the playground.
3 Don't take your books out of your bag.
4 Don't ask the teacher if you want to leave the classroom.
5 Run in the classroom.
6 Talk when the teacher is talking.

3 Listen 60 [CD2 Track 33]

- Learners listen to the recording and complete the library rules using a positive or negative imperative.

Audioscript: Track 60

OK, class. Listen please.

As you can see, we're in the library but there are rules for students who want to use it.

Rule 1: Don't eat in the library – finish your sandwiches or snacks outside.

Rule 2: Look after the books – there are all sorts of books here – encyclopaedias, historical books and novels, but they are not yours, so look after them.

Rule 3: Don't use your mobile phone to text or chat to friends – turn it off!

Rule 4: Bring your books back on time – it costs 20 pence for each day that you don't return the book.

And finally, rule 5: Enjoy the library – there's lots to learn in here and there are tables at the back to do homework together. OK …

Answers
2 Look after   3 Don't use   4 Bring   5 Enjoy

4 Challenge

- Further practice using positive or negative imperatives. Learners choose a place (the swimming pool, the cinema, or home) and write the rules.

Differentiated instruction

Additional support and practice

- There are several new words for describing the superheroes. Pre-teach expressions from the text *(mask, cape, belt, armband, symbol, logo)* by pointing to a pictures. Demonstrate a *stick person* by pointing to the picture in the book, *erase/rub out* and *press hard* by doing it on the board, and mime *is holding*.
- Revise and consolidate the use of *both, too* and *whereas* from **Unit 1**. Write the three words on the board and encourage learners to use them for their comparisons.

Extend and challenge

- Play a game of *Simon Says* to practise giving instructions in a fun way. Learners take turns to say *Simon says* and an instruction (e.g. *Simon says … stand up*) and the others follow the instructions. If necessary, write some useful verbs on the board, e.g. *sit, jump, read.*
- For homework, learners write a paragraph about their favourite story or comic book. Tell them to say what kind of comic/story it is, where it is set and to describe the characters. Encourage the use of the relative clauses studied in the previous unit.

Lesson 4: Planning a story

Learner's Book pages: 26–27
Activity Book pages: 22–23

Lesson objectives

Speaking: Talk about writing stories.

Reading: Read a short story.

Writing: Plan and write a short story.

Critical thinking: How to create a story – looking at the different parts of a story and the use of sequencing words.

Language focus: Punctuation before reporting verbs.

Vocabulary: Sequencing words: *after, the next day, at last, finally, one day*; reporting verbs: *gasp, whisper, exclaimed, smiled*

Materials: Some easy-readers which are suitable for this level and age group, preferably stories that learners are familiar with.

Learner's Book

Warm up

- To generate interest in the topic of story writing, show learners the books you have brought along and ask them if they know what or who any of them are about. Then focus on the pictures and tell them they are going to read the story. Ask what they can see in the pictures.
- Before reading, nominate a learner and ask the class to chant: *Do you ever write stories?* In the case of a positive reply, ask the class to chant: *What or Who do you write about?* (adventures, sporting dreams, young people, my friends)

  Class: *Do you ever write stories?*
  Teacher: (Say a learner's name.)
  Learner: *Yes, I do./No, I don't./Sometimes.*
  Teacher: *What/Who do you write about?*
  Learner: *Adventures.* (Offer help if necessary.)

1 Read

- Focus on the two questions about the story.
- Tell learners to read the story as quickly as possible and look only for these two pieces of information.

2 Read

- **Critical thinking:** Learners read the story again to look for the answers to the five questions. Make sure learners are only looking for the information required and not trying to understand every single word. Discuss their answers (allow quite open answers to questions 3, 4 and 5 as there are variable responses). Help them to see how these elements help form a story.

Answers
1 at Ben's school and at his grandad's house
2 Ben and his grandad.
3 (Possible answer) He is worried about a big competition. He loses his grandad's silver trophy, which he thinks is lucky.
4 (Possible answer) Ben decides he can win the competition without the lucky trophy. He finds the trophy under the bench.
5 (Possible answer) Ben wins the competition and gets his own trophy.

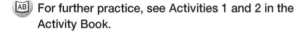 **For further practice, see Activities 1 and 2 in the Activity Book.**

3 Word study

- Tell the class to look at the blue words. Ask what information they give the reader (e.g. when something happens).
- Allow time to read the story again and look for all the other sequencing words.

Answers
one day, just as, then, suddenly, finally, now

Writing tip

- Focus on the sentence 'It was there all the time, he gasped.' Make sure learners understand that *gasp* is a reporting verb and demonstrate its meaning.
- Point to the comma and ask the learners if they know what it is called. Ask them why it is used (to separate *direct speech* from the *subject + reporting verb*).
- Show learners the **Writing tip** and ask them to read the story again to look for other examples.

4 Write

- Tell the class they are going to use what they have just learned to add the correct pronunciation.

Answers
1 'You did really well,' he said.
2 'Here's your trophy,' she smiled.
3 'That's brilliant!' he exclaimed.
4 'Be quiet!' she whispered.

Writing strategy

- Ask the learners to put their hands up if they have ever written a story.
- Discuss the kind of things they included in their story and write them on the board.

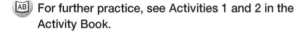 **For further practice, see Activities 3, 4 and 5 in the Activity Book.**

5 Write

- **Critical thinking:** Tell learners they are going to write their own stories and draw their attention to the **Writing strategy** about writing a story plan. Discuss ideas for stories from the learners that answer the four questions.
- Circulate and offer assistance while learners make notes under the four headings.
- Allow learners sufficient time to write their stories in class or set as homework.

Answers
Learners' own answers – Portfolio opportunity.

Wrap up

- When you have corrected the stories, ask for volunteers to read their stories out to the class. You could ask learners to draw a picture for the story and create a class poster. You could also record their readings.
- **Home–school link:** Learners take home stories and read them to their families. Learners ask their families what they like best about the stories.

Activity Book

1 Read

- Focus on **Activity 1** on page 22. Learners read the story and answer the questions to check they have understood the gist.

Answers
A small round creature.

2 Read

- Learners read the story again for information to decide whether the statements are true or false.

Answers
1 false (He found it under the sofa cushions.)
2 true
3 false (He thought it looked angry.)
4 false (It ran upstairs.)
5 false (His brother heard him shouting.)

3 Punctuation

- Learners use the knowledge they have acquired in the **Writing tip** to add the correct punctuation to the sentences.

4 Vocabulary

- Learners complete the summary. To do this, they practise using the sequencing words from the story.

Answers
1 Once   2 Another time   3 This time   4 Then
5 At that moment

5 Challenge

- Learners complete the story. Make sure they use sequencing words where needed. See **Additional support and practice**.

Answers
Learners' own answers.

Differentiated instruction

Additional support and practice

- Offer plenty of opportunities to practise direct speech and reporting verbs. Ask a learner simple questions and then ask another learner to report back, for example:

  Teacher: *How old are you, Brigitte?*
  First learner: *I'm nine.*
  (Write *said* on the board.)
  Second learner: *'I'm nine', Brigitte said.*

- If you are worried that some class members may lack ideas for their story, before writing, you could discuss some ideas.

Extend and challenge

- Encourage learners to look for short stories in English to read at home. They could try on the Internet, in student magazines and newspapers, etc.
- Learners write a paragraph to review a story that they enjoyed.

Lesson 5: *The Seekers*

Learner's Book pages: 28–31

Activity Book pages: 24–25

Lesson objectives

Listening and reading: Listen to and read an adventure story: *The Seekers*.

Speaking: Talk about personal characteristics, predict a story.

Writing: Describe a story scene.

Critical thinking: Use different strategies to understand a story which is difficult for the learners' level because of its length and difficult words.

Language focus: Past simple tense

Vocabulary: Nouns: *(peaceful) Kingdom, stones, journey, path, valley, discover, sound, scream, howl, beast, claws, ravine, rod, flash of light, sword, the ground, breath;* Verbs: *capture, save, protect, back away, leap, blaze, clash, snarl, dig in.* Jobs. (Although there is a lot of new vocabulary in the story, some of the verbs are onomatopoeic and many new words can be demonstrated using the pictures.)

Values: Being brave.

Materials: The books and materials from **Lesson 4**, preferably some adventure stories, **Photocopiable activity 4**.

Learner's Book

Warm up

- To generate interest in the reading, show learners some of the stories you have brought along and explain they are going to read a story. Point to the pictures in the Learner's Book and ask them what kind of story they think it will be. (This is an adventure story.)
- Pre-teach the words *kingdom* and *stones* by pointing to the pictures.
- Ask the class to clap and chant *What's your favourite adventure story?* Nominate volunteers to answer.

1 Talk about it

- Focus on the pictures of the children and ask: *What is his/her name?* Ask if anyone knows why they are called *The Seekers*. If no one knows, help by explaining *seek* means *to look for*. Discuss what the children might be seeking.

Answers
Learners' own answers.

Reading strategy

- Discuss why it is useful to read the text the first time for the gist. (This is to help understand when you read in more detail.) Take this opportunity to remind learners that they do not need to understand every word.

2 Read and listen 8

- Tell learners to read the introduction to the story for gist in order to check the answers to **Activity 1**.
- Then learners listen to the text and read it again.

Audioscript: Track 8
See Learner's Book pages 28–29.

3 Read

- Tell the class they are going to read the introduction again, and this time they need to find more details.
- Allow time for this before giving feedback on the answers.

Answers
1 It was captured by a wicked tribe called the Digons.
2 They could save Raban.
3 Learners' own answers.
4 They chose a special boy or girl to go on a journey to find the stones.
5 His good friends, Bariel and Horaf.

4 Read

- Tell learners that before they listen to the next part of the story, they are going to try and predict what will happen next. Refer to the **Reading strategy** (page 28).
- Tell learners to think about the story so far and look at the pictures to help. Encourage them to make predictions. See the first point in the **Additional support and practice** section.
- Ask learners if they can see the four things in the pictures. Help them out if necessary.

Answers
1 Learners' own answers.
2 ravine – picture g
  sword – all pictures
  flash of light – pictures e and f
  the beasts – pictures b, e, f and g

5 Listen 9

- Play the recording, so learners can check predictions, put the pictures in order and answer the question.
- If necessary play the recording again and pause after each part that corresponds to a picture.

Audioscript: Track 9

Suddenly the children heard a terrible sound. The sound was like the scream of a human and the howl of a crazy dog.
'I knew they would find us in the valley,' Horaf said quietly. Kehan looked around quickly. He was very frightened. There was nowhere to hide.
'Here they come!' Bariel shouted.

The three friends crouched down. Three beasts appeared in front of them. They had heads like dogs, tongues like snakes and bodies like cats, but their bodies were covered in green scales, like fish. They had large feet with huge claws. Their eyes burned like fire.
'What are they?' whispered Bariel.
'They are called Mistraals,' Kehan said.

The beasts crouched down, ready to attack. The children were terrified. Suddenly, Kehan knew what to do.
'Put the swords together!' he shouted, as the animals leapt. The children fell down hard on the rocky valley path. They were very close to the edge of the ravine. As they fell, Bariel's sword clashed with Kehan's. There was a flash of light and the Mistraals backed away. The three children jumped up.
'The swords!' Kehan shouted. 'Bring them together.'
The swords blazed as they clashed together. Snarling, the Mistraals backed away.

'We must lead them to the ravine,' Kehan said. 'Walk slowly towards them. Then, when I give the signal, turn and run. Stop at the edge of the ravine and jump.' He looked at the faces of his friends. They looked confused and worried.
'Trust me,' Kehan said.

The friends moved towards the terrible beasts. They could feel the hot breath of the Mistraals on their faces, Kehan shouted, 'Run!'
They ran quickly towards the ravine. Then, as they came to the edge, Kehan shouted, 'Jump!'
The swords lifted them high into the air. Bariel gasped.
'We're flying!'

Answers
Learners' own answers.
d, b, f, e, c, g
They went left through a thick forest down to the valley.

6 Listen 9

- Tell learners to read the first halves of sentences (1–5) and the mixed-up second halves (a–e).
- Play the recording again and tell learners to listen out for these details and match the two halves. If necessary, pause the recording after each sentence.
- Ask class what they think happened to the beasts.

Answers
1 d   2 e   3 c   4 b   5 a

Language detective

- Look at the past simple sentences in the **Language detective** box. Read the first sentence and ask learners if they know why the verb *captured* ends in *ed*. If they don't know, it's the past simple form for regular verbs. Point to *Long ago*. Check learners know we use this form when we know *when* past actions happened.
- Read the next two sentences and make sure learners know which verbs *chose* and *gave* come from.
- Ask them if they know any more irregular past simple forms and write them on the board.

7 📝 🔤 Use of English

- Ask learners to copy the table for regular and irregular verbs into their notebooks. Tell them to read and listen for past simple tense forms in the story. Make sure they know the infinitives of the irregular verbs and teach the new verbs.

Answers

Learners should provide six of the examples in the table.

regular	irregular
called (call)	gave (give)
captured (capture)	chose (choose)
wanted (want)	came (come)
passed (pass)	said (say)
finished (finish)	found (find)
	can (could)
	has (have)
	was (were)

 For further practice, see the Language detective box and Activities 1, 2, 3 and 4 in the Activity Book.

8 Talk

- Discuss what learners think happens next. Encourage them to use the past forms from the story.
- **Critical thinking:** Tell learners they are going to work in groups and discuss what their group thinks happened next.
- Allow five minutes for this, while you circulate and offer help with vocabulary and past simple forms.
- Ask for a volunteer from each group to tell the class what they think happened next.

Answers

Learners' own answers.

9 Talk

- Focus attention on the first adjective and discuss which child(ren) from the story it describes.
- Repeat for the other adjectives.

Answers

Learners' own answers.

 For further practice, see Activity 5 in the Activity Book.

10 Values

- Discuss what being brave really means. Discuss jobs where people do brave things and write them on the board.
- Ask learners if they know anyone who does these jobs. Encourage suggestions and discuss why these people are brave.

Answers

Suggested answers: firefighter, soldier, sailor, pilot, police officer.
A firefighter is very brave because fire is very dangerous.
Firefighters put themselves in danger to save lives.

11 Read

- Read the sentences and encourage learners to tick the sentences that describe someone they know or have read about. Help them with any new words and expressions (e.g. *stand up for, weaker*).

Answers

Learners' own answers.

12 Talk

- Allow learners time to tell their partner about the sentences they ticked. Circulate and offer help with any vocabulary they might need.

Answers

Learners' own answers.

Wrap up

- Ask for volunteers to report back to the class about their partners, for example: *Helga's uncle is very brave because ...*

Activity Book

Language detective

- Learners use the **Language detective** box to revise the form and the rule for using the *past simple* for talking about actions that happened in the past.

1 Use of English

- Learners put the verbs from the story into two columns according to whether they are regular or irregular.

Answers

Regular	Irregular
captured	could
started	chose
passed	gave
	had

2 Use of English

- Learners use the past simple forms of the verbs from the previous activity to complete sentences.

Answers

1 chose	**2** gave	**3** started	**4** gave
5 passed	**6** captured	**7** could	**8** chose

3 Use of English

- Further practice of the past simple. Learners complete the summary of **Part 2** of the story with the correct verb in the past simple form.

Answers

1 heard	**2** saw	**3** leapt	**4** fell down
5 jumped	**6** ran	**7** jumped	**8** lifted

4 Vocabulary

- Learners use the adjectives to complete sentences using their dictionaries to help them.

> **Answers**
> 1 loyal 2 dangerous 3 adventurous 4 peaceful 5 magical

5 Challenge

- Learners apply and personalise their new knowledge by writing about someone they know using the adjectives and by saying why they have this characteristic.

> **Answers**
> Learners' own answers.

Differentiated instruction

Additional support and practice

- If learners struggle to make predictions about the story, ask questions to help: *Will they save the Kingdom? Where will they go? What will attack them? How will they stop the attack? Will they use their swords?*

- Play games to help learners remember the past simple forms. Give learners a blank piece of paper and tell them to cut the paper in half, and in half again and again until there are 16 pieces of paper. On each piece, ask them to write an infinitive on one side and the past simple form on the other. Put the pieces of paper (infinitive facing up) in a pile and try and guess the past simple form. Turn over to check.

Extend and challenge

- **Photocopiable activity 4:** *Past simple prompt cards – Did you play football last week/month?*
- Put up a list of irregular past simple verbs in the classroom. Encourage learners to read stories in English and add more past simple forms they find to the list.

Lesson 6: Choose a project

Learner's Book pages: 32–33
Activity Book pages: 26–27

Lesson objectives

Speaking: Talk about comics.

Writing: Create a comic strip.

Critical thinking: Use newly acquired knowledge to produce a piece of creative writing.

Language focus: Unit 2 Review

Materials: Comics (and/or tell learners to bring in a comic that they like reading), glue, large pieces of card.

Learner's Book

☞ Warm up

- Revise past simple forms from the last lesson by playing *Past Simple Bingo* – learners choose six irregular verbs from the story and write the infinitive. If you have a list of past simple forms on the classroom wall, you could use these. As you call out the past simple form, learners cross off the verbs they have written.
- Give learners ideas for their comic strip by looking back at characters in the unit and encourage them to show the class the comics they have brought and/or let them look at some comics you have brought.
- Ask learners: *Do you read comics?* (If they have brought one, hold it up.) If the answer is *yes* ask: *Who's your favourite character?*

> **Answers**
> Learners' own answers.

Choose a project

- Tell learners they are going to choose from the two projects and follow the instructions below for the one they have decided on.

1 Create your own comic strip

- Step 1: Tell the class they are going to work in pairs/ small groups to create their own comic strip. Show them the story plan template on page 27 of the Learner's Book and give them a few moments to decide on a title.
- If necessary, help by discussing the sequencing words and adjectives from the unit. If learners lack ideas, ask the class for suggestions and discuss ideas.
- Step 2: Allow learners time to write their own story using the past simple tense, adjectives and linking words. Circulate and offer assistance, encouraging them to look back over the unit.
- Step 3: Once learners have finished writing the story, tell them to divide it into eight parts (offer help if necessary) and ask them the most important thing that happens in each part.
- Step 4: Write the different parts of the story under the pictures.
- Step 5: Make sure they have glue and tell them to stick the story pieces on the card.
- Step 6: Ask the groups to come to the front with their comic strip and present it to the class.

2 Write the ending to *The Seekers* story

- Tell learners they are going to write their ending to *The Seekers* story.
- Refresh their memories by discussing the 'story so far' and then by reading/listening to the story again.
- Ask the class for some suggestions by asking: *Do the children find the stones? How? What dangers do they face?*
- Show the class the story plan template on page 27 of the Learner's Book and tell them to use it as it says in Step 2.

- If necessary, help learners by discussing the sequencing words and adjectives they have learnt in the unit. If learners lack ideas, ask the class for suggestions and discuss ideas.
- Circulate and offer help and advice while they write the rest of the story in their notebooks.
- Groups come to the front with their story ending and present it to the class.

⇨ Wrap up

- Ask learners to vote for their favourite ending/ favourite comic strip and put the story endings/comic strip on the classroom walls.
- **Portfolio opportunity:** If possible, leave the learners' projects on display for a while. Then consider dating and filing the projects, photos or scans of the work, in learners' portfolios.

Reflect on your learning

- Reintroduce the Big question from **Lesson 1:** *What makes a good story?* Discuss learners' responses to the question now and compare them with their comments at the beginning of the unit. Has much changed?
- There are different approaches to these revision activities. If your class is very spontaneous, you could use these activities as oral practice. However, most classes will benefit from being given time to think and write down their answers, which could then be used as future revision notes. You might like learners to work in class individually or in groups or pairs. Alternatively, you could set this task for homework/ self-study.

> **Answers**
> Learners' own answers.

Look what I can do!

- **Aim:** To check learners can do all the things from **Unit 2**.
- Again, there are various different approaches to these revision activities. You could nominate learners, or ask for volunteers to show the class evidence that they can do one of the things on the list. You could turn it into a competition to make it more fun for the learners. Revisit the Big question for the unit here and discuss what they think of it now.

> **Answers**
> Learners' own work – Portfolio opportunity.

Activity Book

Unit 2 Revision

1 Vocabulary

- Open the Activity Book at page 26. Focus on **Activity 1**. Learners revise different ways of speaking about likes and dislikes.

> **Answers**
> a into   b reading   c on   d learning

2 Vocabulary

- Learners revise adjectives for talking about characteristics by sorting letters and writing synonyms.

> **Answers**
> 1 fearless   2 intelligent   3 powerful   4 wicked

3 Word study

- Learners revise relative pronouns by matching sentence halves.

> **Answers**
> 1 e   2 c   3 d   4 b   5 a

4 Over to you

- Learners personalise their new knowledge by completing the sentences so that they are true for them.

> **Answers**
> Learners' own answers.

My global progress

- Learners answer the questions about the unit. This provides useful feedback for the teacher.

> **Answers**
> Learners' own answers.

Differentiated instruction

- 💬 Divide the class into teams and nominate learners from each team to show the relevant part of their notebooks and award them points for the content of what they show. The team with the most points at the end is the winner.

  You might like learners to work in pairs or in groups and show their partner's evidence from their notebooks while you circulate and monitor.

- Have a writing competition – choose *The Best Story* and *The Best Character*. Learners write an adventure story. Choose a title and set a word limit.

Review 1

Learner's Book pages: 34–35

1 Listen 🔟

- Think about the strategies learners have learnt in the first two units and encourage them to apply these to help them understand while listening to the audio. Make sure you include the following: listening for specific words; making predictions about what you are going to hear; using pictures and titles to help. This is especially important for lower-level groups.
- Learners look at the pictures and discuss words they might hear to describe the characters.
- Listen to the first part of the recording and check the answers. Listen to the rest of the recording and give feedback at the end. In lower-level classes, play the recording twice, pausing for feedback between each character.

> **Audioscript: Track 10**
>
> **a** Harry likes doing things outside. He loves walking, climbing mountains and working outside with his family. He's got three brothers and a dog. He likes animals. He lives on a farm.
>
> **b** Freddy is a superhero who isn't very heroic. He isn't very strong. He's scared of everything and he isn't very intelligent. But he is very funny! He's got two little sisters.
>
> **c** Nick is a great athlete. He's very strong and agile. He loves playing football and baseball, doing judo and going water skiing. He likes to try everything. He lives with his mother, father and his grandfather.
>
> **d** Mark loves reading and listening to music. He likes playing tennis with his friends but he's only an average player. He's very good at writing stories. He's got one sister and a cat.

> **Answers**
> 1 Mark
> 2 Freddy
> 3 Nick
> 4 Harry

2 💬 Talk

- Demonstrate the activity by asking a learner to describe the character they have chosen to the class. In lower-level classes, give learners time to think about what to say, offering help if necessary.
- Allow learners time to describe their character to their partners while you circulate and offer support.

> **Answers**
> Learners' own answers.

3 📝 Vocabulary

- Learners work in small groups and have a race to see which group finishes first. Before announcing the winner, check the group's answers are correct.
- Learners from the winning group read out their answers to the class.

> **Answers**
> 1 fearless
> 2 character
> 3 grandfather
> 4 trampolining
> 5 never
> 6 the Olympics
> 7 encyclopaedia
> 8 firefighter

4 📝 Use of English

- Learners are required to apply several different aspects of their grammatical knowledge in this activity. They may find this difficult as it may be the first time they have completed such an activity. Their ability to complete it correctly will help you assess their progress, and decide whether learners are ready to continue or if further revision is necessary.
- In lower-level groups, learners may benefit from a quick revision of frequency adverbs, third person present simple, simple past and relative pronouns before doing the activity.

> **Answers**
> 1 to dance
> 2 but
> 3 works
> 4 always
> 5 Sometimes
> 6 performed
> 7 found
> 8 who
> 9 but
> 10 that

5 💬 Use of English

- Learners work in pairs and ask their partners the questions while you circulate and monitor. Give lower-level learners support by revising the present simple question forms and/or providing examples.

> **Answers**
> Learners' own answers.

6 📝 Punctuation

- It may be useful to do some quick revision of the use of capital letters, especially in lower-level groups.

> **Answers**
> 18 capital letters
>
> Hi Leo,
>
> I watched your dance crew on the TV last week when you performed in Shanghai, China. It was the most amazing show ever. I'm totally into dance but I don't know how you do half of those moves. I see that your next show is in Argentina and then Mexico.
> Hope to see you when you're next in New York.
>
> Your cousin,
>
> Juliette

7 📝 Write

- Work together to come up with ideas for writing an email to a person in another country.
- Allow time for learners to write a short email while you circulate and offer support whenever required.

Answers
Learners' own answers.

8 💬 Talk

- Learners work in teams and try to remember as many things as they can about the two stories in **Units 1** and **2** before reporting back to the class on what they remember.
- Allow learners time to tell a partner which story they liked best and why.
- Learners report back to the class what their partners told them.

Answers
Learners' own answers.

3 Day and night

Big question What is happening when you're asleep?

Unit overview

In this unit learners will:
- read about the Midnight Sun
- talk about and compare Earth's natural landscapes
- learn about our solar system
- write a fact file about a nocturnal animal
- read a poem about night time
- identify words that rhyme.

Learners will explore the idea that something is always happening, even when they are asleep. They will learn about the Midnight Sun in Norway, nocturnal animals, landscapes and the solar system. They will build communication skills by talking about the temperature, landscape and when it gets dark in their countries, as well as describing animals and what happens in a poem.

Learners will improve literacy skills by reading different types of texts including a poem about a nocturnal creature. They will use their newly acquired language and grammar to write a description of their favourite planet as well as comparing it with other planets. They will also write their own *cinquain* poem.

The photocopiable activities provide practice using comparative adjectives, and asking and answering questions about what people do at certain times, using the prepositions *in*, *at*, *on*, *last*.

Language focus

Making comparisons: comparative and superlative adjectives.

Prepositions of time.

Vocabulary topics: time, adjectives, planets, animal body parts.

Self-assessment
- I can understand a text about the Midnight Sun.
- I can talk about and compare natural landscapes.
- I can identify the planets in our solar system.
- I can talk about types of nocturnal animals and describe their features.
- I can write a fact file about an animal.
- I can understand the story described in a poem.
- I can identify words that rhyme.

Teaching tip

It is useful to know whether learners have already studied the subjects in the Learner's Book in other lessons as well as English. If so, you could find out what they know from the teacher of the relevant subject, how much they already know themselves and if they are likely to be interested in the subject.

Lesson 1: Day and night

Learner's Book pages: 36–37

Activity Book pages: 28–29

Lesson objectives

Speaking: Ask and answer questions.

Reading: Read about activities of a child living in Norway. The text is intended to promote interest in other cultures and different routines in other countries.

Writing: Write a sequence of short sentences in a paragraph about daily routines.

Critical thinking: Awareness that there are different time zones and longer or shorter days in different parts of the world.

Language focus: Prepositions for time expressions.

Vocabulary: *get(s) dark/light, (the Sun) sets, to last, to stay up late, to do a hike, to go on a hike, to have a barbecue, to fly → flew (→ flown)*

Materials: Daylight photos and photos of people doing things when it's dark, for example: playing sports with floodlights, **Photocopiable activity 5**.

Note

The use of the 12/24-hour clock and am/pm

In many countries, the 24-hour clock is used in general conversation. In Britain, this is not so. Also am and pm are not usually used to indicate morning, afternoon or night when it is possible to understand the time of day from the context. However, the 24-hour clock is used for talking about bus, train or flight times in the UK.

Learner's Book

Warm up

- Ask learners: *When's your birthday?*
- Give lower-level learners help and support with months and cardinal numbers.
- Focus on the **Amazing fact** at the top of page 37. Read it together and discuss whether the class would like to try it. Learners should understand the question from the context, despite the use of the hypothetical form *flew*.

1 🗣 Talk about it

- Introduce the subject of *darkness* and *light* by showing the class a daytime picture and discuss what time of the day it could be. Ask for reasons why. Repeat for night-time pictures.

- **Critical thinking:** Introduce the Big question: *What is happening when you're asleep?* Discuss this with the learners. Write down their ideas and save them for the end of the unit.
- Focus on the questions. Check learners understand key words: use the picture to help and write *get dark, it's light/dark outside* on the board. Ask a volunteer from the class to explain.
- Ask learners the questions before allowing them time to ask and answer the questions with a partner.

Answers
Learners' own answers.

2 Read

- If you don't expect the learners to know the expressions *to stay up late, to have a barbeque, the Sun sets, hiking,* pre-teach them before asking questions about the picture. Ask: *What time of the day is it? Why is it sunny at midnight? Where do you think they are? Would you like to live there?*
- Allow learners a minute to skim through the blog to find out how Norway is different from most countries. Discuss whether they think they will need to understand every word of the text for this.
- Ask them where they would find a text like this (a blog, on the Internet).

Answers
It has sunlight all day from the end of May to the end of July.

3 Read

- Focus on the true/false questions.
- Explain that learners have two or three minutes to read the text again and say whether the sentences are true or false.
- Give class feedback on the answers.

Answers
1 false (It was last night, and the time was 11.30 pm.)
2 false (It has sunlight all day from the end of May to the end of July.)
3 false (People often have more energy.)
4 false (His dad and grandad are going hiking.)

4 📝 Word study

- Write (*in, at, on* and *last*) __ *Saturday,* __ *night,* __ *week,* ___ *morning* on the board. Ask the class if they know where each preposition can go. Tell them to use the blog and the **Word study** box to help them.
- Pick times and ask the learners to reply with the time expression, for example:

Teacher: *Monday*
Learner(s): *on Monday*

- Ask learners to complete the sentences with the correct preposition.

Answers

1 in   2 at   3 on   4 last

 For further practice, see Activities 1, 2 and 3 in the Activity Book.

5 🖉 🗨 Talk

• Introduce the topic by writing *advantages* and *disadvantages* on the board. Ask if anyone knows which are *good* and which are *bad*.
• Discuss the advantages and disadvantages of living in a place where it never gets dark.
• Give the class time to choose three of each and write them down.
• Ask learners the questions.

Answers

Learners' own answers.

6 🗨 Talk

• Write on the board: *What do you usually do at 6 am?* and *How does this change on holidays?*
• Two learners mime. One mimes the clock and the other the activity that he/she does at that time while the other learners guess the activity.
• Repeat the procedure for the other times (12.30 pm, 4 pm and 9 pm).
• Allow the learners sufficient time to practise asking and answering the questions in pairs.

Answers

Learners' own answers.

 For further practice, see Activities 4 and 5 in the Activity Book.

🖙 Wrap up

• Learners write three or four sentences about their partner on a piece of paper. Mix the pieces of paper up and ask learners to pick them at random. Read the sentences and encourage the class to guess who said what.

Activity Book

1 Vocabulary

• Focus on **Activity 1** on page 28. Learners practise *in, at* and *on* with time expressions by writing the time expressions in the correct column in the table.

Answers

in	at	on
in the morning	at midnight	on Saturday
in the afternoon	at 3 pm	on Thursday
in the evening	at 9.30 am	

2 Vocabulary

• Learners add the months and seasons to the correct column in the table.

Answers

in	at	on
in the morning	at midnight	on Saturday
in the afternoon	at 3 pm	on Thursday
in the evening	at 9.30 am	
in the summer		
in April		
in the winter		
in June		

3 🖉 Challenge

• **Critical thinking:** Learners personalise and practise the time expressions by writing sentences to compare different activities they do in the summer and winter using *whereas*.

Answers

Learners' own answers.

4 Read

• Learners practise using the words from the text about the Midnight Sun by completing a text about Argentina using these words. The text also contains information about location, language, the capital city, climate and neighbouring countries.

Answers

1 second   2 countries   3 language   4 summer
5 sets   6 winter   7 rises   8 at

5 Write

• Learners personalise and practise using this information by completing a similar text about their own country/ies.

Answers

Learners' own answers.

Differentiated instruction

Additional support and practice

• 🗨 Offer extra opportunities to practise the time expressions. Learners make a *Time Expression Game.* Each pair cuts a blank piece of paper into eight pieces and writes different *times of day, specific times,* and *days of the week* on them. They swap the cards with another pair and place them in a pile face down. Then they take turns to pick up a card and read the time word with the correct time expression, for example: *seven thirty – at seven thirty.*

Extend and challenge

- **Photocopiable activity 5:** Learners use present (and past simple) questions to interview each other and do further practice of the time expressions using the Prompt cards: 'Expressing time: *in, at, on, last*'.
- Learners write a paragraph about a place they would like to live and why. Encourage them to find information from books and travel websites in English.

Lesson 2: Planet Earth

Learner's Book pages: 38–39

Activity Book pages: 30–31

Lesson objectives

Listening: Supported narrative, checking ideas on newly familiar topics, listening for specific information, listening strategies: anticipating (guessing) the information they will hear.

Speaking: Ask and answer questions: *Which is longer/wider/taller?*, use comparative adjectives.

Writing: A true/false quiz made up of short sentences containing comparative adjectives.

Critical thinking: Awareness of how landscapes are different in different countries.

Language focus: Comparative adjectives and *than*, long and short adjectives.

Vocabulary: landscapes: *mountains, beaches, (rain) forests, volcano(es), deserts, the North Pole, the South Pole, coral reef, to erupt*

Adjectives, *long → longer, high → higher, hot → hotter, cold → colder, dry → drier, big → bigger, cool → cooler, warm → warmer, wide → wider, old → older, humid → more humid, beautiful → more beautiful*

Materials: Photos of mountains, beaches, (rain) forests, volcanoes, deserts, the North Pole, the South Pole, coral reefs. You could ask learners in the previous lesson to look for some pictures; **Photocopiable activity 6**.

☞ Warm up

- Show the pictures of the landscapes to generate interest in the topic. Pre-teach new vocabulary.
- Ask learners: *Are there any mountains where you live? Where can I see mountains?*
- Learners practise using the vocabulary by telling a partner about the landscape near where they live.

1 � Talk about it

- Generate interest in the topic by asking learners if they know what each photo shows.
- Allow a few minutes for learners to write the answers before giving class feedback.

- Drill pronunciation.
- **Critical thinking:** Compare the landscapes to what learners can find in their own country.

> **Answers**
> a The Amazon Rainforest
> b The Sahara Desert
> c The Great Barrier Reef
> d Mauna Loa Volcano
> e The Amazon River
> f The North Pole

2 Word study

- To help learners make predictions about the content of listening, check they are familiar with the adjectives in the box. Mime and write *hot* on the board. Encourage learners to point to a picture showing somewhere *hot*. Do the same for the other adjectives, starting with *cold*. Ensure learners are completing the table.
- Predict which adjectives could be used to speak about the places in the photos.
- You can give more feedback on the answers after learners have listened to the audio in **Activity 3**.

> **Answers**
>
> | The Desert | The Tropical Rainforest | The Arctic | The Savannah |
> | --- | --- | --- | --- |
> | dry | humid | cold | hot |
> | hot | wet | cool | humid |
> | beautiful | beautiful | | |
> | cold | | | |

[AB] **For further practice, see Activity 1 in the Activity Book.**

3 Listen 🎧11

- Learners use their predictions from the previous activity to help them hear which places are described on the audio.
- Listen to the audio twice and ask learners which places are described.

> **Answers**
> The Amazon Rainforest, the Desert (the three deserts in Africa: the Sahara, the Namib and the Kalahari), volcanoes on Hawaii (Kilauea and Mauna Loa).

> **Audioscript:** Track 11
>
> The Amazon River is 6400 km long and it is very wide too. In some areas the river is almost 11 kilometres wide. Only the River Nile is longer than the Amazon River but the Amazon is wider than the Nile. The Amazon flows through many countries and forms part of a larger area called the Amazon Rainforest which is home to 33% of the Earth's plants and animals. The Amazon River is also home to many interesting mammals and fish such as pink dolphins and piranhas (man-eating fish). There are 950 species of bats too and the Amazon is home to the only real vampire bat, so be careful at night if you are in the Amazon Rainforest!

There are three deserts in Africa: the Sahara Desert, the Namib Desert and the Kalahari Desert. The Sahara Desert is very big; in fact it covers approximately 9 million square kilometres. The Sahara is hotter and drier than the Namib and Kalahari Deserts, which have an average temperature of 30 degrees. Sometimes the temperature is more than 50 degrees centigrade in the hottest months, so you have to use a lot of sun cream. The Namib Desert is older than the others. It's at least 80 million years old!

Hawaii is beautiful but is it more dangerous than you think?! The Kilauea Volcano in Hawaii is always erupting. It is more active than its neighbour volcano, the Mauna Loa (Long Mountain) which has erupted 33 times since 1843. Mauna Loa, however, is much bigger than Kilauea. It is 100 kilometres long and 50 kilometres wide – that's half of the island of Hawaii! At night you can see the beautiful colours of the erupting volcano; the bright orange and yellow of the burning lava and the blues and purples of the gases.

Listening strategy

- Discuss good ways to make listening for specific information easier.
- Focus attention on the **Listening strategy** box. Tell learners they are going to follow the suggestions to help them choose the correct options in **Activity 4**.

4 Listen

- Learners listen and choose the correct answers.
- Give class feedback on the answers.

> **Answers**
> 1 b   2 b   3 a

Language detective

- Use the audio as a starting point to discuss comparative adjectives (and base forms). Write on the board in four columns: **1** short adjectives (e.g *old*); **2** adjectives ending in *er/r*; **3** adjectives ending in *y;* **4** double letters and long adjectives. (**Note:** you will not find examples of all these in the recording.)
- Discuss the rules for forming the comparative of the adjectives.
- Ask learners the comparative form of some common adjectives.
- Learners apply the rule from the **Language detective** box in **Activity 5**. There are also suggestions for more practice in **Additional support and practice** and **Extend and challenge**.

5 🗨 Use of English

- Focus on the example and write the base form of an adjective on the board. Learners say sentences containing comparative forms (e.g. *cold*): *The Arctic is cold. It is (much) colder than the Sahara Desert*.
- Repeat this procedure with more adjectives until learners have understood the activity.
- Allow five minutes to continue the activity in pairs. Circulate and note typical errors.
- Give class feedback on the errors in form and pronunciation you have noted.

[AB] For further practice, see the Language detective box and do Activities 2 and 3 in the Activity Book.

6 ✍ Write

- Tell learners to work in small groups to write a true/false quiz about their country. Make sure they understand that everyone in the group needs to take note of their questions, because later they will be using their quiz in a different group.
- Nominate learners and elicit the kind of things they could include (mountains, beaches, forests, deserts, temperature). Elicit some statements they know are false (as well as true ones) and some examples of comparatives. Check learners realise that some of their statements must be false.
- Allow the learners sufficient time to write at least six statements for the quiz.
- Circulate and monitor, checking learners have enough knowledge to complete the task. Research their countries beforehand if necessary.

> **Answers**
> Learners' own answers – Portfolio opportunity.

7 🗨 Talk

- Learners find another group to practise their quiz with.
- Demonstrate the activity by nominating a learner to read a statement and another to try and say if it is true or false. Repeat this procedure if necessary.
- Allow five minutes for the learners to practise in groups.

> **Answers**
> Learners' own answers.

[AB] For further practice, see Activities 4 and 5 in the Activity Book.

➡ Wrap up

- To finish off, groups use the information they have just learnt to make a factsheet to put up on the wall.
- **Home–school link:** Make a photocopy of the quiz and ask the learners to take it home and see how well their families can do it.

Activity Book

1 Vocabulary

- Open the Activity Book at page 30. Focus on **Activity 1**. Learners revise adjectives for talking about natural landscapes by circling the adjective that best describes the pictures.

> **Answers**
> 1 big/dry   2 humid/beautiful   3 cold/high   4 hot/long

Language detective

- Learners use the **Language detective** box to revise the rules for forming comparative adjectives.

2 Use of English

- Learners practise using comparative adjectives by completing sentences comparing natural landscapes.

Answers
1 is shorter than
2 is cooler than
3 is hotter than
4 is more beautiful than
5 is drier than

3 📝 Write

- Further practice using comparative adjectives. Learners make sentences comparing natural landscapes.

Answers
Learners' own answers.

4 Read

- Learners read a text about Mount Everest. They look for the information to complete the fact file.

Answers
Name: Mount Everest
Location: on the border between Nepal and Tibet (China)
Height: 8850 m
Temperature: between −36°C and −60°C
Curious fact: it grows a few centimetres each year

5 📝 Challenge

- Learners use the information about Mount Kilimanjaro to write a similar text about it.

Answers
Learners' own answers.

Differentiated instruction

Additional support and practice

- Offer extra opportunities to practise sentences with comparatives. Ask two learners to come to the front of the class and write some adjectives on the board, for example: (height) *tall*, *small*; (age) *old*, *young*; (hair) *long*, *dark*, *fair*. The other learners make comparisons about them, for example: *Petra's hair is **longer** (than Sven's)*.
- Compare towns or countries. Write the name of the learners' town or city (e.g. Tokyo) and another town or city (e.g. London). Write base adjectives like *modern*, *small*, *big*, *hot*, *cold* and *wet* and encourage learners to make comparisons.
- **Photocopiable activity 6** provides further practice of comparatives.

Extend and challenge

- Learners research a town or other place that they are personally interested in and produce a piece of writing in English comparing it with the place where they live. It could be a place they studied in their geography lesson, or they can get information from travel websites and holiday brochures.

Lesson 3: Orbits

Learner's Book pages: 40–41
Activity Book pages: 32–33

Lesson objectives

Speaking: Talk about planets.

Reading: Read to check answers to a quiz and complete notes.

Writing: Create your own planet.

Critical thinking: Think about different planets, what they are like and how they are different from each other.

Language focus: Superlative adjectives.

Vocabulary: the solar system: *the planets, Mercury, Venus, Earth, Mars, Jupiter, Saturn, Uranus, Neptune, to orbit, travel around, moon, astronomers, to support life, rings*

Materials: Some interesting pictures of different planets. In the previous lesson, you could ask learners to look for some pictures.

🖙 Warm up

- Generate interest in planets. On the board write *solar system* and *planets* and the numbers 1–8. Show the pictures of planets and ask if anyone knows their names. Write the names on the board in the order of their proximity to the Sun (Mercury, Venus, Earth, Mars, Jupiter, Saturn, Uranus, Neptune).
- Ask the class what they know about planets and ask what they can see in the pictures. Use the opportunity to pre-teach some of the words in this lesson's **Vocabulary** section.
- Cover the names of the planets and have a competition to see who can recite them, preferably in order of proximity to the Sun.

1 💬 Talk about it

- Learners work in groups and they have five minutes to complete the quiz. Explain it is a competition to see which group knows the most about our solar system. Wait to check answers until after **Activity 2**.

Answers
Learners' own answers.

2 📖 Read

- Allow learners two minutes to read the text and calculate their group score. Compare scores to find the winner.

Answers
1 8
2 Mercury, Venus, Earth, Mars, Jupiter, Saturn, Uranus and Neptune
3 The Earth
4 Luna
5 less than 28 days
6 No, it is a dwarf planet.

3 📝 Read

- Use the pictures to demonstrate the words: *rings, lifeless, pale (yellow)* and *rocky*.
- Focus on the notes about Mercury. Tell learners they will read a text and make similar notes on three other planets. Allow them 5–10 minutes for this.

Language detective

- Write the title *Superlatives* on the board and ask the class to look for examples from the reading texts.
- Write examples on the board in columns: **1** short adjectives (e.g. *near*); **2** adjectives ending in *e*; **3** adjectives ending in *y*; **4** double letters; **5** long adjectives.
- Discuss the rules for forming the superlative of the adjectives.
- Have a competition in groups. Give the base form of different adjectives and see which group can say the most superlative forms in one minute.
- See suggestions for more practice in **Additional support and practice** and **Extend and challenge**.

4 💬 Talk

- Ask learners the example question about the planets using: *Which + superlative?*
- Then ask other similar questions: *Which is the largest/ fourth largest / nearest to / farthest from the Sun?*
- Allow learners two minutes to practise these questions in pairs.

Answers
Learners' own answers.

[AB] **For further practice, see Activities 1, 2, 3, 4 and 5 in the Activity Book.**

5 📝 Write

- Tell learners they are going to create their own planet. To generate interest, write questions on the board, for example: *What's its name? What colour is it? Is it rocky? How many moons has it got? Has it got any rings?*

- Allow learners time in pairs to think of ideas, before asking each pair: *What's your planet's name?*
- **Home–school link:** Allow learners 10–15 minutes to write about their planet. This task could be set for homework.

Answers
Learners' own answers – Portfolio opportunity.

📤 Wrap up

- To finish off, after correcting the errors in the writing activity, the learners' compositions can be displayed on the wall as a poster.

Activity Book

1 📖 Read

- Open the Activity Book at page 32. Focus on **Activity 1**. Learners practise superlative adjectives by completing a text with the superlative form of the adjective in brackets.

Answers
1 largest   2 longest   3 biggest   4 smallest   5 fastest

Language detective

- Learners use the **Language detective** box to revise the rule for forming superlative adjectives before they complete **Activity 2**.

2 Use of English

- Learners practise using superlative adjectives by writing superlative sentences about the planets.

Answers
2 Saturn is the most beautiful planet in the solar system.
3 Mercury is the nearest planet to the Sun.
4 Mercury is the smallest planet in the solar system.
5 Earth is the fifth largest planet in the solar system.

3 Vocabulary

- Learners practise using adjectives to talk about natural landscapes. Learners match an adjective with a picture.

Answers
1 high
2 hot
3 long
4 beautiful
5 cold
6 dry

4 Use of English

- Learners use the superlative form of the adjectives in the previous activity to complete sentences about the pictures.

5 Write

- Learners personalise their knowledge by writing a text about landscapes in their country using superlative adjectives.

Differentiated instruction

Additional support and practice

- Offer extra opportunities to practise using superlative adjectives. Write prompts on the board like *the best actor, the fastest car, the most exciting film* and ask learners for suggestions using sentences like: *The best actor is ....*
- Do an informal class survey. Write base forms on the board like *old, young* and *tall.* Ask questions with superlatives, for example: *Who is the tallest in the class?*

Extend and challenge

- **Home–school link:** Learners look for ten interesting facts, each with superlatives. They can ask family members, look on the Internet and look at fact books. Use these facts as the basis of a *Ten interesting facts* quiz.
- Vote for the most interesting facts and create a class poster to put up on the wall to remind learners of the superlative forms.

Lesson 4: Nocturnal nature

Learner's Book pages: 42–43
Activity Book pages: 34–35

Lesson objectives

Listening: Listen to facts about animals, listen for specific information, predict content.

Speaking: Talk about and describe animals.

Writing: Write a fact file.

Critical thinking: Awareness of the existence of nocturnal animals, their characteristics and their habitats.

Language focus: Order of adjectives.

Vocabulary: Animals: *barn owl, rattlesnake, springhare, racoon;* animal body parts: *claws, feathers, fur, pointed nose, paws, scales, bushy tail, habitat*

Materials: Night-time landscape picture to demonstrate *nocturnal,* pictures of savannah and rainforest animals and birds (e.g. gorilla, chimpanzee, spider monkey, jaguar, poison dart frog, parrot, macaw, toucan, anaconda). You could give learners the names of the animals in a previous lesson and ask them to look for pictures of them to bring in.

Learner's Book

👉 Warm up

- Demonstrate the meaning of *nocturnal* by showing a picture of a dark landscape. Show pictures of animals you or the learners have brought in and teach their names.
- On the board write the names of the nocturnal animals and birds on page 43 (*owl, rattlesnake, springhare* and *racoon*). Demonstrate meaning by pointing to the pictures.
- Ask: *Do owls come out at night? Have you seen one?* Repeat with other nocturnal animals.

1 💬 Talk about it

- Ask learners the questions. Work together to come up with a list of names of nocturnal animals.
- **Critical thinking:** Speculate about why these animals come out at night.

2 Listen 12

- Tell learners they are going to check their ideas (predictions) from the previous exercise.
- Listen to the text and give class feedback on the answers.

Audioscript: Track 12

Why do animals come out at night?

Animals that come out at night are called nocturnal animals. Nocturnal means 'night-time'. For a lot of animals, the night time is the best time to hunt and look for food. For small animals, like mice, it is safer to look for food at night because the darkness protects them from other animals. For animals that live in hot places, like the desert, the night time is the coolest time.

3 📝 Listen 13

- Focus on the text. Before listening, learners read it carefully and think about what they might hear.
- Learners listen to the audio and fill in the gaps. If necessary listen again, pausing the audio for the learners to write.

Audioscript: Track 13

Here we are in the dead of night, trying to catch sight of the extraordinary Giant Pangolin. This wonderful mammal makes its home here in the rainforests and savannahs of Africa. It really is the most extraordinary looking animal! There it is! Can you see? It has a small head, a long pointed nose and large brown scales on its body. It walks mainly on its back legs because its front legs have very long, sharp claws. It has a very long tongue but no teeth. It also has no ears that you can see, but it can hear very well!

This animal is a nocturnal creature. It sleeps during the day. At night it uses its strong sense of smell to find insects to eat. It loves to eat ants and uses its long thin tongue to scoop them up!

Look at the pangolin's scales! Did you know that they are made of the same material as human fingernails? These scales are very sharp and protect the pangolin from other animals. When it is asleep or afraid, it curls itself into a ball. This creature has many strange and wonderful features. Did you also know that its tongue can be 25 cm long?

Now let's have a look and see what's going on over here ...

Answers

1	Giant Pangolin	9	tongue
2	mammal	10	teeth
3	rainforests	11	ears
4	head	12	sleeps
5	nose	13	eat
6	scales	14	tongue
7	legs	15	scales
8	claws	16	tongue

4 Talk

- To generate interest, show the learners the pictures of the savannah and rainforest animals again. Have a competition to see who can say the most names in a minute. Write the animal names on the board.
- Ask learners the three questions before allowing two minutes for them to practise the dialogue in pairs.

Answers
1 Learners' own answers.
2 Learners' own answers.
3 A savannah is an area of grassland with widely spaced trees.

5 Match

- Point to one of the animal photos. Ask the class if they know what it is. Do the same for the other animals.

Answers
a owl   b rattlesnake   c springhare   d racoon

6 Word study

- Use the photos to demonstrate the meaning of the words in the box. Ask learners to point to the *wings*. Repeat the procedure for the other words in the box.

Answers
Learners' own answers.

 For further practice, see Activities 1, 2 and 3 in the Activity Book.

7 Talk

- Tell learners they are going to practise using adjectives to describe the animals in the pictures.
- Point to different features and ask for volunteers to describe them.
- Focus learners' attention on the **Writing tip**. Elicit the rule about the correct order by asking learners what each adjective describes, i.e. size, shape or colour.

Answers
Learners' own answers.

8 Write

- Tell learners they are going to choose an animal and write a fact file about it using the following headings: *Name*, *Habitat*, *Features*, *Night-time habits* and *Interesting facts*.
- Ask each learner which animal they have chosen.
- **Home–school link:** Allow learners 15 minutes to write their fact file. Offer advice if needed. This could be set for homework in a higher-level class.

Answers
Learners' own answers – Portfolio opportunity.

 For further practice, see Activities 4 and 5 in the Activity Book.

Wrap up

- To finish off, learners can present their fact files to the class. Learners could bring in a photo of their animal.
- **Home–school link:** Learners make posters to display at home.

Activity Book

1 Read

- Open the Activity Book at page 34. Focus on **Activity 1**. Learners practise the words they have learnt in the lesson for talking about animals by reading animal descriptions and matching them with pictures.

Answers
1 d   2 a   3 c   4 b

2 Vocabulary

- Revision of new words from the Learner's Book for talking about animal parts.

Answers
2 scales   3 tail   4 paws   5 claws   6 wings

3 Word study

- Learners practise using the words for animal parts. Learners say which parts animals use for various activities.

> **Answers**
> 2 eyes   3 wings   4 paws, claws   5 legs   6 teeth, fangs

4 Use of English

- Learners practise word order of adjectives which they learned in the **Writing tip** in the Learner's Book.

> **Answers**
> 2 Some owls have large wings.
> 3 Racoons have paws with short, sharp claws.
> 4 Racoons have short, black noses.
> 5 Springhares have long, brown, pointed ears and brown tails.

5 📝 Challenge

- Learners apply their newly learned vocabulary about animal parts to write a description of the animal in the picture.

> **Answers**
> Learners' own answers.

Differentiated instruction

Additional support and practice

- 🗨 Offer extra opportunities to practise the order of the adjectives. Learners have 12 pieces of paper. They each write three adjectives about size, shape and colour, and three nouns (animal parts). Then they swap with another group and practise different combinations of adjectives and nouns.
- Discuss the words they have just learnt to describe animals. Learners invent their own animals and write sentences about them using these adjectives. Encourage them to be as creative as possible.

Extend and challenge

- Children this age are often fascinated by animals. Learners could research an animal that particularly interests them using information from books or wildlife websites.
- 🗨 Alternatively, divide learners into groups and choose a country like Australia or South Africa for each group. Ask learners to look for pictures and information about typical wildlife and produce a group poster.

Lesson 5: Afraid of the dark

Learner's Book pages: 44–47

Activity Book pages: 36–37

Lesson objectives

Speaking: Talk about what happens in a poem, talk about poems in general, pronunciation: rhyming words.

Reading: Read a poem.

Critical thinking: Forming opinions about poetry.

Language focus: Review of past simple (including new irregular verbs: *sent, ate, told, shook, thought, blew, grew, heard*).

Vocabulary: Adjectives: *unwelcome, slick, clever, quick, drastic, camouflage, killer, crafty, sure, true, hairy*; verbs (and regular past simple forms): *lift, charge, snort, suck, vacuum, dress, welcome, scream, pick up, stagger, cough, collapse, accuse, curl, roll, turn out*

Materials: Illustrated books of poetry suitable for learners of this age. If any learners have previously read poems in English, encourage them to bring in poems they have enjoyed. Also, some pictures of things people are afraid of (e.g. spiders, snakes, dogs).

Note: It will not be necessary to pre-teach much of the new vocabulary as there are pictures to help learners and they should be encouraged not to worry about words they don't know. The following words will be covered in the **Word study:** *hoover, nudge, bust, cross, move, spread.*

Learner's Book

👉 Warm up

- Learners work in groups and have a competition to see who can remember the most animal words from the previous lesson (names for animals, animal body parts or adjectives used to describe them).
- Give them a time limit, before asking each group to read their lists, checking words and pronunciation are correct and announcing the winners.

> **Answers**
> Learners' own answers.

1 🗨 Talk about it

- Show learners pictures of things people might be afraid of. Compile a list and write on the board.
- Ask learners: *Are you afraid of spiders/the dark?*
- Allow learners time to ask and answer the two questions with a partner.

> **Answers**
> Learners' own answers.

Reading strategy

- Before reading, generate interest in poetry by showing the books you have brought along and encourage any learners who have enjoyed a poem in English to talk to the class about it.
- Focus attention on the poem on pages 44–46 and in particular the pictures. Discuss what the pictures show.
- Discuss with learners which strategies they have been using to read for general understanding (gist). Allow learners time to read only for gist, emphasising they do not need to worry about new words.

2 Read 14

- Focus attention on the two questions. Make sure learners understand that they are going to look only for this information and that the pictures are there to help them.
- Learners read and listen to the poem.
- Allow time to look for the answers to the question.

Audioscript: Track 14
See Learner's Book pages 44–46.

Answers
1 a creature   2 He threw a gym sneaker under the bed.

3 Word study

- Focus on the word *vacuum cleaner*. Make sure learners know the meaning and ask what part of speech it is to establish that they are going to look for a noun in the text.
- Focus attention on the blue words and encourage learners to read the sentences around them. Ask for suggestions about which word could have the same meaning. If it proves difficult, try a process of elimination, e.g. *It can't be **budge** or **bust**, because they are verbs.*
- Repeat for the other blue words.

Answers
1 Hoover   2 nudge   3 bust   4 'cross   5 budge   6 spread

4  Read

- Focus on **1**. Tell learners you are going to read the text together to look for 'He ate the insects with cheese and biscuits'. Tell them the wording might not be exactly the same.
- Read the text aloud until 'He ate them with crackers and cheese'. Write **1** next to this line in the text.
- Repeat for **2**: 'He smelt the gym shoe and fell over' stopping at 'he still wouldn't budge'.
- Learners work in pairs to find the other actions in the text and put them in the correct order. In lower-level classes, offer more support.

Answers
6, 3, 4, 1, 2, 5.

5 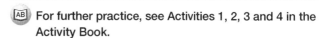 Talk

- Focus on the first question, discuss with the class and encourage learners to write answers in their notebooks.

Answers
1 He hears the creature at night.
2 He is worse than an unwelcome guest.
3 He hides under his spread.
4 The creature rolls across the floor, smashing right through the door.
5 It hides under the boy's brother's bed.
6 The creature is slick, clever and quick.

6 Pronunciation

- Read the verses, pausing at the end of each line. Encourage learners to pick out words that rhyme and write these rhyming words on the board.
- Drill pronunciation of rhyming words.

Answers
Verse 1: *night* with *light; bed* with *instead; away* with *stay.*
Verse 2: *go* with *no; guest* with *pest; nudge* with *budge.*
Verse 3: *slick* with *quick; manoeuvre* with *Hoover; spread* with *bed.*
Verse 4: *nose* with *hose; plug* with *rug; dust* with *bust.*
Verse 5: *sore* with *war; fleas* with *bees and cheese; ants* with *pants; in* with *grin.*
Verse 6: *enough* with *tough; said* with *bed; threw* with *true.*
Verse 7: *sneaker* with *weaker; air* with *fair; sneezed* with *wheeze.*
Verse 8: *nose* with *toes; ball* with *all; floor* with *door.*
Verse 9: *night* with *light; head* with*h bed; brother* with *mother.*

For further practice, see Activities 1, 2, 3 and 4 in the Activity Book.

7 Talk

- **Critical thinking:** Learners work in pairs to discuss their opinions about this and other poems. Circulate and offer support when necessary.

Answers
Learners' own answers.

Wrap up

- Finish off by asking learners to tell the class what they have learnt from their partners. Write the names of poems they have read, especially the ones they enjoyed, on the board.

Activity Book

1 Read

- Focus on **Activity 1** on page 36 of the Activity Book. Learners read the sentences about each verse before reading the poem again in the Learner's Book and matching each sentence with a verse.

Answers
1 Verse 3   2 Verse 5   3 Verse 6   4 Verse 2

2 Word study 61 [CD2 Track 34]

- Learners read verse 7 again and answer the questions. They guess the meaning of the highlighted words by looking at the pictures and imagining how the creature felt.

- Learners underline the rhyming words before listening again to the verse to check.

Audioscript: Track 61
See Activity Book page 36

- Learners look for words in the poem that match the definitions. Lower-level learners will need more guidance.

> **Answers**
> 1 Learners' own answers.
> 2 Learners' own answers.
> 3 sneaker/weaker, sneezed/wheeze, air/fair
> 4 a gasp for air b cough c stagger d collapse e sneeze

3 Write

- Learners read the last verse of the poem again and make notes about other ways to get rid of the creature, what the creature might do and who it might visit next.

> **Answers**
> Learners' own answers.

4 Challenge

- Learners apply and personalise their new knowledge. They think of rhyming words and use their notes from the previous activity to write the next lines of the poem. Offer lower-level learners more guidance.

> **Answers**
> Learners' own answers.

Differentiated instruction

Additional support and practice

- Add the irregular past simple forms to the list from **Unit 2 Lessons 5–6**.
- In **Activity 4** of the Learner's Book, some learners may require extra help because the wording in the text is often different from the wording in the activity. Circulate and monitor, offering help if necessary.
- Make some *Rhyming Words Cards*. Learners cut up an A4 sheet into 16 pieces ('cards') and write a word from the poem on each one. Learners take eight cards each and keep them face down and play a game that is similar to 'Snap'. Players take turns to put down a card face up; when the last two cards rhyme, players say *Snap*.

Extend and challenge

- **Home–school link:** Learners choose and memorise a short poem to recite for the class and at home.
- Encourage children to read more similar poems. Look on children's websites, or in the library.
- Have a competition to hunt for the *Best Poem*. Photocopy the best three and put them on the classroom wall for children to read and enjoy.

Lesson 6: Choose a project

Learner's Book pages: 48–49
Activity Book pages: 38–39

Lesson objectives

Listening: Listen to class presentations.
Speaking: Present a project to the class.
Reading: Read a poem.
Writing: Write a *cinquain* poem.

Language focus: Unit 3 review

Materials: Some photocopies giving extra information about the planets. They should contain basic information on the planets' characteristics.

Note: A *cinquain* poem is a simple poem with five lines. The poem in the example shown has a syllabic pattern of two, four, four, nine, four. However there are different kinds of *cinquain* poems with other syllabic patterns. Any five line poem with a syllabic pattern reasonably close to the example is acceptable.

Learner's Book

Warm up

- Learners should have information about their favourite planet from Lesson 3 and homework. Ask questions like: *What's your favourite planet? Have you got a picture? What do you know about it?*

> **Answers**
> Learners' own answers.

Choose a project

- Tell learners they are going to choose from the two projects and follow the instructions for the one they have decided on.

1 My favourite planet

- Explain that learners are going to tell the class about their favourite planet. Ask them to choose one and think about why it is their favourite. Prepare some photocopies with information about different planets and distribute them accordingly. Encourage learners to find out information for themselves as well on the Internet and in books from their other subjects. They should draw a picture of their chosen planet and make notes.
- Ask for a volunteer to come to the front of the class with his/her planet picture and notes.
- This learner holds up the picture for the class to see. Encourage the class to ask questions about the planet and guess which it is.
- Make a note of any new vocabulary.
- When the learner has finished, write new words on the board for the class to copy and give class feedback on errors with form and pronunciation.
- Repeat the procedure with other learners.

2 Create your own poem

- You are going to read a *cinquain* poem together and analyse the function of each line, thus providing a framework for learners to write their own poem.
- Direct learners' attention to the poem. Before you read, revise the following words from **Lesson 4**: *owl* (noun), *grasp* (verb), *prey* (noun), *sharp* (adjective), *claw* (noun).
- Read the poem slowly, demonstrating meaning by miming actions like *silent* and *grasp*.
- Project/write the poem on the board and point to the first line. Ask learners what is contained in it (the name of the subject). Repeat the procedure for the other lines, before looking at the outline in Step 2.
- Next, explain to learners that they are going to write their own poem. Tell them to look at Step 1. Elicit suggestions about each topic, before telling them to choose a subject.
- Tell the learners to write their choice down and that this is to be the first line of the poem.
- Then point out Line 2 in Step 2 and give them time to choose two adjectives to describe their chosen subject.
- Circulate and check that the first two lines reasonably resemble the pattern of the example poem.
- Repeat for Lines 3–5 from Step 2. Encourage learners to draw on their own knowledge, but offer assistance if they ask for new words and make a note of them.
- When the poems are finished, encourage learners to decorate their poems with pictures (Step 3).
- Learners read their poems to the class, or if time is short, learners exchange poems or read them out to their group.
- **Home–school link:** Learners take their poems home and read them to their families.
- Write new words on the board for the class.

⤷ Wrap up

- Learners present their work to the class.
- **Portfolio opportunity:** If possible, leave the learners' projects on display for a while. Then consider dating and filing the projects, photos or scans of the work, in learners' portfolios.

Reflect on your learning

- Reintroduce the Big question from **Lesson 1**: *What happens when we sleep?* Discuss learners' responses to the question now and compare them with their comments at the beginning of the unit. Has much changed?
- In higher-level classes use these activities as oral practice. Lower-level classes will benefit from being given time to think and write down their answers, which could then be used as future revision notes. You might like learners to work in class individually or in groups or pairs. Alternatively, you could set this task for homework/self-study.

> **Answers**
> Learners' own answers.

Look what I can do!

- **Aim:** To check learners can do all the things from **Unit 3**.
- As in **Unit 2**, there are various different approaches to these revision activities. You could nominate learners, or ask for volunteers to show the class evidence that they can do one of the things on the list. You could turn it into a competition to make it more fun for the learners.
- You might like learners to work in pairs or in groups and show their partner(s) evidence from their notebooks while you circulate and monitor.

> **Answers**
> Learners' own answers.

Activity Book

Unit 3 Revision

1 Crossword

- Open the Activity Book at page 38. Focus on **Activity 1**. Learners solve the puzzle by completing the sentences with information from each lesson. If they don't know the answers, encourage them to look back at the unit.

> **Answers**
> **Across: 3** fifty **4** at **5** long **7** on **8** nearest **11** Pluto
> **Down: 1** hotter **2** all **3** fangs **6** forest **9** Reef **10** tail

2 ✑ Challenge

- Learners make their own crossword using clues to revise what they have learned so far. Give lower-level learners extra guidance.

> **Answers**
> Learners' own answers.

My global progress

- Learners think about what they liked about **Unit 3** and what they found challenging. In addition they think about what else they could learn and how what they have learned relates to their other school subjects. This activity is a step towards independent learning and provides useful feedback for the teacher.

> **Answers**
> Learners' own answers.

> **Differentiated instruction**
>
> 🗨 Divide the class into teams and nominate learners from each team to show the relevant part of their notebooks. Award them points for the content of what they show. The team with the most points at the end is the winner.

4 Homes

Big question What do people build?

Unit overview

In this unit learners will:
- talk about different types of homes
- talk and read about places in town
- write about a landmark in their town or city
- understand and enjoy an extract from children's literature.

Learners will learn about different kinds of buildings, building materials and parts of a house. They will use this new knowledge to design their own novelty house. They will continue to develop listening skills by hearing other learners talking about their homes, and about other buildings and speculating about what buildings might be used for. Learners will develop their speaking abilities by describing their home and asking about other people's homes.

Learners will practise and extend their vocabulary by reading an extract from *The Hobbit*. At the end of the unit, learners will apply and personalise what they have learned by creating their dream home or writing about a landmark in their town.

Language focus
Question tags

Modals of prohibition

Present perfect

Vocabulary topics: Houses and building materials, places in a town and landmarks, adjectives to describe personal appearance.

Self-assessment
- I can express an opinion about different types of homes.
- I can identify the materials used to build a house.
- I can talk about the places in my town.
- I can identify world landmarks.
- I can write about a famous landmark in my country.
- I can understand an extract from children's literature.
- I can talk about how to be a responsible person.

Teaching tip

Review learners' performance in the **Reading strategy** and reading exercises to see if they are developing the necessary strategies for reading for specific information or if they need more revision of reading strategies. Remind them that if they develop the skill of looking for specific information effectively, reading will be easier and more fun.

Lesson 1: Homes

Learner's Book pages: 50–51
Activity Book pages: 40–41

Lesson objectives

Listening: Describe homes.

Reading: Read about eco-homes.

Speaking: Talk about different types of house.

Critical thinking: Awareness of different kinds of homes and different building materials.

Vocabulary: *detached house, terraced house, high-rise flat, eco-house, bungalow, hut, stairs, tree house, stone, mud, wood, natural resources, materials found in the rubbish tip, wood burner, to heat*

Materials: Some pictures of homes from around the world, including eco-houses (if possible, pictures of Simon Dale's hobbit house which are available on the Internet) – you could ask learners to bring in a picture of their home or another home they find interesting.
Photocopiable activity 7.

Learner's Book

☞ Warm up

- To raise interest in the topic of the unit, show learners some pictures of houses. Use the opportunity to pre-teach words like *(semi-)detached house, terraced house, high-rise flat, eco-house,* and *bungalow.*
- Ask learners: *Do you live in a house or a flat? Is it a high-rise flat? Is it a (semi-)detached, terraced house? Is it a bungalow? Is it an eco-house?*

1 ☾ Talk about it

- **Critical thinking:** Introduce the Big question: *What do people build?* Discuss this with the learners. Write down their ideas and save them for the end of the unit.
- Focus on the words and the pictures. Ask learners which type of home goes with which picture.
- Allow learners a few moments to ask and answer questions about the pictures with their partners.

Answers
a detached house
b bungalow
c hut
d high-rise flats
e eco-house
f terraced house

2 ▨ Listen 15

- Ensure learners use the strategies they know to help with listening. Help them make predictions about what they might hear by asking them what they can see in the pictures (building materials, size and number of floors). In lower-level classes, ask learners what they like about these types of homes, so that they will have ideas about what they might hear on the recording.

- Listen to the first speaker and pause the audio. Check learners have understood the kind of information they are listening for before listening to the other speakers.

Audioscript: Track 15

1: I live in a bungalow which has only got one floor. The kitchen, living room, dining room and office are at the front of the house and all the bedrooms and the bathroom are at the back. I love it because I don't have to walk up and down the stairs all the time!

2: I live in a hut, with my family. It's a type of shelter made of mud, stones and wood. In my community all the families live in these types of shelters. We live very close together. I like where I live because there are lots of children to play with.

3: I live in an ecological home. It has a low impact effect on the environment because we use solar energy to heat our water and our house. I like it because it's very modern and comfortable.

4: I live in a small, terraced house with my family. It forms part of a long line of houses along a road. I love it because there's a park at the back and lots of my friends live in the same street.

5: I live very high up, in a high-rise flat on the 25th floor. I live with my family and my cat. I like where I live because we have incredible views of Tokyo and Mount Fuji.

6: I live in a large, detached house with my family in a green, leafy area of Boston. I love where I live because I can ride my bike in the street and my best friend lives next door.

Answers
1b A bungalow. He loves it because he doesn't have to walk up and down the stairs.
2c A hut. She likes it because there are lots of children to play with.
3e An eco-house. He likes it because it's very modern and comfortable.
4f A terraced house. She loves it because there's a park at the back and lots of her friends live in the same street.
5d A high-rise flat. He likes it because the flat has incredible views of Tokyo and Mount Fuji.
6a A detached house. She loves where she lives because she can ride her bike in the street and her best friend lives next door.

3 ☾ Talk

- Talk through different expressions for describing homes from the beginning of the lesson and the audio.
- In lower-level classes, check learners can manage the activity by asking the questions as a class before allowing time to work in pairs.

Answers
Learners' own answers.

4 ☾ Talk

- Come up with adjectives that learners could use to compare different kinds of homes and revise comparative forms. Try to include short adjectives like *small* and longer adjectives like *comfortable.*
- Again, in lower-level classes, check learners can manage the activity before working in pairs.

For further practice, see Activities 1, 2 and 3 in the Activity Book.

5 Read

- **Critical thinking:** Show pictures of *eco-houses*, if possible, including Simon Dale's hobbit house. Discuss what might make a house 'ecological' and make predictions about what the text might say to make reading easier.
- Learners read the text quickly to check if they were right.

Answers

It is a house which uses natural resources like water and energy efficiently.

6 Read

- Make sure learners understand the specific information they are looking for and allow them time to check their ideas and look for the relevant parts of the text.

Answers

recycled materials, rubbish tip, local materials like stone, metal, wood and mud, built into the hillside, natural resources, wood burner, big windows, solar panels, collect rain water

7 Word study

- Learners read the text again and look for the words for the materials the family used.
- Have a competition to see who can remember the most materials used for building the eco-house. Cover the text and give learners one minute in pairs to write.

Answers

recycled materials, stone, metal, wood, mud, wooden beams from trees

8 Talk

- **Critical thinking:** Think about some good and bad things about living in the hobbit house.
- Allow time for learners to discuss the questions with a partner. Tell them to remember their partner's answers.

Answers

Learners' own answers.

 For further practice, see Activities 4, 5 and 6 in the Activity Book.

Wrap up

- To finish off, ask learners to tell the class about what they have found out from their partners.

Activity Book

1 Vocabulary

- Open the Activity Book at page 40. Focus on **Activity 1**. Learners revise the words they have learnt for the different kinds of homes.

Answers

1 detached house   2 bungalow   3 hut   4 eco-home

2 Listen 62 [CD2 Track 35]

- Learners listen to Talya and say what kind of home she lives in.

Audioscript: Track 62

Hello, my name's Talya and I live in Turkey. I live in a city called Istanbul. It's a very big and busy city. Ten million people live in this city and it has got the biggest sea port in Turkey. I live near my family and friends and I visit my grandparents a lot. They live in the old part of the city – their house is traditional and it's made of wood. I love their house because it's big and old. My friend Nadide lives in the city centre – I go to her house after school sometimes to do our homework. I like her house because it's very modern and comfortable, but I love my house the most because my bedroom is cool and we've got a football net in our garden! I live outside the city in an eco-home, so it uses energy efficiently. We have solar panels on the roof to heat the house and to give us electricity. It's very modern and has big windows – my favourite room is at the top because there are big windows in the roof. I can watch the clouds in the sky.

Answers

Talya lives in Turkey. She lives in an eco-home.

3 Listen 62 [CD2 Track 35]

- Learners listen for more information about Talya and choose the correct answer.

Answers

1 b in a big city   2 b 10 million   3 b wooden
4 c modern

4 Read

- Revision of vocabulary connected to eco-homes. Learners complete the text using words from the lesson.

Answers

2 recycled   3 energy efficient   4 natural resources
5 solar panels

5 Vocabulary

- Learners unscramble anagrams to make words for materials that they have learned in the lesson.

Answers

1 stone   2 glass   3 metal   4 wood

6 📝 Challenge

- Learners apply and personalise the newly learned vocabulary about building materials and parts of a building to describe a castle.

> **Answers**
> Learners' own answers.

Differentiated instruction

Additional support and practice

- Using the information from the **Activity 2** in the Learner's Book as a model, learners write about their homes. They should include what kind of home it is, a drawing, some information about building materials, and why they like (or dislike) living there. Mix up the descriptions, and ask learners to guess which house belongs to who.
- Practise talking about where people live using **Photocopiable activity 7: *Questions about people's homes***.

Extend and challenge

- Have a competition to find the most interesting eco-building. Encourage learners to look on websites and in libraries. Give a word limit and write a paragraph beginning *I think this is the most interesting eco-building because ... .*
- 📢 Learners work in groups and design their own eco-home. Encourage the use of materials from the rubbish tip. Make sure learners provide a drawing and label the parts of the house and the materials they have used. Make posters and ask groups to present their homes to the class.

Lesson 2: Strange buildings

Learner's Book pages: 52–53
Activity Book pages: 42–43

Lesson objectives

Reading: Read for information needed to label the parts of a house.

Listening: Listen for information to complete sentences.

Writing: Describe a strange building.

Critical thinking: Novelty buildings and what they are used for.

Language focus: Modals of probability.

Vocabulary: Parts of buildings: *roof, well*; what buildings are used for: *spaceship, museum, shopping centre, petrol station, library*

Materials: Pictures of novelty buildings in different parts of the world.

Photocopiable activity 8.

Learner's Book

👉 Warm up

- Have a competition in teams to see how many words about homes learners can remember from the previous lesson.
- Show learners pictures of novelty buildings and ask questions using the words from the last lesson. *Is it a detached/terraced house/bungalow/hut/castle? Is it a high-rise flat/eco-home/tree house? Is it built of stone/mud/wood/natural resources/ materials found in the rubbish tip? Are there any stairs/windows/solar panels? Is there a roof/a garden?*
- If the building looks like a plane, coffee pot, doughnut, etc. ask: *Does it look like a ...? What does it look like?* Start to introduce the concept of *It must be a ...* when something is almost certain and *It might/ could be a ...* when something is possible but not certain.

1 💬 Talk about it

- Focus on the photos of strange buildings on page 52 of the Learner's Book. Ask learners the questions.
- **Critical thinking:** Ask why people would want buildings that look so different.

> **Answers**
> Learners' own answers.

2 📝 Listen 16

- Focus on the sentences and tell learners they are going to listen to some children talking about the buildings in the photos.
- Write the modals *must, might* and *could* on the board.
- Tell learners to listen for these verbs and choose the correct one to complete each sentence.

> **Audioscript:** Track 16
>
> **a**
> – Well, I think this building is in a city because I can see tall buildings to the right of the picture. What do you think it could be?
>
> – Well, I can see lots of books, so it must be a library.
>
> **b**
> – It's a very small building and it looks like a teapot! What do you think it could be?
>
> – I can see three petrol pumps in front of it, so it can't be a house.
>
> **c**
> – Wow, this building is really strange! It's very sci-fi, isn't it? What do you think it could be?
>
> – Well, it looks like a spaceship to me, but perhaps it could be a museum.

d

– This building must be in the country because we can see some green grass. What do you think it could be?

– I think it might be a house, but it must be very small inside. Those rocks are enormous!

e

– Wow! This building doesn't look real to me. What do you think it could be?

– Well, it's very modern. I think it could be a shopping centre.

Answers
a must **b** can't **c** could **d** might **e** could

 For further practice, see Activities 1, 2, 3 and 4 in the Activity Book.

Language detective

- Look back at the sentences from the previous activity. Read out each sentence and then look at the pictures they refer to in order to encourage learners to guess the meaning from the context.
- Focus on the sentences in the **Language detective** box in the Learner Book (page 53) and check learners understand the phrase *It can't be a house.*
- For practice of modals, see **Additional support and practice**.

3 Talk

- Before allowing learners to work in pairs, demonstrate the activity with an example. Focus on photo **e** (bottom right-hand corner). Discuss how the building is probably a shopping centre.
- In lower-level classes, more examples may be necessary.

Answers
Learners' own answers.

4 Listen 17

- Learners listen to the recording to check their predictions about what the buildings are used for.

Audioscript: Track 17
Teacher: Children, be quiet, please.

Photo **a** is in Kansas City, USA. The face of the building is decorated with large multi-coloured books. What kind of building do you think it is?

Pupil 1: It must be a library.

Teacher: That's right. Well done! Photo **b** is a small petrol station located in Zillah in the USA. It was built in 1922 and is believed to be the oldest petrol station in the country. It is curious because of its teapot-shaped office behind the petrol pumps.

Photo **c** is The Atomium monument in Brussels. What do you think it is?

Pupil 2: It looks like a space station to me.

Teacher: Well it's not a space station. It's an example of futuristic architecture and was built for the World Fair in 1958. It is now a museum and holds many exhibitions every year.

Photo **d** is a very peculiar house in Portugal. It has been built between two enormous rocks and if you look closely you can see the small window and door. Would you like to live in this house David?

Pupil 3: Oh no Miss! I'd probably get crushed by the big rocks!

Teacher: Photo **e**: This is the National Theatre of Beijing in China. It is a dome-shaped building which is surrounded by an artificial lake. People say it looks like an egg floating on water!

Pupils: Yes, it does!

Answers
a a library
b a small petrol station
c a museum
d a house
e a theatre

5 Read

- Focus on the picture of the mushroom house. Ask questions like the ones in the **Warm up**.
- Allow learners time to read the text and write labels for the house. Circulate and check they have done so correctly.

Answers
a solar panel **b** roof garden **c** large windows **d** well

6 Over to you

- Tell learners they are going to draw and write about their own strange building. Talk about ideas for the form of the building and what it is made from. Build up a list on the board.
- Ask learners about the building they have decided on, what it's made from and its special features.
- Learners draw a picture and write about the building by answering the questions in the activity.
- Circulate and offer help and suggestions.

Answers
Learners' own answers – Portfolio opportunity.

7 Talk

- Demonstrate the activity with an example. Ask a learner to describe his/her building to the class. More examples may be necessary in lower-level classes before learners work together in pairs. Make sure learners know they should remember their partners' descriptions.

Answers
Learners' own answers.

🖙 Wrap up

- Display learners' work where it can be seen by everyone.
- Ask for volunteers to say what they remember about their partners' buildings. The class guess which picture they are describing.

Activity Book

1 Vocabulary

- Focus on **Activity 1** on page 42 of the Activity Book. Learners unscramble the anagrams to revise words for places from the Learner's Book.

> **Answers**
> **1** school **2** museum **3** library **4** shop **5** theatre **6** house

Language detective

- Learners revise the use of modals of probability to think about possible situations in the present.

2 Use of English

- Practise using modals of probability to think about possible situations in the present. Learners choose the correct modal for each situation.

> **Answers**
> **1** might **2** can't **3** must **4** could

3 Use of English

- This activity provides further practice using modals of probability. Learners complete the sentences with the correct modal.

> **Answers**
> **2** might **3** can't **4** might **5** might **6** must

4 Word study

- Learners use the words they have learned to complete a description of a novelty building.

> **Answers**
> Learners' own answers.

Differentiated instruction

Additional support and practice

- Give learners more practice with modals. Ask them to speculate about the use of the other buildings in the photographs you have brought.
- **Home–school link:** For extra practice about the parts of a house, learners draw a picture of their house and label it. They can take the picture home to share with parents/carers.

Extend and challenge

- 🗨 Use **Photocopiable activity 8 to** play *Modal Dominoes.*
- Novelty buildings can be fascinating for children of this age. Have a competition to find the best novelty building. There is plenty of information on the Internet – try searching under *Buildings that look like animals/ships.* Alternatively try the library.

Lesson 3: Out and about

Learner's Book pages: 54–55
Activity Book pages: 44–55

Lesson objectives

Listening: Listen for gist.

Speaking: Talk about places in town.

Pronunciation: Intonation in question tags.

Reading: Read a quiz, complete a chart.

Critical thinking: Classify information.

Language focus: Question tags: *I'd like, I'd prefer.*

Vocabulary: places: *town hall, box office, castle grounds, sports centre;* entertainment: *fairground rides, carnival, musicians, magicians, bands, events, dressing up, charities, funds raised, outdoor*

Materials: Pictures of children of 8–10 years participating in sports days, carnivals, and other outdoor summer activities like concerts. You could encourage learners to bring in pictures of their own.

Photocopiable activity 8(ii).

Note

Sports Days

There are sports days in many countries; some are organised by schools. In primary schools, often traditional games are played. In the UK, typical games are the *sack race* or the *egg and spoon race.*

Learner's Book

🖙 Warm up

- Talk through the modal verbs from the previous lesson and write them on the board.
- Show pictures of children participating in different activities and write the names of these on the board.
- Learners mime the events they have seen. The class guesses what the event is. Encourage learners to use the modal verbs on the board.

1 🗨 Talk about it

- Discuss the questions as a class, building up a list of *Places* learners go and *Activities* they do and *Dates* (with *on*) and *Times* (with *at*) on the board.
- To prepare learners for the reading exercise, ask *Why?* questions similar to the ones they will be answering in the table in **Activity 2**.

- Allow learners time to ask and answer questions with a partner.

> **Answers**
> Learners' own answers.

Reading strategy

- Discuss when and how we read for specific information and why this skill is useful.

2 📝 Read

- Generate interest by asking learners what they can see in the photos in the Learner's Book. Write up any new words they need to describe the photos.
- **Critical thinking:** Learners read the adverts and look for the specific information that is missing from the table.

Answers

	Advert 1	Advert 2	Advert 3
What?	Outdoor summer concert	Blue Box Sports Day	Carnival
Where?	Penleave Castle	Ralley Road Sports Centre Field	Town Park
When?	26th June	5th July	10th July
What time?	7 pm	11 am	11 am
Other information	Free parking in the castle grounds	Food, drink and fairground rides. All funds raised go to charity.	The theme of the Carnival is our favourite cartoon characters! Fun and entertainment with musicians, magicians and bands.

 For further practice, see Activity 1 in the Activity Book.

3 💬 Talk

- Demonstrate the activity by asking a few learners the questions before allowing time to ask and answer with a partner.
- For extra practice using *I'd prefer/I'd like,* see **Additional support and practice** and **Extend and challenge**.

> **Answers**
> Learners' own answers.

4 📝 Listen 18

- Check learners understand they need to listen only for the gist of the conversations.
- If necessary, re-play the recording, pausing after each speaker.

> **Audioscript:** Track 18
>
> **1**
>
> **Girl 1:** You're going to the carnival, aren't you, Faye?
>
> **Girl 2:** Yes, I am. Your sister is dressing up, isn't she?
>
> **Girl 1:** Yes, I think so. Oops, there's the bell. I've got to go to Maths class, now. See you later!
>
> **2**
>
> **Boy 1:** You've got a brother who plays for the local football team, haven't you?
>
> **Boy 2:** Yes, I have. He's a striker and a good one too! He's playing at the Blue Box Sports Day. You play football, don't you?
>
> **Boy 1:** No, not much. I prefer basketball. I've just been playing on the indoor court. Do you fancy doing some shooting practice?
>
> **Boy 2:** OK then, let's go!
>
> **3**
>
> **Girl:** I'm going to the outdoor concert this week.
>
> **Boy:** Really? It starts at 7 o'clock, doesn't it?
>
> **Girl:** Yes. Why don't you come? Your mum won't mind, will she?
>
> **Boy:** I'll ask her tonight. The Sting Ray Rappers are playing, aren't they? I love them.
>
> **Girl:** I know – I can't wait.

> **Answers**
> **1** Carnival   **2** Blue Box Sports Day   **3** The outdoor concert

Language detective

- Write an example of a sentence with a question tag on the board. Check learners understand what they are used for.
- Work together to come up with a list of examples from the listening activity. Drill pronunciation, including correct intonation.
- Focus on the **Language detective** box and ask learners for new examples.
- For extra practice using question tags, see **Additional support and practice** at the end of the lesson.

5 Pronunciation 19

- Learners listen to the recording carefully and repeat. Insist on correct intonation.

> **Audioscript:** Track 19
>
> 1 You're going to the carnival, aren't you?
>
> 2 Your sister is dressing up, isn't she?
>
> 3 You play football, don't you?
>
> 4 It starts at 7 o'clock, doesn't it?

6 📝 💬 Talk

- Ask a learner to say sentences about his/her partner and write them on the board. Help learners form a question by eliciting the correct question tag. For example:
  Yolanda is going to the carnival, isn't she?
  Chanta plays football, doesn't she?
- Learners write five statements about their partners and add tags to make them into a question. Circulate and check they have formed the question tags correctly.
- Allow learners time to ask and answer questions with a partner. Circulate and monitor.

> **Answers**
> Learners' own answers.

📖 For further practice, see the Language detective box and Activities 2, 3 and 4 in the Activity Book.

🔁 Wrap up

- Learners report back to the class as follows:
  Learner 1 reads out a statement about his/her partner.
  Learner 2 makes a tag question and asks Learner 1.
  Learner 1 replies.

  Learner 1 (Yolanda's partner) *Yolanda is going to the carnival.*

  Learner 2 (from another pair) *Yolanda is going to the carnival, isn't she?*

  Learner 1 (Yolanda's partner) *Yes, she is./No, she isn't.*

Activity Book

1 📝 Read

- Open the Activity Book at page 44. Focus on the sentences in **Activity 1**. Learners read the advertisements and find out if the sentences are true or false.

> **Answers**
> **2** false (Admission is free.)
> **3** true
> **4** true
> **5** false (It's about a school like no other.)
> **6** false (He is a local footballer.)
> **7** true
> **8** false (Everyone is welcome.)

Language detective

- Learners use the **Language detective** box to revise the form and use of question tags.

2 Listen 63 [CD2 Track 36]

- Learners listen to the children and say where they decide to go at the weekend.

> **Audioscript:** Track 63
> **Aiden:** What do you want to do at the weekend?
> **Cali:** I don't know. *School Rocks 3* is on at the cinema, isn't it?
> **Aiden:** Hmmm, I don't want to see that. There's a street dance class at the town hall.
> **Cali:** You can dance, can't you?
> **Aiden:** Yes, but it starts at 5pm, doesn't it?
> **Cali:** Yes, you're right. We could go to the bowling alley. It's open all day, isn't it?
> **Aiden:** Yes, it is. Let's go bowling then!

> **Answers**
> They decide to go to the bowling alley.

3 Pronunciation 64 [CD2 Track 37]

- Learners complete the dialogues with question tags. They then listen to the correct intonation.

> **Answers**
> **1** isn't it? **2** can't you? **3** doesn't it? **4** isn't it?

4 📝 Challenge

- Learners apply and personalise what they have learned from **Activities 1** and **3** by writing a dialogue making plans for the weekend.

> **Answers**
> Learners' own answers.

> **Differentiated instruction**
> **Additional support and practice**
>
> - 💬 If learners enjoyed playing dominoes with **Photocopiable activity 8**, make some *Question Tag Dominoes*. Use the same format for the dominoes. On the right-hand side of each domino, write a statement, for example: *You are going tomorrow,* followed by a comma. On the left of the next domino write the corresponding question tag, in this case *aren't you?* Photocopy one set for each pair of learners. Learners cut the cards up carefully! To play, instead of matching numbers, players play a domino which completes the question.
> - Give extra opportunities to practise: *I'd like to ...* and *I'd prefer ... .* Write prompts on the board like: *eat: chocolate or cheese? travel: by car or train?* Use these prompts to help learners form sentences: *I'd like/prefer to eat chocolate.*

Extend and challenge

- Learners research what happens at school sports days at primary schools in different countries. They look for pictures and descriptions of a traditional game that is played. They present the information to the class and the class guess the country. Alternatively they could find information about what happens at carnivals around the world.
- For extra practice using *I'd like to*, learners write a paragraph with the title: *What I'd like to do at the weekend.* They say *what, where, when* and *why*.

Lesson 4: Famous places

Learner's Book pages: 56–57

Activity Book pages: 46–47

Lesson objectives

Speaking: Interview a partner.

Reading: Read about how to get to Machu Picchu.

Writing: Write about a famous landmark.

Language focus: Present perfect.

Vocabulary: Scenery: *mountain, peak, lush forest, spectacular, landmark;* people: *emperor, explorer,* travel: *region, trek, route, discovered, spiritual*

Materials: A world map, some adhesive and some labels; some pictures of beautiful and varied scenes, preferably showing vocabulary from the unit like *mountain, peak, lush forest, spectacular, landmark.*

Learner's Book

Warm up

- Generate interest in the topic of famous places by showing the class photos of famous landmarks from around the world. Ask what you can see in the photos and pre-teach some of the lesson's vocabulary.
- Ask learners about the places in the photos, for example: *Have you been to China? Have you seen the Great Wall of China?* In the case of a positive answer, attach a label with the learner's name to the world map.
- If no one has visited any of the places, you could change the question to: *Have you heard about the Great Wall of China?* or *Would you like go to ... ?*

1 Read

- Focus on the tour guide leaflet. Ask questions about what you can see in the picture. Check learners know the words *mountain, peak* and *spectacular views.* Encourage learners to guess where it is before showing them on the world map.
- If you and your class are not familiar with this area of the world, ask if anyone has been to Peru, or if anyone knows anything about Peru or the Incas.

- Allow time for learners to read and find the answers to the questions in the text.
- Learners tell the class their answers to the questions.

> **Answers**
> Learners' own answers.

2 Read

- Focus on the three questions and discuss which reading strategy learners should use before allowing them time to read the text again and look for the information.

> **Answers**
> 1 Old Mountain
> 2 It was discovered by American explorer Hiram Bingham in 1911
> 3 the Inca Trail

 For further practice, see Activities 1, 2 and 3 in the Activity Book.

Language detective

- Focus attention on the question: *Have you been to Peru?* Ask learners if they know what the name of this verb tense is and if the present perfect refers to a specific time. Make sure they understand it is used because it is a general question about all time up until now, not a specific time.
- Focus on the **Language detective** box and elicit more examples of the present perfect.
- Practise using the present perfect by asking learners to give examples of things they have done and by asking them present perfect questions.

 For further practice, see the Language detective box and Activity 4 in the Activity Book.

3 Talk

- Ask learners the past participles of the five verbs in the activity (*visited, seen, climbed, been,* and *travelled*). Ask how to form the question (*Have you visited/been ...?*).
- Circulate and monitor learners as they ask and answer questions in pairs.

> **Answers**
> Learners' own answers.

Writing tip

- Focus on the **Writing tip.** Talk through a list of adjectives which learners can use later in the writing activity. Ask questions to check learners know the position of the adjective in the sentence.

4 Word study

- Check learners know the meaning of the adjectives in blue. Encourage them to work out any meanings they don't know from the context and by using the pictures.
- Focus on the photographs and ask learners for suggestions.

5 📝 Over to you

- Learners choose a landmark. Ask which one they have chosen, before they look for information and write their paragraphs for homework.
- Encourage learners to use the reading text in **Activity 1** about Peru as a model for their writing.

Writing strategy

- Make sure learners use the **Writing strategy** to help. You could demonstrate with an example.

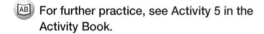 For further practice, see Activity 5 in the Activity Book.

📢 Wrap up

- Learners present their writing to the class who guess which landmark they are talking about.

Activity Book

1 Read

- Open the Activity Book at page 46. Focus on **Activity 1**. Learners practise paragraph summarising skills by reading a text about the Pyramids and matching each heading with a paragraph.

2 Vocabulary

- Learners replace the simple adjectives in the text with more sophisticated adjectives from the list.

3 Read

- Learners read the text again and look for specific information about the Pyramids.

Language detective

- Learners use the **Language detective** box to revise the form and use of the present perfect to speak about experiences when it is not important to specify when we did something.

4 Use of English

- Learners practise forming sentences using the present perfect.

5 📝 Write

- Learners write an account of a famous place they have visited. If necessary, use **Activity 1** in the Learner's Book as a model to show learners the kind of things they can include about the history and travel information.

Differentiated instruction

Additional support and practice

- 💬 Practise adjectives more by talking about scenery and landmarks. Distribute one of the pictures you have brought to each group of learners. Learners describe the pictures and then swap pictures with other groups.

Extend and challenge

- Start a list of past participles for the classroom wall with the title: *Have you been to ... ?* Leave plenty of space to add new verbs to the list as learners encounter them.
- Make some **Question prompt cards**. Talk through common irregular past participles. Help learners if they don't know them. Learners cut up an A4 piece of paper into eight pieces and choose eight verbs. Write an infinitive on each piece of paper. Use the cards as the basis for mini dialogues: learners take a card and read the verb, for example: *climb → Have you climbed a mountain? No, I haven't.* The cards can be used for other grammatical structures, for example: present simple, past simple.

Lesson 5: *The Hobbit*

Learner's Book pages: 58–61

Activity Book pages: 48–49

Lesson objectives

Listening and reading: Listen to and read a story extract from *The Hobbit*.

Speaking: Talk about ways of being responsible.

Critical thinking: Identify and understand fantasy stories.

Study skills: Answer multiple-choice questions.

Values: Being a responsible person.

Vocabulary: Revision and expansion of vocabulary from the unit.

Materials: A copy of *The Hobbit* by J.R.R. Tolkien.

Learner's Book

Warm up

- Revise words for talking about buildings, materials and parts of a house. Have a competition between teams to see how many they can think of in a limited time.

1 🗪 Talk about it

- Discuss the questions as a class. Discuss what learners know about hobbits.
- **Critical thinking:** Discuss what a fantasy story is. Do learners like fantasy stories? Why? Why not? What makes a fantasy story? Do they think *The Hobbit* is a fantasy story?

> **Answers**
> Learners' own answers.

2 Read and listen 🔊

- Explain that this is a famous story that was written many years ago. Over time, writing styles change. This style might be unfamiliar to learners and will have new words but this is part of the challenge and pleasure of reading new stories.
- As there are high-level words in the text, discuss strategies for dealing with any difficulties this may cause.
- Focus on the paragraph headings and discuss what information might be in each paragraph. Use the pictures to help discuss ideas about what the hobbit's house might look like. Encourage the use of modals and words from the **Warm up**.
- Allow sufficient time for learners to read and listen to the extract and match the headings.

> **Audioscript:** Track 20
> See Learner's Book pages 58–60.

> **Answers**
> a 2 b 1 c 3

3 Read

- Learners read multiple-choice questions 1–5. Remind them to look only for the specific information and then allow time to read the story again quickly to find the answers.

> **Answers**
> 1 b and c
> 2 c
> 3 c
> 4 a

4 📝 Read

- Learners skim the text to look for the adjectives to describe what Baggins is like.

> **Answers**
> well-to-do, respectable

5 📝 Read

- Read the definitions. Ask questions to check learners have understood them. Focus on the words in blue in the text.
- Demonstrate strategies for the activity with an example. Look at the first of the blue words *oozy*. It is likely learners will not know this word. Use the context to help learners guess.
- Ask questions to check learners know *oozy* is an adjective. Eliminate the definitions which are not adjectives.
- With lower-level classes, more examples will be necessary.

> **Answers**
> 1 oozy   2 time out of mind   3 respectable
> 4 well-to-do   5 meadows   6 porthole

6 📝 Read

- Focus on the questions. Allow learners time to re-read and look for the answers.

> **Answers**
> 1 It's comfortable.
> 2 These were the best rooms and the only rooms to have windows.
> 3 A hall, bedrooms, bathrooms, cellars, pantries, kitchens and dining rooms.
> 4 A long time
> 5 They never had any adventures or did anything unexpected.

📖 For further practice, see Activities 1, 2, 3 and 4 in the Activity Book.

7 🗨 Talk

- Discuss some ideas as a class about the characteristics of the hobbit house and adjectives to describe hobbits before allowing learners time to answer the questions in pairs.

Answers
Learners' own answers.

8 Values

- Talk about things that responsible people do and make a list on the board.
- Focus on the list of values. Check that learners understand all the words in the activity and discuss which sentences best describe a responsible person.
- See **Additional support and practice** for more practice of speaking about being responsible.

Answers
Learners' own answers.

9 🗨 Talk

- Discuss some ideas as a class before allowing learners time to answer the questions in pairs. Tell them to make notes.

Answers
Learners' own answers.

 For further practice, see Activities 5 and 6 in the Activity Book.

🗳 Wrap up

- Learners tell the class about how they are responsible.

Activity Book

1 Read

- Focus on **Activity 1** on page 48 of the Activity Book. Learners reread the text from *The Hobbit* on pages 58–60 of the Learner's Book and write whether the sentences are true or false.

Answers
2 true
3 false (They had neighbours.)
4 false (They liked them because they never had any adventures.)

2 Vocabulary

- Learners read the sentences and match the words in bold with their opposites.

Answers
1 worst 2 dull

3 Vocabulary

- Learners are to complete the description of *The Hobbit* and draw a picture.

Answers
1 height 2 fat 3 shoes 4 brown 5 heads 6 fingers

4 Values

- This activity tests learners' understanding of what is meant by being responsible.

Answers
Learners' own answers.

5 📝 Challenge

- Learners explain why they think one of the people mentioned in **Activity 4** is responsible.

Answers
Learners' own answers.

Differentiated instruction

Additional support and practice

- Practise talking about why and how people are responsible. Choose the names of jobs, for example *teachers, police officers*. Talk about why and how they are responsible.

Extend and challenge

- Watch scenes from the film *The Hobbit* in English.
- Learners write a review of the film *The Hobbit* or another film they have seen. They should include information about actors, the plot and where it is set. They read the description to the class who guess which film it is.

Lesson 6: Choose a project

Learner's Book pages: 62–63
Activity Book pages: 50–51

Lesson objectives

Speaking and writing: Talking and writing about *My dream home* or *A landmark in my town*.

Language focus: Unit 4 Review

Materials: Some pictures of interesting houses that could be considered dream homes, pictures of local landmarks.

Learner's Book

Warm up

- Tell learners they are going to choose one of the projects: *My dream home* or a *Landmark in my town*.

Choose a project

- Give learners ideas for **Project 1** and revise vocabulary for kinds of buildings, parts of buildings and building materials. Show the learners the *dream home* pictures and ask them to describe them. Ask: *Would you like to live there? Why? Why not?*
- Give learners ideas for **Project 2** and revise vocabulary for landmarks, their history and travelling to them. Give a time limit and have a competition to see who can think of most landmarks in their town. If learners come from villages, they could think about their village, or if this is too limiting, landmarks in their province, county or region. Learners with the most landmarks read their list, so the others can check.
- Learners can work on these individually or in pairs or small groups.

1 My dream home

- Divide the board in half horizontally. On half of the board, talk through a list of features a dream home might have and possible locations.
- Focus on the four steps. Give learners support by choosing a picture of a dream home and asking learners the questions from the four steps. Write some ideas on the board.
- Learners use these ideas to write about the home they have chosen. Circulate and give help and advice, especially about paragraph structure.

2 A landmark in my town

- If learners are interested in this project, tell them to find information in one of the ways listed in the Learner's Book.
- Give support by providing an example of a landmark and showing a picture. Focus on the four steps in the Learner's Book and discuss suggestions for each step.
- Learners use these ideas to write about the landmark they have chosen. Circulate and give help and advice, especially about paragraph structure.

Wrap up

- Learners present their ideas to the class.
- **Portfolio opportunity:** If possible, leave the learners' projects on display for a while. Then consider dating and filing the projects, photos or scans of the work, in learners' portfolios.

Reflect on your learning

- Reintroduce the big question from **Lesson 1:** *What do people build?* Discuss learners' responses to the question now and compare them with their comments at the beginning of the unit. Has much changed?
- Learners work in pairs and make notes about the things people build. In a lower-level class, discuss together and write ideas on the board.

> **Answers**
> Learners' own answers.

Look what I can do!

- **Aim:** To check learners can do all the things from **Unit 4**.
- Whichever approach you choose for these revision activities, remember to give support to lower-level learners and use the activities as an opportunity to assess what learners have learnt. As always, use this information to customise your teaching as you go on to **Unit 5**.

> **Answers**
> Learners' own answers.

Activity Book

Unit 4 Revision

- Open the Activity Book at page 50. Learners revise what they have studied in **Unit 4** by choosing the correct words to complete the sentences. If they don't know the answers, encourage them to look back at the unit.

> **Answers**
> 1 c   2 a   3 c   4 c   5 b   6 a
> 7 b   8 c   9 a   10 b   11 c   12 b

My global progress

- Learners think about the topics and activities they enjoyed in this unit and what they found challenging. They think about what else they would like to learn and how what they have learned relates to the other school subjects. This is a step towards independent learning and provides useful feedback for the teacher.

> **Answers**
> Learners' own answers.

Review 2

Learner's Book pages: 64–65

1 📝 Listen 21

- Think up words that rhyme with the words in the activity. Build up a list on the board.
- Learners listen to the recording and write the words that they hear. Check that learners have spelt the words correctly.

Audioscript: Track 21

1 tall
2 trees
3 doors
4 Sun
5 bold
6 said
7 house
8 dad

My old house is big and tall
It's detached with five windows on every wall.
Around the house are five wide trees
And in each tree are fifty bees!

My old house has got squeaky doors
That open onto creaking floors.
The roof lets in both rain and sun
So we can have showers on the run.

Some say as an eco-home it's very bold
I'd say only live there if you like the cold.
It has great charm it must be said
But not when the cupboards smack your head (ouch!)

Many things live in my house
Like the long-winged bats and the furry mouse
But I live there too with my mum and dad
And that very fact makes me very glad.

Answers
1 tall, wall
2 trees, bees
3 doors, floors
4 sun, run
5 bold, cold
6 said, head
7 house, mouse
8 dad, glad

2 💬 Talk

- Learners answer the questions about the poem they have heard. In lower-level classes, offer more support, for example: ask learners for the opposite adjectives *cold/warm*. Check learners understand the meaning of *alone,* and that they know that *bats* and a *mouse* are animals.

Answers
1 Yes, it is.
2 Yes, it is.
3 No, it isn't.
4 No, it isn't.
5 No, she doesn't.
6 Yes, there are.

3 Vocabulary

- Learners work in groups of four and have a race to see who can guess all the words from **Units 3** and **4** the quickest. Before announcing the winner, check the answers are correct.
- Learners from the winning group read out their answers to the class.

Answers
1 solar system
2 terraced house
3 scales
4 Earth
5 flat
6 feathers
7 paw
8 beautiful

4 📝 Use of English

- Learners read the text and choose the correct word from a choice of three words. The activity tests prepositions of time, modals, auxiliary verbs, and comparatives and superlatives. It provides an opportunity to see if extra revision of any of these is necessary before moving on.

Answers
1 in
2 can
3 better
4 have
5 have
6 at
7 have learned
8 in
9 might
10 more

5 📝 💬 Use of English

- Have a competition. See which pair of learners can correctly ask and answer the most questions using *Where, When* and *What time?* In lower-level groups, give learners the chance to practise first.

Answers
Learners' own answers.

6 📝 Write

- Learners write a quiz about houses using the comparative form of the adjectives, for example: *What is more comfortable – a warm house or a cool house?*

Answers
Learners' own answers.

7 📝 💬 Talk

- Learners use the quiz to interview their partners.

> **Answers**
> Learners' own answers.

8 💬 Talk

- Learners contrast **Units 3** and **4**. They discuss which was more amusing, interesting and exciting. This provides the teacher with useful feedback about learners' interests.

> **Answers**
> Learners' own answers.

5 Getting around

Big question How can we stay safe when we are not at home?

Unit overview

In this unit learners will:
- talk about getting to school
- read about road safety
- design a sign
- talk about cities and give directions
- write a description of a famous person
- read a short story
- identify *-ed* endings.

Learners will explore different ways of getting to various places and awareness of the dangers involved, including reading about how Daisy from Colombia crosses the jungle to get to school. They will read about Neil Armstrong's historic moon landing. Learners will build communication skills and language for giving directions.

Learners will continue to build on their literacy skills by reading and listening to a story about Rabin who got lost in the desert. They will develop an awareness of how to keep safe when out of their home.

Learners will apply and personalise what they have learned by writing an itinerary for a two-day visit to their town, including information about where to stay, what to see and how to travel.

Finally, at the end of the unit, they will use what they have learned to design a safety poster for a vehicle.

Language focus

Zero conditional for giving information and directions;

Past continuous

Vocabulary topics: ways of travelling, uses of *get,* adjective opposites, verbs of movement.

Self-assessment
- I can talk about how I get to school.
- I can understand issues about road safety.
- I can design a road safety sign.
- I can give directions using a street map.
- I can write a description of a famous person in history.
- I can understand a short story.
- I can pronounce the three sounds that come at the end of regular past simple verbs.
- I can talk about the importance of taking advice.

Teaching tip

While learners are doing speaking activities using newly acquired expressions or grammar, remember to monitor how effective they are in applying their new knowledge. You can do this by circulating as learners are participating in the activity. Try to do this without interfering with their confidence or their freedom to express ideas.

Lesson 1: Getting around

Learner's Book pages: 66–67

Activity Book pages: 52–53

Lesson objectives

Listening: Listen for meaning and specific information.

Reading: Read an article about an unusual journey to school.

Speaking: Discuss advantages and disadvantages of different transport.

Critical thinking: Awareness of different ways of getting to school, developing opinions about these.

Vocabulary: Uses of *get*

Materials: Photos of learners travelling to school (preferably in uniform) by different methods in different countries, pictures of unusual ways to travel, **Photocopiable activity 9**.

Learner's Book

Warm up

- Show learners photos of children travelling to school and discuss what you can see.
- Ask learners questions like: *How do you get to school? How long does it take?*

1 Talk about it

- Focus on the pictures on page 66 of the Learner's Book. Discuss the questions as a class and, in a higher-level group, allow learners time to ask and answer questions with a partner.
- **Critical thinking:** Introduce the Big question: *How can we stay safe when we are not at home?* Discuss this with the learners. Write down their ideas and save them for the end of the unit.

Answers
Learners' own answers.

2 Listen 22

- Review strategies for listening for gist before playing the audio for learners to match each speaker to a picture.

Audioscript: Track 22

1: I live in Bangkok, in Thailand. There are a lot of cars in my city and the roads are very busy. That's why I go to school by tuk tuk. It's faster than walking and you don't get stuck in traffic jams! The tuk tuk driver can drive between cars, so we don't have to wait behind them. The only problem is that tuk tuks are open on each side, so you breathe in the traffic fumes!

2: In Manila, in the Philippines, where I live, we get to school by jeepney. Jeepneys have two benches in the back so a lot of kids can travel at once. It's really good fun travelling with all my friends like this. But the ride is often very bumpy because the benches are quite high up and sometimes it's a bit of a squash!

3: My dad takes me to school on his motorbike. I live in Ho Chi Minh City, in Vietnam, and everybody here travels by motorbike! I like it because it is fast and I get to spend time on my own with my dad. But during the Monsoon it can rain really hard and then it is not so much fun travelling by motorbike. Even with our waterproof clothing, we still get wet!

4: I live on a small island in Hong Kong and I get the ferry to school every day. I like travelling by ferry because, when the weather is good, you can stand on the deck and look at the lovely views of the harbour. But during the winter time it gets really cold, even if you sit inside in the cabin.

5: I live in Hiroshima in Japan and I go to school by tram. It's quite fast and it stops right outside my school, so I don't have to walk far at all. But it often gets really crowded and sometimes I don't get a seat. I have to hang on tight when it goes around corners, otherwise I fall over!

Answers
1 f   2 a   3 e   4 h   5 b

3 Listen 22

- Discuss strategies for listening for specific information. Encourage learners to make predictions using what they know about the methods of transport and the pictures.
- Talk about where the various photos are from. If necessary, use an atlas to show the countries.
- **Critical thinking:** Learners decide what are good points and bad points about the various forms of transport.

Answers

Transport	Good points	Bad points
Tuk tuk	Good fun It's faster than walking You don't get stuck in traffic jams! You don't have to wait behind cars	Open on both sides, so you breathe in exhaust fumes
Jeepney	A lot of kids can travel at once Good fun	Often very bumpy A bit of a squash
Motorbike	Fast Gets to spend time alone with his dad	You get very wet when it rains in the Monsoon
Ferry	Can look at lovely views	Very cold in winter
Tram	Quite fast Stops right outside school	Often really crowded Sometimes don't get a seat Can fall over if you don't hold on tight

AB For further practice, see Activity 1 in the Activity Book.

4 Talk

* Talk through some good and bad points about methods of transport and write some examples on the board. To challenge higher-level learners, put learners in pairs to ask and answer questions with a partner.

> **Answers**
> Learners' own answers.

5 Read

* Check the learners remember strategies for reading for specific information before allowing time to read the text and find the answers to the two questions.

> **Answers**
> She takes a ride on a zipwire. It takes one minute.

6 Read

* Allow learners more time to read than in **Activity 5** as they need to find out more information. Discuss the answers as a class. The discussion should include areas such as safety and helping the family. Encourage different ideas for question 1.

> **Answers**
> 1 She could take a two-hour hike through the jungle. Learners' own answers.
> 2 She has to help her two younger brothers get safely to the other side.
> 3 30 mph.
> 4 She feels nervous.

7 Word study

* Discuss the two different meanings of *get* in the examples in the **Word study** box.

8 Read

* Learners re-read the text and look for examples of the two different uses of *get*. Encourage learners to guess the different meanings from the context.

> **Answers**
> There are only two ways she can **get** to school… ; help her two younger brothers **get** safely to the other side… .

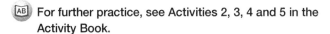 For further practice, see Activities 2, 3, 4 and 5 in the Activity Book.

9 Talk

* Discuss ideas together before giving learners time to work in pairs. See **Additional support and practice**.
* Point to the photograph of Daisy and elicit suggestions. If you have photos of unusual ways of travelling to school, show the class and discuss these before asking for ideas.

> **Answers**
> Learners' own answers.

Wrap up

* To finish off, learners write about their journeys to school. They answer the questions: *How? How long does it take? Who do you travel with? Do you like it? Is it dangerous? Would you like to travel another way?*

Activity Book

1 Word study

* Focus on **Activity 1** on page 52. Learners revise the methods of transport by matching the words with the pictures.

> **Answers**
> 1 train   5 tram
> 2 ferry   6 motorbike
> 3 rickshaw   7 tuk tuk
> 4 jeepney   8 car

2 Vocabulary

* Learners practise the expression *get to work/school* by talking about the people in the pictures.

> **Answers**
> 2 Sam and Bo get to school by ferry.
> 3 My best friend gets to school by rickshaw.
> 4 Lucia and her sisters get to school by jeepney.
> 5 I get to school by tram.
> 6 Mr Diaz gets to work by motorbike.
> 7 Patti gets to school by tuk tuk.
> 8 Ms Roy gets to work by car.

3 Use of English

* Learners read a short text containing expressions with *get* + adjective to indicate a change in something/someone. They tick the expressions that are true for them.

> **Answers**
> get bored, get travel sick, get nervous, get worried, get stuck

4 Read

* Learners apply and personalise their knowledge by practising using *get* + adjective to answer questions about themselves.

> **Answers**
> Learners' own answers.

5 Challenge

* **Home–school link:** Further practice of using the expression *get to work/school*. Learners ask a member of their family the questions in **Activity 4** and write a paragraph using their answers and the phrases in **Activity 3**.

Differentiated instruction

Additional support and practice

- Learners will be becoming familiar with the kind of speaking activities in the Learner's Book. To get the most out of the speaking activities in lower-level classes give extra support, for example discuss ideas as a class and write up examples before allowing time for pair work. In higher-level classes, give less support and more encouragement for learners to become independent.
- To practise asking and answering questions about getting to places see **Photocopiable activity 9:** *Did you ... ?*

Extend and challenge

- Learners find out more ways of travelling to school. If you brought in some unusual pictures, they could choose one of these to research. Alternatively, they could ask their parents/grandparents about when they were young.
- Learners make comparisons about three or more different methods of transport. Encourage the use of comparative and superlatives as well as *whereas, but, however*.

For the next lesson: Ask the children to bring in things that help them stay safe: helmets, reflective arm bands, bright clothes.

Lesson 2: Staying safe on the road

Learner's Book pages: 68–69
Activity Book pages: 54–55

Lesson objectives

Reading: Read road safety advice.

Speaking: Talk about road safety.

Critical thinking: What we can do to be safe while travelling?

Language focus: Zero conditional.

Vocabulary: Road safety: *safe behaviour, main road, helmet, reflective armbands, see clearly, reverse into, pedestrian crossings, cross busy roads, corners, wear/put on a seatbelt*

Materials: Products for improving road safety for example: reflective vest/stripes/armbands, a cycle helmet; road safety information aimed at children of this age – leaflets, posters, and pictures of road signs; **Photocopiable activity 10.**

👉 Warm up

- Have a competition between groups of learners. Allow one minute to write down as many methods of transport from the previous lesson. Write a list on the board.
- **Critical thinking:** Tell learners to rank the methods of transport according to how safe/dangerous they are: 1 = the safest ways to travel, 5 = the most dangerous.
- Discuss as a class, for example:
  Learner 1: *I think the zipwire is the most dangerous, because you can fall (off).*
  Learner 2: *I disagree. Walking through the jungle is more dangerous, because there are dangerous animals.*

1 💬 Talk about it

- If learners have road safety products with them (e.g. reflective vests, cycle helmets) ask them to show the class. Otherwise, show the road safety products you have brought with you. Show posters or leaflets that highlight specific dangers like avoiding lorries or crossing roads carefully.
- Ask learners the two questions and build up a list of things they can do to travel safely by bike, foot and car. Try to include some of the new vocabulary from the lesson.

> **Answers**
> Learners' own answers.

2 Read

- Tell learners they are going to read a text about road safety and ask for predictions about the kinds of things they will read (i.e. ideas from the previous activity).
- Read the text quickly to see if their predictions were right.

> **Answers**
> Learners' own answers.

3 📝 Read

- Allow time for learners to copy the table into their notebooks before giving them plenty of time to make notes of specific information from the text.

Answers

What keeps you safe?	When?
a helmet	when you ride your bike
reflective armbands	when you walk home from school at night
not going near lorries	at any time
use pedestrian crossings	when crossing busy roads
wear seatbelts	in a car

4 📝 Read

- Give feedback on the previous activity. Tell learners the things they have written in the left-hand column are examples of safe *behaviour*. Check they understand *behaviour* is the way we *act* or the things we *do*.
- Allow time for learners to think of two more examples of safe behaviour.

Answers
Learners' own answers.

Language detective

- Learners skim the text to look for sentences that begin with *If* or *When*. Write an example of each on the board. Learners do not need to write at this stage – they will have the opportunity to do so later.
- Help learners to make similar sentences about themselves beginning with an *If* or *When* clause.
- Help learners understand the difference between *If* and *When*. Ask concept-check questions like *Which sentences are more certain?* (Ones that begin with *When.*)
- Ask learners which tense the verbs in the two clauses are in and ask *why*.
- See **Additional support and practice** and **Extend and challenge** for more practice, including giving orders or advice.

5 📝 🗚 Read

- Read the text on page 68 again and complete the sentences.

Answers
2 I walk home at night   **3** I cross the road   **4** we are in a car

🗚 For further practice, see Activity 1 in the Activity Book.

6 💬 Talk

- If you have pictures of road signs, show them to the class and ask if they recognise any.
- Focus on the text and ask learners for suggestions about what the signs mean to drivers, cyclists and walkers (pedestrians). In a higher-level group, learners could discuss in groups first.

Answers
a It is safe to cross the road.
b Drive carefully as children may cross the road.
c You must not drive at over 40 km/h.

7 📝 💬 Over to you

- **Critical thinking:** Talk about the dangers for drivers, cyclists and pedestrians near the school or learners' homes. Choose one particular danger and talk about ideas for a sign. Give extra support in lower-level classes.

- Pairs of learners choose a danger that concerns them.
- Ask pairs which idea they have chosen and discuss the questions from the activity.
- Allow learners time to design their sign.
- Learners present their signs to the class.

Answers
Learners' own answers.

🗚 For further practice, see the Language detective box and Activities 2, 3, 4 and 5 in the Activity Book.

☞ Wrap up

- Put the signs up on the classroom wall and discuss which one(s) are the most useful.

Activity Book

1 Vocabulary

- Open the book at page 54. Focus on **Activity 1**. Learners revise words for road safety items by reading the definitions and writing the words.

Answers
1 helmet   **2** reflective armbands
3 pedestrian crossing   **4** seatbelt

Language detective

- Learners use the **Language detective** box to revise the form of the zero conditional to talk about things that are always true.

2 Word study

- Learners practise using the zero conditional by matching sentence halves.

Answers
2 e   **3** d   **4** b   **5** a   **6** c   **7** f

3 Use of English

- Revision of road safety advice. Learners choose the correct verbs to complete the text.

Answers
2 ride   **3** chat   **4** cross   **5** see   **6** find

4 Use of English

- Learners personalise the expressions by completing sentences with their own ideas.

Answers
Learners' own answers.

5 **Challenge**

- Further practice of giving advice. Learners choose a situation and write sentences giving safety advice and draw a safety sign to warn of the dangers.

> **Answers**
> Learners' own answers – Portfolio opportunity.

Differentiated instruction

Additional support and practice

- Offer opportunities to practise giving orders or advice using the *zero conditional* following the example in the **Language detective** box. Write *If* or *When* clauses on the board, for example: *If you can't find a pedestrian crossing, ...* . Learners work in groups to see how many suggestions they can think of.

- **Home–school link:** Learners choose one danger which is important to them. On a large piece of paper, they draw a picture and write a caption using the *zero conditional* to give advice, for example *be seen when..., always...* or *wear a cycle helmet when... .* Vote for the best one.

Extend and challenge

- To encourage learners to become more independent users of the *zero conditional* with *if* and *when*, use **Photocopiable activity 10: *Zero conditional*.**

- Learners choose another situation which is interesting to them – for example at the fairground, at the swimming pool. They look for advice on keeping safe in these places on posters, the Internet and by asking relatives.

Lesson 3: Getting around big cities

Learner's Book pages: 70–71
Activity Book pages: 56–57

Lesson objectives

Listening: Listen to information and directions.
Speaking: Give directions, plan a visitor's itinerary.
Critical thinking: Categorise transport.

Language focus: Language for directions.
Vocabulary: Ways of travelling: *by car, by bike, by bus, by taxi, by tram, by plane, on foot, by underground, by motorbike, by helicopter, by ferry, by land, by air, by water*

Materials: Some pictures of the different methods of transport.

🖙 Warm up

- Ask: *How do you travel?* Learners mime the answers and other learners guess. Build up a list on the board and ask for more information like: *Is it fast? slow? cheap? expensive?*

- Learners put the ways of travelling in order according to which is the cheapest/most expensive and which is the fastest/slowest.

1 🗨 Talk about it

- In lower-level groups, discuss the questions together, using the information from the **Warm up**, before allowing learners to ask their partners.

- In higher-level groups, learners ask and answer questions in pairs, and then tell the class their partners' opinions.

> **Answers**
> Learners' own answers.

2 Word study

- Focus on the word box and choose the ways of travelling that the class talked about.

> **Answers**
> Learners' own answers.

3 Notebook

- **Critical thinking:** Write the headings *By land, By air* and *By water* on the board. Look at the ways of travelling and decide which heading they come under before adding more ways of travelling to the list.

Answers

By land	By air	By water
car	plane	ferry
bike	helicopter	boat
bus		
taxi		
tram		
on foot		
underground		
motorbike		

 For further practice, see Activity 1 in the Activity Book.

4 Listen 23

- Tell learners they are going to listen to two conversations in the Tourist Office. Discuss the kind of questions people ask in a Tourist Office.

- Check learners understand they just need to answer the general questions and that they don't need to understand everything. See **Listening strategy** below.

- Listen to the recording.

Audioscript: Track 23

1 LONDON

Speaker 1: Hello, could you give us some information about places to visit in central London? We are looking for somewhere interesting to spend the afternoon ... and somewhere inside, I think, because it looks like it might rain.

Speaker 2: OK ... How about the Natural History Museum? There is something for everyone there ... amazing exhibitions and films and a wonderful wildlife garden which you could visit if the rain stays away.

Speaker 1: That sounds perfect – how do we get there?

Speaker 2: I'll show you on this map. You take the underground to this station here; it's called South Kensington. From here you can walk to the museum, it's not very far – about five minutes ...

Speaker 1: And where's the nearest underground station from here?

Speaker 2: Go out of this office at the exit on the left. Then turn right and walk across the road towards the post office. Turn left just after the post office and walk up that street. The entrance to the underground station is on the right, it's called ...

2 SAN FRANCISCO

Speaker 3: Hi there. Could you tell us how we get to Alcatraz Island?

Speaker 4: Yes, certainly. Let's have a look on this map. This area of San Francisco is called Fisherman's Wharf. To get to Alcatraz Island, you have to take a boat from this pier here – Pier 33. From this information office, you need to take a bus or a tram to the pier. Then walk along the pier until you get to the boat terminal. You can buy a ticket for the boat when you get there. There's a ticket office on the left-hand side.

Speaker 3: That's great, thanks. Sounds quite straightforward ... Would you recommend it as a place to visit?

Speaker 4: Yes, definitely. You can do guided history tours, visit special exhibitions at the famous prison and go on nature walks too. The island has lots of interesting wildlife.

Speaker 3: And what about other things to do in this area?

Speaker 4: Oh, there's loads to keep you entertained, and it's all quite nearby too. How about the Aquatic Park over here? Or you could visit the Submarine Museum at Pier 45? Look, take this map to give you some ideas ...

Speaker 3: Thanks very much for your help.

Answers
1 London and San Francisco
2 London: underground, on foot;
   San Francisco: boat, bus, tram, on foot

Listening strategy

- Discuss ways of making it easier to listen for specific missing information. Make sure learners understand the importance of reading the notes before listening and making predictions.

5 Read and listen 24

- Before listening to the recording, learners read the gapped text and make predictions about what they will hear. Write some predictions on the board. Listen to check these predictions, thus completing *Dad's notes*.

Audioscript: Track 24
See Track 23 opposite – London section.

Answers
1 History
2 garden
3 walk
4 five
5 left
6 underground station

6 Listen 25

- Focus on the second conversation and read the questions. Learners listen to the San Francisco section of the recording again and make a note of the information requested.

Audioscript: Track 25
See Track 23 opposite – San Francisco section.

Answers
1 You can do guided history tours, visit special exhibitions at the famous prison and go on nature walks.
2 A map.

Language detective

- Focus on the prompts in the **Language detective** box. Listen to the recording (Track 23) again for the full sentences.
- Mime expressions like *go out of the door, walk towards, walk across* to check learners understand.
- Practise using the expressions. Ask learners about how to get to places from the classroom/school.

7 Talk

- Using the examples from the **Language detective** box, help learners give directions to one of the places on the map. For lower-level learners, give more examples and write them on the board.
- Learners work in pairs and ask and give directions. Circulate, offering help and support if necessary.

Answers
Learners' own answers.

 For further practice, see Activity 2, the Language detective box and Activities 3 and 4 in the Activity Book.

8 Over to you

- Give plenty of support, especially to lower-level learners. Discuss where visitors could stay, places they could visit and how they could travel to the different places. Write some ideas on the board.
- Learners write their itinerary using these ideas. In lower-level classes, they could work in pairs. In mixed classes, lower-level learners could be paired with higher-level learners.
- Learners present their ideas to the class.
- **Home–school link:** Keep a copy at home for visitors.

> **Answers**
> Learners' own answers.

Wrap up

- Learners compare their itineraries and say which they would prefer to follow.

Activity Book

1 Vocabulary

- Focus on **Activity 1** on page 56. Learners find forms of transport in the word search and write the names of the transport they have used.

> **Answers**
> | | |
> |---|---|
> | car | plane |
> | ferry | bike |
> | tram | boat |
> | underground | taxi |
> | bus | motorbike |

2 Read

- Learners practise following instructions. Learners read the instructions and draw the route on the map and say which building is the swimming pool.

> **Answers**
> B = swimming pool

Language detective

- Learners use the **Language detective** box to revise the use of prepositions of direction.

3 Use of English

- Learners practise giving instructions by completing a text about getting to the library.

> **Answers**
> **2** from **3** towards **4** on the right **5** left **6** across
> **7** right **8** up **9** on the left

4 Challenge

- Learners personalise their new knowledge by choosing a place near the school and writing instructions for getting there. They can illustrate this by drawing a map.

> **Answers**
> Learners' own answers.

Differentiated instruction

Additional support and practice

- Offer extra opportunities to practise speaking about methods of transport. Learners work in groups of three or four. They create flashcards by cutting an A4 blank piece of paper into eight and writing a way of travelling on each. Place the flashcards face down in the middle and take turns to pick one. The group talks about it. For example: *by underground – I often/never travel by underground. It's very fast/expensive.*
- For extra opportunities to practise asking and giving directions, learners draw a map of their area, or find one on the Internet. Then, they ask and give directions in pairs using these maps.

Extend and challenge

- Learners choose a place they would like to visit. They look for information about it in holiday brochures, on the Internet, etc. They then write an itinerary and give a PowerPoint presentation to the class.
- Higher-level learners use the imperative forms they have seen in the lesson to give instructions for other functions, for example a recipe for *how to do* something they are interested in.

Lesson 4: One giant leap

Learner's Book pages: 72–73
Activity Book pages: 58–59

Lesson objectives

Reading: Read a description of a famous person.

Writing: Plan and write a description.

Critical thinking: Learners read and analyse a description of a famous historical figure before planning and writing their own description along similar lines.

Vocabulary: Adjective opposites

Materials: Pictures of spaceships, astronauts and Moon landings, pictures of some famous people in history.

Learner's Book

Warm up

- Show some pictures of spaceships and astronauts. Ask learners questions about what they can see.
- Ask learners: *Would you like to be an astronaut? fly to the Moon? fly in a spaceship? visit another planet?*

1 Talk about it

- **Critical thinking:** Focus on the questions and give learners a few minutes to think about their answers in groups.
- Talk through suggestions and write them on the board.

> **Answers**
> Learners' own answers.

2 Read

- Focus on the picture of Neil Armstrong and ask if learners know who he was. Can they guess how long ago he was an astronaut?
- Allow learners time to read the text quickly and check their ideas. Make sure learners only look for this one piece of information and don't worry about higher-level vocabulary.

> **Answers**
> He was the first man to walk on the Moon.

3 Read

- Discuss the best strategy for looking for the information about the dates.
- Allow learners just enough time to scan the text for the dates and note the relevant information.

> **Answers**
> 1 Neil Armstrong became the first man to step on the Moon.
> 2 Neil Armstrong became an astronaut.
> 3 Neil Armstrong was born.
> 4 Neil Armstrong died.

4 Read

- Tell learners they are going to look more closely at each paragraph.
- Focus on description **1**. Make sure learners understand the word *achievement*. Look for clues in the text to help match the description with a paragraph.
- Learners read the descriptions **1–4** before reading the text again to match each description with the paragraph it describes.

> **Answers**
> **1** D **2** A **3** B **4** C

5 Read

- Demonstrate the activity by reading the first paragraph again together and asking learners the three questions about it.
- Allow learners time to answer the questions for the other paragraphs. Check answers together.
- **Critical thinking:** Discuss what Armstrong achieved and why it was important. What do the children think about space travel now?

> **Answers**
> Learners' own answers.

Writing tip

- Read out the sentences from the **Writing tip**. Emphasise the point by reading them again, substituting the pronouns with the nouns they represent. This will make the sentences sound very repetitive. Ask learners which version they would prefer to read.

6 Read

- Read the text again and look for the first underlined word *he*. Discuss what *he* refers to.
- Repeat for the other words. Ask learners why we use these words. If there is any doubt, read the sentences substituting the pronouns with the nouns they represent as you did in the **Writing tip**.

> **Answers**
> 1 Neil Armstrong
> 2 Neil Armstrong
> 3 flying
> 4 the spacecraft
> 5 landing on the Moon

For further practice, see Activities 1, 2, 3 and 4 in the Activity Book.

7 Write

- Show some pictures of familiar famous historical figures and ask learners who they are and why they are famous. Encourage them to add names of more historical figures they have studied in history lessons.
- On the board, build up a list of adjectives to describe these people.
- Think through ideas for the learners' descriptions by asking questions from **Activity 5** about the famous people.
- Encourage learners to use the reference words. Circulate, giving help and support, especially to lower-level learners.

For further practice, see Activity 5 in the Activity Book.

 Wrap up

- To finish off, mix up the descriptions and read them to the class. Don't say the name of the person.
- Learners guess who the description is about.

Activity Book

1 Read

- Focus on **Activity 1** on page 58. Learners practise their reading skills by reading the story of Amelia Earhart and matching each paragraph with a description.
- Ask the learners to comment on her achievements. Ask: *Why was she important?*

Answers
1 B **2** C **3** D **4** A

2 Read

- Learners read the text again and answer the questions.

Answers
1 She flew alone across the Atlantic.
2 1897
3 when she was 20 years old
4 She made daring flights and set many aviation records.
5 It disappeared over the Pacific Ocean.

3 Word study

- This activity checks whether learners understand who or what *she, he, it, her* and *that* refer to in the text.

Answers
1 Amelia Earhart
2 Amelia's love of flying
3 flying
4 her first flight
5 her last flight

4 Word study

- Learners apply their knowledge of referencing words to replace the underlined words with a pronoun.

Answers
2 her **3** she **4** He **5** her **6** it **7** She

5 Challenge

- Learners apply and personalise what they have learned in the unit by writing a description of someone who did something special.

Differentiated instruction

Additional support and practice

- Offer extra opportunities to practise saying dates (e.g. 1962) as these often prove tricky for learners. Write some dates on the board and ask learners to say them until you are satisfied they feel comfortable with them.
- To become more familiar with how to use reference words, look at other reading texts and identify what the reference words represent. Texts from previous units of the Learner's Book can be used.

Extend and challenge

- For extra practice with dates have fun with a quiz called: *When did it happen?* Learners research the years that important historical events happened. They write down the event and the date and use this information for a class quiz. They can get information from other school subjects, teachers, encyclopaedias, the Internet, etc.
- Learners look for information about other famous transportation firsts, for example: the first (trans-Atlantic) flight, the first (trans-Atlantic) balloon flight, the first dirigible and the first woman pilot.

Lesson 5: *Lost in the Desert*

Learner's Book pages: 74–77
Activity Book pages: 60–61

Lesson objectives

Reading: Read a short story – *Lost in the Desert.*
Pronunciation: -*ed* verb endings.
Critical thinking: Giving advice.
Values: Taking advice.

Language focus: Past continuous.
Vocabulary: Verbs of movement

Materials: Pictures of things you might find in or near a desert (e.g. scenery, insects, snakes).

Learner's Book

Warm up

- Check learners understand the expression *get lost.* Have a competition in groups. Allow one minute to think of as many places as possible where you could get lost.
- Write a list of places on the board.
- Have a quick class survey. Choose a few places and ask: *Have you ever got lost in the supermarket?* Learners raise their hands if they have.
- Think about ways of finding your way again (e.g. asking a police officer, calling parents).

1 Talk about it

- Ask learners individually the question: *Have you ever got lost somewhere away from home?* In the case of a positive answer, ask the second question about finding your way again.

> **Answers**
> Learners' own answers.

2 Read

- Tell learners they are going to read about a girl who got lost in a desert. Ask them what they can see in the pictures. Allow learners time in pairs to discuss ideas and make predictions about what might have happened to Rabin.

> **Answers**
> Learners' own answers.

3 Read and listen 26

- Focus on the questions after the first part of the story. Tell learners to look out for specific information and to check their predictions. Make it clear they do not need to understand every word.
- Read and listen to the first part of the story. Check learners' understanding. See **Additional support and practice**.
- Read and listen to the rest of the story. Check learners' answers to the questions and whether any of their predictions were correct. Include a discussion of the story and values.

> **Audioscript:** Track 26
> See Learner's Book pages 74–76.

> **Answers**
> 1 She lived in a small village in the desert, southwest of Cairo.
> 2 She lived in a tent.
> 3 She wanted to follow a rabbit.
> 4 no
> 5 no
> 6 She saw a large beehive.
> 7 She jumped up and ran as fast as she could **or** She ran into the bushes and realised she was lost **or** She sat down on a rock and started to cry.
> 8 She saw a cobra.
> 9 She was very frightened.
> 10 She hopped off the rock and started running back to the riverbed.
> 11 She felt tired, hungry and afraid.
> 12 It was evening and the sun was setting.
> 13 She lay down and fell asleep.
> 14 The rabbit showed her the way to go.
> 15 He was worried.
> 16 She was very sorry and walked back home.

[AB] For further practice, see Activity 1 in the Activity Book.

Language detective

- Focus on the **Language detective** box. Read the sentence and ask learners if they can remember a similar sentence in the story.
- If they can't produce one, write a sentence, for example: *...they <u>were walking</u> along a sandy trail, when they <u>came</u> to an area of trees.*
- Discuss why the writer uses these two different verb forms and help learners produce some more examples.
- See **Additional support and practice**.

4 Language detective

- Now look at the sentence halves. Learners try to match them using logic and memory before reading the text again to check they were right.

> **Answers**
> 1 b   2 d   3 a   4 c

5 Word study

- Look at the first verb in blue – *skipped off*. Learners use the clues from the words around it to try and guess the meaning. If is not possible to guess from the context, ask learners to look in the dictionary. In the case of the dictionary giving more than one meaning, they should look again at the context and choose the most appropriate.
- Learners look for the other blue verbs and follow the same procedure. In lower-level classes, be prepared to offer more support. In a mixed class, learners work in pairs; make sure lower-level learners are paired with a higher-level learner.

> **Answers**
> Learners' own answers.

6 Pronunciation 27

- Write the verbs *dropped, raised* and *landed* on the board. Ask learners if they can remember the pronunciation. Ask for more examples of *past simple* verbs pronounced the same way.
- Learners listen to the recording and write the verbs in the correct column.

Audioscript: Track 27

dropped

landed

laughed

raised

looked

skipped

loved

wanted

jumped

listened

started

watched

hopped

arrived

moved

stopped

Answers

/t/	/d/	/ɪd/
dropped	raised	landed
laughed	loved	wanted
looked	listened	started
skipped	arrived	
jumped	moved	
watched		
hopped		
stopped		

 For further practice, see Activities 2, 3, 4, the Language detective box and Activity 5 in the Activity Book.

7 Values

- Check learners understand *advice* by asking what sort of advice their teachers give them at school. Ask why they give this advice and if learners follow it.
- Discuss the answers to the questions as a class.

Answers
1 Her mother told her not to leave the path because it was very dangerous.
2 She got lost and met dangerous animals.
3 She felt tired, hungry and afraid.
4 She said she would never leave the path again.

8 🗩 Talk

- Talk through a list of types of advice that learners' parents or family members give them.
- Check learners understand *ignore advice* before allowing time to answer the questions with their partners. Circulate and offer support where necessary. Tell them to remember their partners' answers.

Answers
Learners' own answers.

🗣 Wrap up

- To finish off, ask learners to report back to the class about what their partners told them.

Activity Book

1 Read

- Open the Activity Book at page 60. Learners read the story on pages 74–76 of the Learner's Book again and say whether the sentences are true or false.

Answers
2 true
3 true
4 false (Her mother had told her not to leave the path.)
5 true
6 false (Her friends didn't go with her.)
7 false (She didn't catch the rabbit.)
8 false (She started to cry because she was lost.)
9 false (It slithered away across the sand.)
10 false (She was very frightened.)

2 Vocabulary

- Learners practise using verbs of movement by matching the verbs with pictures.

Answers
1 a 2 e 3 c 4 d 5 b

3 Pronunciation 65 [CD2 Track 38]

- Learners listen to the pronunciation of the past simple verbs and write /t/, /d/ or /id/ according to the pronunciation of -ed.

Audioscript: Track 65
1 Rabin hopped off the rock.
2 She started to cry when she saw the snake.
3 Rabin realised she was lost.
4 She looked up and noticed the bees.
5 She watched the rabbit run away.

Language detective

- Learners use the **Language detective** box to revise the use of the *past continuous* and *past simple* for interrupted actions.

4 Use of English

- Learners practise using the *past continuous* and *simple past* to complete a summary of the last part of the story.

Answers
2 woke up   3 standing   4 following   5 saw   6 ran off

5 📝 Challenge

- **Critical thinking:** Learners practise giving advice. They give advice to help other children stay safe when they are not at home.

Answers
Learners' own answers.

Differentiated instruction

Additional support and practice

- *Lost in the Desert*, Learner's Book (pages 74–76): After the first part of the story, if you see that learners are having problems, offer them more support. First revise the reading strategies they need for reading for specific information and checking predictions. Then after each part of the story, stop the recording and check their understanding.
- Offer extra opportunities to practise sentences with past simple and past continuous. Write two headings on the board: *Short action* and *Longer action*. Write verbs underneath and help learners make sentences, for example: *Short action: phone rang* and *Longer action: have dinner* becomes *I was having dinner when the phone rang.*

Extend and challenge

- To practise the verbs of movement and storytelling, make up a new story as a class using the blue verbs. Learners take turns to make up lines. When they say one of the verbs of movement, the other learners act out the verb.
- Make class posters which give advice in various different situations. For example *not talking to/ not accepting lifts from strangers, diet.* Display the posters in the classroom.

Lesson 6: Choose a project

Learner's Book pages: 78–79

Activity Book pages: 62–63

Lesson objectives

Writing: Design a safety poster or a vehicle.

Speaking: Make a presentation.

Critical thinking: Uses of a vehicle and keeping safe when you are not at home.

Language focus: Unit 5 Review

Materials: Large pieces of card for the posters, pictures of innovative or unusual vehicles, safety posters.

Learner's Book

👉 Warm up

- Generate interest by showing some pictures of innovative or unusual vehicles to the class. Check learners understand the word *purpose* and discuss the purpose of the vehicles.
- Show some safety posters and discuss the kinds of advice they give.
- Revise words and expressions from the unit that could be useful for the two projects. Learners work in teams and have a competition.
- For the first round, set a time limit. Write *car, plane, train* on the board. Learners write as many sentences beginning: *I use the car/plane/train to get to ... .* Before announcing the winner, check the sentences are correct.
- For the second round, team members take turns to say a way of staying safe outdoors. When a player from a team can't think of a suggestion, they are eliminated from the round, until only one team is left.
- For the third round, learners mime something they do to keep safe. The first team to guess scores a point.

Answers
Learners' own answers.

Choose a project

- Learners work in pairs. Allow time to choose one of the projects. Ask for a show of hands to indicate which project each pair has chosen and ask relevant questions about their choices.

1 Design your own vehicle

- If learners have chosen the first project, ask the purpose of their vehicles and compile a list on the board.
- Ask if it is a vehicle for land, air or water before discussing special features, etc.
- Learners can do a picture of the vehicle but they could also make a model of it for homework.

- Circulate and offer help and suggestions while learners complete their work.
- Learners present their designs to the class and answer any questions.

2 Design a safety poster

- Tell the learners to raise their hands if they have chosen the second project. Talk through suggestions to answer the questions.
- Circulate and offer help and suggestions while learners complete their posters. Make sure learners have made eight suggestions and are using appropriate grammatical structures from the unit.
- **Critical thinking:** Compare the advice given on the various posters.

Wrap up

- To finish off, learners present their posters to the class.
- **Portfolio opportunity:** If possible, leave the learners' projects on display for a while. Then consider dating and filing the projects, photos or scans of the work, in learners' portfolios.

Reflect on your learning

- Reintroduce the Big question from **Lesson 1:** *How can we stay safe when we are not at home?* Discuss learners' responses to the question now and compare them with their comments at the beginning of the unit. Has much changed?
- Choose whether to use these activities as oral practice or as an opportunity to show learners how to make effective revision notes, etc. Depending on the level and on how homogenous your class is, choose whether learners work in class individually, in groups or pairs. Depending on time constraints or how much self-study is expected, you also could set these tasks for homework.

> **Answers**
> Learners' own answers.

Look what I can do!

- **Aim:** To check learners can do all the things from **Unit 5**.
- As in previous units, choose the most suitable approach(es) for your class. Nominating learners to show the class they can do one of the things on the list will help learners become more spontaneous.
- However, if lower-level learners need more support, showing their partner(s) evidence from their notebooks will help them to understand the importance of taking clear notes for revision.
- Making the activity into a competition will encourage participation and make learning more fun.

> **Answers**
> Learners' own answers.

Unit 5 Revision

1 Vocabulary

- Learners revise transport vocabulary by reading the definitions and sorting the letters to write the words.

> **Answers**
> **1** ferry **2** tram **3** rickshaw **4** motorbike **5** underground

2 Vocabulary

- Learners practise using verbs of movement by completing the sentences with a phrasal verb describing movement.

> **Answers**
> **1** plodded along
> **2** ran away
> **3** leapt over
> **4** jumped up
> **5** jumped into

3 Use of English

- Learners complete a mini-story about a road accident using the verbs.

> **Answers**
> **1** was walking
> **2** saw
> **3** was crossing
> **4** was riding
> **5** changed
> **6** called
> **7** helped
> **8** arrived

4 Over to you

- Learners practise using the zero conditional by completing sentences that are true for them.

> **Answers**
> Learners' own answers.

My global progress

- Learners think about the topics and activities they enjoyed in this unit and what they found challenging. They think about what else they would like to learn and how what they have learned relates to the other school subjects. This is a step towards independent learning and provides useful feedback for the teacher.

> **Answers**
> Learners' own answers.

Differentiated instruction

Suggestions for further reading

A wealth of information on transport inventions and transportation firsts can be found on websites, in history books, encyclopaedias, etc.

6 School lunch

How do people eat in different places?

Unit overview

In this unit learners will:
- read about school lunches around the world
- identify what objects are made of
- talk about quantities of food and drink
- read about how chocolate is made
- read and listen to an extract from *Charlie and the Chocolate Factory*
- identify and practise connected speech.

Learners will develop an awareness of what people eat in different countries by reading about lunches around the world and listening to information about the celebrity chef Jamie Oliver. There are speaking exercises for learners to compare their school lunch with that of learners in other countries. They will learn about how chocolate is produced, explore 'recycling art' and talk about what objects are made of/from. Learners will use quantity expressions to talk about how much/many.

Learners will apply their new knowledge and further improve their literacy skills by reading and listening to extracts from Roald Dahl's *Charlie and the Chocolate Factory*. They will practise writing skills by planning their own party.

At the end of the unit, learners will apply and personalise what they have learned by designing their own new type of sweet or writing their own version of Augustus Gloop's accident from *Charlie and the Chocolate Factory*.

Language focus

Some and *any*

Vocabulary topics: families, daily routines, chores, phrasal verbs (relationships).

Self-assessment
- I can talk about what children eat around the globe.
- I can talk about what objects are made of.
- I can write about quantities of food and drink.
- I can understand the processes of basic food production.
- I can read and understand an extract from children's literature.
- I can write about a new type of sweet.

Teaching tip

Guessing meaning from context
Help learners develop this very useful strategy for dealing with difficult words. First, encourage learners to read the whole sentence as often it is possible to understand it without knowing every word. Encourage learners to use the context to understand the meaning of the new word.

Use the vocabulary matching activities in the Learner's Book. If it is not possible to understand the meaning from the context, help learners to develop other strategies. Ask questions to check learners know if the new word is a noun, adjective, etc. and use this information to help understand meaning. Give extra support and practice. In lower-level classes, more examples will be necessary.

Lesson 1: School lunch

Learner's Book pages: 80–81

Activity Book pages: 64–65

Lesson objectives

Reading: Read about school lunches.

Speaking: Talk about junk food versus healthy food.

Critical thinking: Classify food.

Language focus: *Some* and *any*.

Vocabulary: Food: *cookbook, cooking programmes, school dinners, to feed, fish, a piece of chocolate cake, chips, chicken, (too much) fat, salt, sugar, crisps, sweets*

Materials: Pictures of different things people have for lunch (e.g. rice, spaghetti, sandwiches), preferably food eaten in different ways, e.g. with fingers, knives and forks, a spoon, chopsticks.

Learner's Book

👉 Warm up

- Show pictures of different foods people eat for lunch and ask learners what they can see in the pictures. Build up a list of useful vocabulary on the board.
- Play a mime game. Learners pretend they are eating lunch. Ask: *What is she/he eating?* If you live in a country where everyone eats the same kind of food, learners pretend to eat other things, for example: foods from the pictures.

1 💬 Talk about it

- Write *healthy* (adjective), and *too much fat/sugar/salt* on the board and ask for suggestions about what *healthy* means and which foods could be considered healthy and unhealthy.
- Learners answer the questions. If learners all say the same things, use prompts: *Do you ever have a pudding/ any vegetables/dairy products/grains/fruit/fish/meat/rice?* Ask about other mealtimes.

> **Answers**
> Learners' own answers.

2 Read

- Look at the pictures of lunches around the globe.
- **Critical thinking:** Introduce the Big question: *How do people eat in different places?* Discuss this with the learners. Write down their ideas and save them for the end of the unit.
- Ask learners what they can see in the pictures. Match the countries with the dishes. Use an atlas to show where the people are from.

> **Answers**
> a France: salad, fish, meat, pasta, rice, cheese, fruit.
> b Brazil: *queijadinhas* (a muffin made from cheese and coconut), green salad, rice and beans, meat, vegetables, banana.
> c Japan: *kyuushokuas*, salad, carrots, onions, soya bean soup, pork, rice and black bean.

3 Read

- **Critical thinking:** Learners copy the table into their notebooks. Check they understand the headings by asking for examples from each column. Use pictures to show learners foods they are not familiar with.
- Allow time for learners to read the text again and fill in the specific information.

> **Answers**
>
> | Vegetables | Fruit | Dairy products | Grains | Protein |
> |---|---|---|---|---|
> | salad | coconut | cheese | pasta | pork |
> | carrots | banana | | rice | fish |
> | onions | | | | |
> | beans | | | | |
> | soya beans | | | | |
> | black beans | | | | |

 For further practice, see Activities 1, 2 and 3 in the Activity Book.

4 💬 Talk

- Write some useful words on the board (e.g. *we both, but, whereas*) from **Unit 1**. Learners use these to help them compare their lunch with one of the pictures.

> **Answers**
> Learners' own answers.

5 💬 Talk

- Focus on the two pictures. Learners say what they can see in the pictures. Help them out with new vocabulary.
- Learners use the words: *both, and, but, whereas* to say what is similar and different about the pictures.
- Add adjectives like *healthy, nice, tasty, good.* Encourage use of comparatives to make comparisons.

> **Answers**
> Learners' own answers.

6 Listen 28 [CD2 Track 1]

- Focus on the picture of Jamie Oliver. Ask if anyone has heard of him. If not, ask what he's doing in the picture and what learners think his job is. (See audioscript paragraphs 1 and 2 for background information about Jamie Oliver.) Ask learners about the food they can see and if they think it's healthy or unhealthy.

- Tell learners they are going to listen to some information about Jamie Oliver and talking about the two pictures. Make sure learners know they do not need to understand every word and they will have the chance to listen again.
- After class feedback, ask learners to discuss the final question in the audio *Do you know where the food on your plate comes from?* Ask if they agree/disagree with Jamie Oliver's opinion of school dinners. Ask: *Can you buy crisps, sweets and fizzy drinks at your school?*

Audioscript: Track 28

Jamie Oliver is a famous chef in Great Britain. He has written a lot of cookbooks and has done cooking programmes for television.

Jamie was very worried about the food children were eating at school in the UK. His TV show *Jamie's School Dinners* showed the poor quality of typical school dinners. This started the 'Feed me Better' campaign which helped change school dinners from photo one to photo two.

In photo one, there are some chips and some fish. There aren't any vegetables and there isn't any fruit.

In photo number two, on the other hand, there are some vegetables, two pieces of bread and some chicken.

Children were eating food with too much fat, salt and sugar and they didn't have enough vitamins and minerals to help them concentrate at school, so now children can't buy crisps, sweets or fizzy drinks any more at school because they are bad for our health. Can you buy crisps and sweets at your school?

Jamie wants children to learn about where the food on their plates comes from – where it is grown and how it is cooked. Jamie suggests having food gardens at school, so children can grow their own vegetables, and cooking lessons, so they can learn to prepare healthy meals. Do you know where the food on your plate comes from? Think about it when you next have lunch at school or home.

Answers
Learners' own answers.

7 Listen 28 [CD2 Track 1]

- Focus on the questions. Help learners apply the listening strategies they have practised. Ask learners to make predictions about the answers by asking questions like: *What do you think children eat too much of?* Make sure they remember to listen out only for specific words or expressions that will answer the questions.
- Play the recording. If necessary play it again, pausing after each answer, so learners can make notes.

Answers
1 He is a chef.
2 because they were poor quality
3 'Feed Me Better'
4 fat, salt and sugar
5 where the food on their plates comes from

Language detective

- Try to elicit the rule from the learners. Write the words *some* and *any* on the board.
- Play the descriptions of the two lunches again. Learners say which words they heard with *some* (*chips, fish, vegetables, potatoes*) and which they heard with *any* (*vegetables, fruit*).
- Ask concept-check questions, for example: *Are the nouns countable? Are they plural? positive? negative?*
- Ask learners if they know whether we usually use *some* or *any* in questions.

8 Talk

- Demonstrate by asking what *there is/isn't/are/aren't* in the pictures. Ask questions using: *Is/Are there ...?*
- Learners continue describing the pictures in pairs. See **Additional support and practice**.

Answers
Learners' own answers.

 For further practice, see the Language detective box and Activities 4 and 5 in the Activity Book.

Wrap up

- Assess how well learners use the new language. Ask learners to describe a picture to the class.

Activity Book

1 Vocabulary

- Open the Activity Book at page 64. Direct learners' attention to the word search grid. Learners revise food words by finding ten words in the grid.

Answers

cheese	fruit
chicken	onions
pasta	banana
salad	carrots
rice	meat

2 Vocabulary

- This activity tests if learners know the meaning of the words from the first activity.

Answers
2 banana   3 carrots/onions   4 chicken   5 rice   6 fruit

3 Listen 66 [CD2 Track 39]

* Learners listen to the recording and write or draw what Pablo chooses for lunch.

Audioscript: Track 66

Speaker 1: What would you like for lunch today, Pablo? We've got soup, pasta or salad to start. For the main course, there's chicken with rice and mixed vegetables or fish and chips with a green salad.

Pablo: Hmm... I'm not sure. I quite like soup. What kind of soup is it?

Speaker 1: It's carrot soup.

Pablo: Oh, I don't like carrots very much! What's in the pasta?

Speaker 1: Sweetcorn, tuna, pepper and cheese.

Pablo: Yum! I think I'll have the pasta then.

Speaker 1: And the main course?

Pablo: I like both the chicken and the fish. The fish is with chips, isn't it?

Speaker 1: Yes it is.

Pablo: Well, I'll have the fish then, please.

Speaker 1: For dessert, there's fruit or apple pie.

Pablo: What kind of fruit is it?

Speaker 1: Pears.

Pablo: Apple pie for me then, please. I don't like pears very much.

Answers
Starter pasta **Main course** fish and chips **Dessert** apple pie

Language detective

* Learners use the **Language detective** box to revise the rule for using *some* and *any* in positive and negative sentences and in questions.

4 Listen 67 [CD2 Track 40]

* Learners practise using *some* and *any* by completing a dialogue, before listening to check their answers.

Audioscript: Track 67

Marie: Hi Pablo, what did you have for lunch today?

Pablo: I had some pasta.

Marie: Were there any vegetables in the pasta?

Pablo: Yes, there were and there was some melted cheese too.

Marie: Hmm, delicious! What about the main course?

Pablo: There wasn't any pizza today, so I had fish instead.

Marie: What about dessert? I didn't see any ice cream on the menu today and it's my favourite!

Pablo: You're right – there wasn't. I'm not keen on pears, so I had some apple pie.

Answers
1 some   2 any   3 some   4 any   5 any   6 some

5 Challenge

* Learners personalise what they have learned by designing and writing their favourite menu.
* **Home–school link:** Learners take a copy of their menu home and try to make it with their families.

Answers
Learners' own answers – Portfolio opportunity.

Differentiated instruction

Additional support and practice

* Practise *some* and *any* with food – **Activity 1** (Activity Book). Learners describe other pictures of meals from around the world.
* Play the *Shopping Game*. Think up a list of words for food you can buy at the grocer's. Learners copy 16 words. Each pair of learners cuts a sheet of A4 paper into 16 pieces and writes the name of one food item on each. One learner plays the shopkeeper and writes 'sold out' next to six food items on the list. The other learner is the customer and picks six cards from the pile. The customer asks the shopkeeper:
  Is/are there a/any? according to the cards chosen. The shopkeeper replies: *Yes, there is/are* or *No there isn't/aren't a/any* according to his/her list.

Extend and challenge

* If learners are interested in food, find one of Jamie Oliver's (or another celebrity chef's) videos and watch it. Pause the video after each step and ask questions about what learners can see.
* Learners find a typical recipe from their country in cookery books, the Internet or from relatives. They bring their recipes to class and learners ask questions using *some* and *any* and *How much?* (non-count nouns) or *How many?* (count nouns)

Lesson 2: Recycled art

Learner's Book pages: 82–83
Activity Book pages: 66–67

Lesson objectives

Speaking: Talk about recyclable materials.

Reading: Read about recycled art.

Critical thinking: Consider why we need to help the environment, design sculptures from recycled items.

Language focus: *Made of/made from.*

Vocabulary: Materials (that can be recycled): *paper, types of metal, wood, plastic, reuse, recycle, containers, recycling bin, unwanted*

Materials: For **Additional support and practice 1**, pictures of objects that are made from other objects, **Photocopiable activity 11:** *Flashcards*.

Learner's Book

⮞ Warm up

- **Critical thinking:** Allow learners time in small groups to make a list of things they do to help the environment. Ask: *Why is it important to help the environment? Why is throwing things away harmful to the environment?*
- Learners come to the front and mime one of the things from their list, for example: *sorting rubbish into different containers to be recycled, turning off the tap when brushing teeth to save water, turning off the light when leaving a room.* The class guesses what they are doing. Write the expressions on the board.

1 🗨 Talk

- Write *reuse* and *recycle* on the board and discuss the difference between the two.
- Allow learners time to think of things you can recycle. Learners compare their list with their partner.
- Use learners' ideas to create a list on the board.

> Answers
> Learners' own answers.

2 🗨 Talk

- Look at the boy in the picture and ask: *What he is doing?*
- Focus on the list. Learners tell their partners the things they do.

> Answers
> Learners' own answers.

Reading strategy

- Discuss the different reading strategies that learners know. Ask which strategies learners should use to find information quickly to complete a task. Make sure learners know they should look for specific words and, in this case, use the pictures to help predict the information they will read.

3 Read

- Focus on the pictures and ask questions to check learners understand the word *sculptures*.
- Ask learners what they can see in the pictures. Make a list of the recycled materials on the board before allowing an appropriate time limit to look for the information in the text.

4 📝 Read

- Learners read the text again this time more slowly. If there are some words they don't understand, demonstrate how to use clues in the text and the pictures to help, for example: if they don't understand *brush,* refer to *His hair is made from an old brush* in the text.

> Answers
> 1 wood – face   2 brush – hair
> 3 combs – mouth   4 handle – nose
> 5 blue tubes – hair 6 wheel – head
> 7 plastic – eyes   8 door handles – ears
> 9 metal springs – earrings

[AB] For further practice, see Activities 1, 2 and 3 in the Activity Book.

Language detective

- Write the headings *made of* and *made from* on the board.
- Learners look for examples in the text. Write the materials on the board under the correct heading, for example: *made of wood,* and *made from an old brush, two red combs, the handle of the brush and blue tubes.*
- Ask learners concept-check questions to check they understand the difference: *Which is a 'pure' material? Which are existing objects made into others?*
- See **Additional support and practice 1** for ideas to practise the expressions.

[AB] For further practice, see the Language detective box and Activity 4 in the Activity Book.

5 📝 Create it!

- Write parts of the sculpture on the board like *hair, nose, mouth, arms* and *legs.* Have a competition to see which team can come up with the most different objects to make these things out of. Write ideas on the board.
- **Critical thinking:** Allow learners time to draw their sculptures using these ideas.
- Learners label the reused/recycled objects on their drawing.
- If you have suitable materials at school, learners make their sculptures. If not, learners can look for the materials for their sculptures at home.

[AB] For further practice, see Activity 5 in the Activity Book.

Wrap up

- To finish off, learners present their sculptures to the class, explaining what reused/recycled materials they are made from. If learners haven't made their sculptures because they don't have the materials, they present their drawings instead.

> **Answers**
> Learners' own answers – Portfolio opportunity.

Activity Book

1 Vocabulary

- Direct learners' attention to the picture on page 66 in the Activity Book. Learners revise vocabulary by identifying the items they can see on the beach.

> **Answers**
> Learners' own answers.

2 Read

- Learners read the text and write the items that are found on beaches around the world.

> **Answers**
> **1** cigarette ends
> **2** plastic bottles
> **3** plastic bags.
> **Others:** car tyres, umbrellas, clothing

3 Read

- Learners read the text again and circle the correct word in sentences 1–5 in the Activity Book. Note that the exact words will not be found in the text. Learners will need to interpret the information and choose the best synonym.

> **Answers**
> **1** many   **2** around   **3** typical   **4** can   **5** in one year

Language detective

- Learners use the **Language detective** box to revise the use of *made of* and *made from*.

4 Use of English

- Learners practise using *made of* and *made from* by completing sentences about objects.

> **Answers**
> **1** made from a carrot
> **2** made of wood
> **3** made from a can
> **4** made of metal
> **5** made of rocks/stones
> **6** made from a bottle

5 Challenge

- **Critical thinking:** Learners think of something original they can create from a plastic bottle. They draw and describe their design.

> **Answers**
> Learners' own answers.

Differentiated instruction

Additional support and practice

- Practise *What is/are____ made of?* Ask learners questions about classroom objects, for example: *What is this chair/desk/window made of?* Show pictures of things made from other objects to practise: *What is/are____ made from?*
- For extra practice of: *What is/are____ made of?* see **Photocopiable activity 11: *Flashcards*.** Learners match typical products with the main materials they are made of. They then ask questions using the question: *What is/are____ made of?*

Extend and challenge

- **Home–school link:** Learners ask their families to help them look for ideas on how to reuse and recycle objects to make useful or decorative objects for the home (e.g. pen holders, picture frames). There are many children's websites and libraries that contain useful books with innovative ideas.
- Have a competition to find the most interesting sculpture/picture from recycled art. Learners look in the library, museum catalogues and on the Internet. They make a PowerPoint presentation to the class, giving information about the artist and the materials used.

Lesson 3: Party plans

Learner's Book pages: 84–85
Activity Book pages: 68–69

Lesson objectives

Listening: Listen to a recording about shopping for a party.
Writing: Write a list.
Pronunciation: Connected speech.

Language focus: Quantifiers: *any, a bottle, a can, a cartoon, a cup, a few, a little, a loaf, many, much, a packet, some, a tub.*
Vocabulary: Food

Materials: Pictures of children having fun at birthday parties, preferably with food (including a birthday cake and candles) and drink. Learners could bring in pictures from their parties. **Photocopiable activity 12.**

Learner's Book

👉 Warm up

- Show the pictures of children having fun at birthday parties to generate interest in the lesson.
- Have a competition in teams. Learners think of as many names as they can for food and drink that they eat and drink at parties. Each team reads out the words, so you can check they are correct and announce the winning team. Help learners with new words.
- Ask and answer questions about food from **Lesson 1**, for example: *Do you eat pasta/rice/fish at parties?*

1 🗨 Talk about it

- Learners ask and answer the questions in pairs. Circulate and help them with words they don't know.
- Ask learners to tell the class what they have learnt about their partners.

> **Answers**
> Learners' own answers.

2 📝 Listen 29 [CD2 Track 2]

- Make predictions about the things Fred and his mum will need for the party.
- Learners listen to the recording and check their predictions.

> **Audioscript:** Track 29
>
> **Mum:** How many friends do you want to invite to the party Fred?
>
> **Boy:** I want to invite 12 from my class. Is that too many?
>
> **Mum:** No, that's OK. Let's write a list of the food and drink we need to buy.
>
> **Boy:** OK. Well, there isn't any bread for sandwiches.
>
> **Mum:** So we need to buy three loaves of bread and two packets of cheese. How many cans of cola are there?
>
> **Boy:** There are only a few left.
>
> **Mum:** Six cans of cola then.
>
> **Boy:** We need to buy some water too. Four bottles should be enough.
>
> **Mum:** Is there any ice cream?
>
> **Boy:** There are two tubs. One of chocolate and one of vanilla.
>
> **Mum:** Mmm ... That should be enough.
>
> **Boy:** How about crisps?
>
> **Mum:** OK. Are four packets of crisps enough?
>
> **Boy:** Yes, we don't need to buy any crisps.
>
> **Mum:** Anything else you can think of?
>
> **Boy:** There's only a little orange juice left.
>
> **Mum:** OK ... and two cartons of orange juice. That's it then. Let's go shopping.

> **Answers**
> loaves of bread, cheese, cola, water, orange juice.

3 📝 Listen 29 [CD2 Track 2]

- Focus on the quantity words. Ask learners if they know which nouns they can go with, or if they remember any from the recording.
- Play the recording again and check.

> **Answers**
> 1 three loaves
> 2 two packets
> 3 six cans
> 4 four bottles
> 5 two tubs
> 6 four packets
> 7 two cartons

4 Pronunciation 30 [CD2 Track 3]

- Focus on the expressions. Listen to the recording, paying particular attention to the pronunciation of the word *of* /əv/ which is unstressed.
- Learners listen and repeat. Drill pronunciation.

> **Audioscript:** Track 30
> 1 A packet of crisps.
> 2 A tub of ice cream.
> 3 A can of cola.
> 4 A bottle of water.
> 5 A carton of orange juice.

📒 **For further practice, see Activities 1 and 2 in the Activity Book.**

5 Use of English

- Learners focus on the five sentences and choose the correct expression. Ask questions to check learners understand why each expression is correct or incorrect.

> **Answers**
> 1 many   2 a little   3 plenty of   4 much   5 plenty of

Language detective

- Focus on the first sentence of the previous activity and the **Language detective** box. Check learners understand why *many* is correct and *a little* is incorrect. Ask questions like: *Is the word 'sandwiches' countable/plural? Can 'a little' be used with countable nouns/plurals?*
- Repeat for the other sentences. Remember to ask questions to check learners understand why one expression is correct and the other incorrect, for example: *Can 'much' be used with positive nouns? Can 'a few' be used with uncountable nouns?*
- Ask learners which expressions indicate a small quantity and which indicate a large quantity.

6 Use of English 31 [CD2 Track 4]

- Circulate and monitor while learners complete the dialogue. Ask concept-check questions as in the previous activity if learners are undecided about the missing words.

> **Answers**
> **1** a few **2** many **3** much **4** a little

 For further practice, see the Language detective box and Activities 3 and 4 in the Activity Book.

7 Write

- Show pictures of children having fun at birthday parties. Ask learners what they can see in the pictures.
- Help learners to think about their plans by discussing who they could invite to their parties, what kinds of things they could do, and what they could eat and drink.
- Write: *I'm going to invite ... I'm going to ... We're going to eat ... We're going to ... .* Ask concept-check questions to check learners know why they are using this future form. Ask learners about their parties before giving them time to finish planning and writing about their birthday parties.

> **Answers**
> Learners' own answers.

 For further practice, see Activity 5 in the Activity Book.

Wrap up

- To finish off, learners tell their partners about their parties.

Activity Book

1 Vocabulary

- Open the Activity Book at page 68. Direct learners' attention to the quantity expressions. Learners circle the correct word for talking about the food and drinks.

> **Answers**
> **1** packet **2** can **3** loaf **4** carton **5** bottle **6** packet

2 Pronunciation 68 [CD2 Track 41]

- Learners practise the pronunciation of the words in the first activity.

Language detective

- Learners use the **Language detective** box to revise the use of quantifiers.

3 Use of English

- Learners practise using the quantifiers by completing sentences.

> **Answers**
> **2** many **3** plenty of **4** a little **5** much **6** a few

4 Quantifiers

- Further practice of quantifiers by circling the correct words.

> **Answers**
> **1** many **2** a little **3** much **4** plenty of **5** a lot of **6** a few

5 Challenge

- Learners draw a fridge with items of food. Then they write about what they have got in the fridge.

> **Answers**
> Learners' own answers.

Differentiated instruction

Additional support and practice

- For an extra opportunity to practise speaking about food, learners mime eating at parties and other learners guess (for example: *Are you eating ice cream?*)
- **Photocopiable activity 12**: Learners practise shopping dialogues. First they read and match the dialogues to the shop where they take place, and then they fill in the gaps and use the quantity expressions: *any, a bottle, a can, a carton, a cup, a few, a little, a loaf, many, much, a packet, a slice* (new), *some, a tub.*

Extend and challenge

- Make party invitations for learners' parties.
- Learners find out about birthday parties in different parts of the world. If they have a penfriend who lives in another country, they could write a letter/email to ask about this. Alternatively, they could find information on children's websites. Use the information to create a class poster.

Lesson 4: All about chocolate!

Learner's Book pages: 86–87

Activity Book pages: 70–71

Lesson objectives

Reading: Read for comprehension.

Writing: Write about food growth and production.

Critical thinking: How things are processed.

Vocabulary: Chocolate, food growth and production: *melt in our mouths, harvested, cut down, cacao pods, shells, cracked, roasted, paste, mixture*

Materials: Chocolate bars or pictures of different chocolate bars, preferably white, milk and dark varieties.

Learner's Book

👉 Warm up

- Generate interest in the topic by showing learners the chocolate bars (or pictures) you have brought.
- Ask learners: *Do you like chocolate? Do you prefer white, dark or milk chocolate? How often do you eat chocolate?*

1 💬 Talk about it

- **Critical thinking:** Learners ask and answer the questions in pairs. You may need to pre-teach the expression *melt in our mouths.*

> **Answers**
> Learners' own answers.

2 Read

- Learners read the text to check their ideas from the previous activity. There are some high-level words describing the process of making chocolate. Discuss which reading strategies learners can use to avoid any difficulties this may cause so that they can find the specific information requested.
- Help learners by looking at the pictures and asking what they can see and by writing new words on the board. Several words can be demonstrated by miming or looking at the pictures, for example: *harvested, cut down, cacao pods, shells, cracked, roasted, paste* and *mixture.*

Note: Learners may need help with the question: *How is it made?* as they need to understand and summarise a long process described in several sections of the text.

> **Answers**
> – Chocolate is made from cacao beans. It's harvested, fermented, dried in the sun, roasted in big ovens and then the shells are cracked and the beans inside are crushed into a paste and mixed with sugar, cocoa butter, vanilla and milk, then cooled.
> – Joseph Fry in 1847.
> – Because the melting point of cocoa butter is lower than the human body temperature.

 For further practice, see Activities 1 and 2 in the Activity Book.

3 Read

- Read the statements together, checking learners remember the words *harvested, cut down, cacao pods, shells, cracked, roasted, paste* and *mixture.* Encourage learners to make predictions.
- Learners read the text to check if the sentences are true or false.

> **Answers**
> **1** true
> **2** false (They are harvested twice a year.)
> **3** false (They use long sticks to cut down the pods.)
> **4** false (The beans are roasted in big ovens; then the shells are cracked.)
> **5** true
> **6** false (When it is cooled we have the final product.)

Writing tip

- Discuss words learners know to link ideas when writing.
- Write *linkers of purpose* on the board. Help learners understand that after *linkers of purpose*, they will find a reason for an action. Ask concept-check questions about the information that follows, for example: *Does it say what, how or why something is done?*

4 📝 Read

- Learners read the text again and look for expressions that give a reason for actions.

> **Answers**
> The workers use a long stick with a machete (a type of knife) to cut down the pods **so as not to** break the tree which is very fragile.
> They open the pods with their hands, **so that** the beans inside don't break.
> After that, they go to the factory **in order to** be turned into chocolate.
> **In order to** make the paste sweet, it is mixed with sugar, cocoa butter, vanilla and milk.

5 📝 Write

- Practise using the *linkers of purpose* from the text. Learners copy the beginning of the sentences into their notebooks. Look for the first expression in the text and tell learners to write the rest of the sentence in their notebooks.

- Ask learners for predictions about the other sentences before using the text to help them to complete the second half.

> **Answers**
> 1 so as not to break the tree
> 2 so that the beans inside don't break
> 3 so that they can dry
> 4 in order to make the paste sweet
> 5 in order to make the final product

 For further practice, see Activity 3 in the Activity Book.

6 Write

- Discuss what learners know about the food products, before choosing one to find out more information about.
- Discuss what kind of information learners should look for, for example: *Where/How is it made? When was it first used? Are there different varieties?*
- **Home–school link:** For homework, learners research and write about the product they have chosen. In lower-level classes, encourage learners to use the text about chocolate as a framework. In higher-level classes, learners plan a PowerPoint presentation.

> **Answers**
> Learners' own answers – Portfolio opportunity.

> **Audioscript:** Track 31
> See Learner's Book page 85.

 For further practice, see Activity 4 in the Activity Book.

Wrap up

- Learners present the product they have chosen to the class.

Activity Book

1 Vocabulary

- **Critical thinking:** Learners focus on the photo and say what they think the product is.

> **Answers**
> Learners' own answers.

2 Read

- Learners read the text and check their answers. Lower-level learners may have difficulties with the vocabulary.

> **Answers**
> c, a, e, b, d

3 Word study

- This activity tests learners' understanding of the process by matching sentence halves.

> **Answers**
> 1 b   2 c   3 a

4 Word study

- Learners write about the process of bread-making. Lower-level learners may need help with vocabulary.

> **Answers**
> 1 yeast/salt
> 2 mix/ingredients
> 3 knead/loaf
> 4 add/nuts/seeds
> 5 baked

> **Differentiated instruction**
>
> **Additional support and practice**
> - If your class has difficulties understanding the process of making chocolate, look for photos on the Internet, books, etc. to help demonstrate it. Ask learners to describe what is happening in the photos.
> - Offer extra opportunities to practise talking about the process of making chocolate. Learners mime a stage in the process and the class guesses which stage it is.
>
> **Extend and challenge**
> - Learners find out about how to make products using chocolate, e.g. cakes.
> - If your class enjoyed miming the process of making chocolate, ask them to mime a stage in the process of the other products they have researched. The class guesses which product and stage it is.

Lesson 5: *Charlie and the Chocolate Factory*

Learner's Book pages: 88–91
Activity Book pages: 72–73

> **Lesson objectives**
>
> **Reading and Listening:** Read and listen to extracts from *Charlie and the Chocolate Factory*.
>
> **Vocabulary:** Food, landscapes: *meadows, valley, river, steep cliffs, waterfall, whirlpool, muddy, trees, bushes, grass, buttercups;* adjectives: *generous, helpful, greedy, selfish, mean*
>
> **Values:** Being generous.
>
> **Materials:** A copy of *Charlie and the Chocolate Factory*, pictures of a chocolate factory – real photos, film sets or cartoon pictures.

Learner's Book

Warm up

- Have a competition in groups to try and remember the stages in making chocolate. If groups forget any stages, mime or show the pictures to remind them.

- To generate interest in the text about the chocolate factory, show the pictures you have brought. Ask learners what they can see.

1 ✑ Talk about it
- Learners ask and answer questions in pairs before telling the class about their ideas of what a chocolate factory would look like inside.

> **Answers**
> Learners' own answers.

2 ✑ Read and listen 32 [CD2 Track 5]
- Focus on the questions and encourage learners to make predictions about what they are going to read.
- Learners read and listen to the first extract and check their ideas.
- **Note:** There are some high-level expressions like *screwed the little caps on to the tops of the tubes of toothpaste, they could afford,* etc. Tell learners to focus on the words they *do* know, especially for question 1. For example, they should understand the family was poor because of *is never paid much* and *there wasn't enough money.*

Audioscript: Track 32
See Learner's Book page 88.

> **Answers**
> 1 Because he lived in a small, uncomfortable house and his family were very poor.
> 2 He ate bread and margarine for breakfast, boiled potatoes and cabbage for lunch and cabbage soup for supper.
> 3 It was the largest and most famous chocolate factory in the world.
> 4 Because he won a competition which meant he could visit the factory and have a lifetime's supply of sweets and chocolate.

3 ✑ ✑ Read and listen 33 [CD2 Track 6]
- Learners read and listen to the second extract *Inside the Chocolate Factory*.
- Demonstrate the activity by doing an example together. Find the first green word *steep*. Read the sentences around it and help learners predict which meaning is most likely. Lastly, check in the dictionary.
- Learners work in pairs to find the meaning of the words. Circulate and check they are using the context to help them. In lower-level classes, it may be necessary to do more examples together.

Audioscript: Track 33
See Learner's Book page 89.

> **Answers**
> 1 b 2 c 3 a 4 b

4 ✑ Read
- Learners practise using the words in blue to describe the Chocolate Room with a partner.
- Cover up the text and have a competition to see who can describe the Chocolate Room best without looking at the blue words.

> **Answers**
> Learners' own answers.

5 ✑ Read and listen 34 [CD2 Track 7]
- Focus on the questions and discuss strategies for finding this information. Ask learners if they have any ideas about what the answers could be.
- Read and listen to the third text extract, Augustus Gloop's Accident. If lower-level learners have difficulties, listen again and point to where the information is found in the text.
- Learners answer the questions. After class feedback, ask questions to elicit learners' reaction to the texts: *Would you like to live in a place like this? Why/why not?*

Audioscript: Track 34
See Learner's Book page 90.

> **Answers**
> 1 because he touches the chocolate in the river
> 2 He falls into the river.
> 3 Learners' own answers.

6 ✑ Talk
- Focus on the pictures and ask learners which one comes first in the story. Re-read the beginning of the third extract if necessary.
- Allow learners time to put the pictures in order and check.
- Ask learners to describe the pictures in order, before allowing time in pairs to practise using the prompts to tell the story.

[AB] **For further practice, see Activities 1 and 2 in the Activity Book.**

> **Answers**
> b, d, c, a
> Learners' own answers.

7 Vocabulary
- Focus on the words in the word box. Ask learners their meaning and discuss which word best describes Augustus.

> **Answer**
> greedy

8 📝 💬 Adjectives

- Help learners make sentences about people they know. Write some examples on the board.
- Allow learners time in pairs to make more sentences about the people they know. Circulate and offer help and support.

> **Answers**
> Learners' own answers.

9 Values

- Read the description together, and discuss the kinds of things people like to keep for themselves and the kinds of bad things they might do to satisfy their greed.

> **Answers**
> Learners' own answers.

10 Vocabulary

- Look at the adjectives in the word box in **Activity 7**. Discuss which one is the opposite of greedy.

> **Answer**
> generous

 For further practice, see Activities 3, 4 and 5 in the Activity Book.

11 💬 Talk

- Learners work in pairs and try and think of ways of being generous.
- Learners tell the class their ideas. Build up a list on the board.

> **Answers**
> Learners' own answers.

👉 Wrap up

- To finish off, ask learners to talk together about what they would do if they went in the Chocolate Room.

> **Answers**
> Learners' own answers.

Activity Book

1 Read

- Open the Activity Book at page 72. Learners read the story on pages 88–90 of the Learner's Book again and test their understanding by circling the correct sentence endings.

> **Answers**
> 1 b   2 b   3 a   4 a   5 a   6 a   7 b   8 a & b

2 Word study

- Learners focus on the role of the waterfall in the chocolate-making process and use a dictionary to help them choose the correct verbs.

> **Answers**
> mixes, churns, pounds, beats

3 Vocabulary

- Learners focus on *The Chocolate Room* extract and find the adjectives in the box. They use the context to match the words with the definitions. Lower-level learners may need more support.

> **Answers**
> 1 amazing/astonishing
> 2 enormous
> 3 graceful
> 4 tremendous

4 Vocabulary

- Learners use the context to match the adjectives in the box to people, places and things, according to what they describe in the story. Lower-level learners may need more support.

> **Answers**
> Suggested answers
> **People:** young, graceful, lucky, deaf, famous
> **Places:** steep, muddy
> **Things:** large, light, wooden, melted, frothy
> Learners' own answers.

5 📝 Challenge

- Learners use the story and their imagination to describe what they can see in the Chocolate Room.

> **Answers**
> Learners' own answers.

> **Differentiated instruction**
>
> **Additional support and practice**
>
> - Learners practise using adjectives to describe people. Without looking at the texts, they write a sentence about some of the characters in the stories from the Learner's Book.
> - Learners work in groups and write a summary of the extracts they have read.
>
> **Extend and challenge**
>
> - If your learners liked the extracts, encourage them to read the rest of *Charlie and the Chocolate Factory* or other books by Roald Dahl.
> - Watch the film version of the story. Look for a version in English or with English subtitles.

Lesson 6: Choose a project

Learner's Book pages: 92–93
Activity Book pages: 74–75

Lesson objectives

Speaking and writing: Project 1 Invent a new type of sweet or chocolate, or **Project 2** Write about what happened to Augustus Gloop.

Language focus: Unit 6 Review

Materials: Some pictures of different types of sweets and chocolates, some images of Augustus Gloop which can be found on the Internet.

Learner's Book

⇨ Warm up

• Tell learners they are going to choose one of the projects: **1** Invent a new type of sweet or chocolate, or **2** Write about what happened to Augustus Gloop.

Choose a project

• The learners can work in pairs or individually.

1 Invent a new type of sweet or chocolate

• Give learners ideas for **Project 1** and revise vocabulary for chocolate, its ingredients and how it is made. Have a competition in teams to see who can come up with the most words.
• Show learners the pictures of different types of sweets and chocolates and ask them to describe them. Ask: *Would you like to try them? Why? Why not?*
• Discuss ideas for new kinds of sweets and chocolates. Divide the board in half horizontally. On half of the board, make a list of suggestions about what they could be made of and how they could be made.
• Then discuss some ideas for names and write them up on the other half of the board.
• Focus on the steps in the Learner's Book and make sure learners follow these to create their piece of writing.
• Circulate and give help and advice, especially about paragraph structure and sequencing words.
• **Home–school link:** If possible, the learners can try to make their sweets with the help of adults at home and bring them in to try.

2 Write about what happened to Augustus Gloop

• Revise vocabulary about Augustus Gloop's accident. See who can recall the most facts from the story.
• Learners re-read the extract about Augustus Gloop's accident (see Learner's Book page 90), paying particular attention to the end of the story.
• Discuss ideas about what could have happened to Augustus after falling in the river, making sure learners use the past simple. If necessary, show some pictures of Augustus to help give learners ideas.

• Focus on the steps in the Learner's Book and make sure learners follow these to create their piece of writing.
• Circulate and give help and advice, especially about paragraph structure, sequencing words and on the past simple.

⇨ Wrap up

• Learners present their work to the class.
• **Portfolio opportunity:** If possible, leave the learners' projects on display for a while. Then consider dating and filing the projects, photos or scans of the work, in learners' portfolios.

Reflect on your learning

• Reintroduce the Big question from the start of the unit: *How do people eat in different places?* Discuss learners' responses to the question now and compare them with learners' comments at the beginning of the unit. Has much changed?
• In higher-level classes, learners work in pairs to do the activities. Circulate and assess their progress.
• In a lower-level class, give more support when necessary.
• In **Activity 3**, make sure learners use the past simple and in **Activity 5** check the pronunciation of the unstressed *of*.

> **Answers**
> Learners' own answers.

Look what I can do!

• **Aim:** To check learners can do all the things from **Unit 6**.
• Remember, whichever approach you choose for these revision activities (asking for volunteers to show the class evidence that they can do one of the things on the list, making them into a competition, etc.) give support to lower-level learners and use the activities as an opportunity to assess what learners have learned. As always, use this information to customise your teaching as you go on to **Unit 7**.

> **Answers**
> Learners' own answers.

Activity Book

Unit 6 Revision

1 Crossword

• Open the Activity Book at page 74. Learners revise vocabulary from the unit by solving the crossword puzzle.

2 📝 Challenge

- Learners make a revision crossword to test their friends. Lower-level learners may need extra support with writing the definitions.

My global progress

- Learners answer the questions about the unit. This provides useful feedback for the teacher.

Review 3

Learner's Book pages: 94–95

1 Listen 35 [CD2 Track 8]

- Revise expressions for asking for directions from **Unit 5** and build up a list on the board.
- Focus on the map and ask learners what they can see.
- Learners listen to the dialogues and say where the people are going.
- For an extra challenge in higher-level groups, draw/use a more sophisticated map and give more complicated directions. You could prepare the map beforehand and photocopy it or draw it on the board. Alternatively, show an authentic town map, or ask learners to draw a map on the board.

> Answers
> The girl is going to the pizza restaurant.
> The boy is going to the snack bar.
> Granny is going to the ferry boat.

Audioscript: Track 35

Traffic cop: OK young lady. You need to walk across the street and go straight on for two streets then turn right. You'll see it on the left.

Traffic cop: Now, young man. Let's see ... go across the park. Take the second road on your right. Go straight on and it's on your right.

Traffic cop: Hello Granny! Be careful with that! OK now slowly go straight on. Don't turn left at the first road. Turn left at the third street, go straight over the roundabout and it is right in front of you. Now drive carefully!

2 Talk

- Learners work in pairs and answer the questions about the picture. In lower-level classes, it may be useful to demonstrate the activity by asking the class the first two questions before learners work independently in pairs.

> Answers
> 1 Granny travels by motorcycle.
> 2 The boy travels in a tuk tuk.
> 3 The girl travels on a scooter.
> 4 The sign near the bookshop means that pedestrians can cross here.
> 5 The sign near the train station means that the speed limit is 30 mph/kph.
> 6 The sign near the school means that pedestrians can cross here.

3 Vocabulary

- Focus on the words from **Units 5** and **6**. Lower-level learners work in teams of four and try and think of the opposites to the words in the boxes on page 94. Higher-level learners work independently. Check answers by looking at the word box at the bottom of the page.
- If learners are having difficulties remembering the opposites, make a card game to help them practise in the class or at home. Each learner cuts an A4 sheet of paper into eight pieces. On each piece, learners write a word. On the back, they write its opposite in a different colour. Learners play the game by guessing the opposite and turning the card over to check.

> Answers
> 1 selfish
> 2 safe
> 3 right
> 4 sit down
> 5 slowly
> 6 a lot
> 7 healthy
> 8 savory

4 Use of English

- This activity revises quantity expressions, the zero conditional and the past simple. It provides an opportunity to assess whether learners can use these in a conversation. If necessary, in lower-level groups, you could do some quick revision before the activity. Alternatively, use the activity to assess if any revision is necessary before moving on to **Unit 7**.
- Focus on the dialogues. Learners choose the correct option from a choice of three.

> Answers
> 1 wear
> 2 doesn't
> 3 explain
> 4 decided
> 5 bottles
> 6 packet
> 7 a little
> 8 so as not to
> 9 a lot of
> 10 plenty

5 Use of English

- This activity revises linkers of purpose from the **Writing tip** on page 87 in the Learner's Book. Learners complete the sentences giving reasons for the things people do in the previous activity.
- For extra practice, write sentences containing the linkers, photocopy them, cut them in half and distribute them to the class. Learners match the sentence halves.

> Answers
> 1 not upset her brother
> 2 hurt himself
> 3 protect him

6 📝 Write

- Learners practise writing about how one of the products in the text is made using the expressions from the words in the box.
- Encourage higher-level learners to add extra information using the linkers from the previous activity.

7 💬 Talk

- Learners contrast **Units 5** and **6**. They discuss what they liked better and which unit taught them more new things.

7 Australia

Unit overview

In this unit learners will:
- talk about extreme weather
- read a country fact file
- listen to a report about endangered animals
- write a blog about an adventure trip
- read a traditional story.

Learners will develop an awareness of the climate, animals, facts and figures and geographical features of Australia. To do this, they will read a fact file about Australia, information about endangered animals and a trip to Australia. They will expand their knowledge of endangered species and practise listening skills by listening to a report on the subject.

Learners practise communication skills by comparing Australia with their own countries and presenting their ideas about why animals are endangered and what we can do to protect them.

Learners will further develop their literacy skills by reading a traditional Aborigine story – *Why emus can't fly.* At the end of the unit, learners will apply and personalise what they have learned by writing either a country fact file or a report about an endangered animal.

Language focus

Infinitive of purpose

Present perfect simple

Vocabulary topics: weather, geographical features, endangered animals, synonyms and words describing movement.

Self-assessment
- I can talk about the weather in my country.
- I can understand a weather report about a weather incident.
- I can give examples of facts about Australian geography, climate, animals and other general information.
- I can explain at least two reasons why animals become endangered and what people do to help them.
- I can distinguish and pronounce the sounds that come at the end of numbers with -*teen* and -*ty*.
- I can write a blog or journal about an adventure trip.
- I can understand a traditional story.

Teaching tip

Review learners' performance in the writing exercises and the project at the end of the unit to see how well they are remembering the information presented in the Learner's Book and applying skills like planning and structuring in their written work. If learners are having problems with recalling information, review note-taking skills and encourage learners to review their notes, before going on to **Unit 8**. If they are having trouble planning and structuring their writing, give extra help and make sure they use the texts in the unit to help structure their own work.

Lesson 1: Australia

Learner's Book pages: 96–97

Activity Book pages: 76–77

Lesson objectives

Listening: Listen to a radio report.

Speaking: Talk about extreme weather.

Critical thinking: Develop an awareness of different types of weather in different countries.

Vocabulary: Weather: *hot, humid, sunny, mild, cold, rainy, stormy, thunder, lightning, hot, dry, snowy, frosty*

Learner's Book

Warm up

• Ask: *What's the weather like?* Mime different types of weather. Learners reply: *It's hot/rainy*, etc. Build up a list of weather words on the board.

1 ✎ Talk about it

• Introduce and discuss the Big question: *What can we learn about one country?* Think about and note learners' ideas.
• Learners read and choose the phrases that describe the weather in their country and then tell a partner what they have chosen.

> **Answers**
> Learners' own answers.

2 ✎ Talk

• On the board write __ *January*, __ *the spring*, __ *May to July*. Ask learners which prepositions they need to use.
• **Critical thinking:** Learners imagine they are talking to someone from another country and tell their partners about the weather in their country. Encourage the use of the frequency adverbs studied in previous units.

> **Answers**
> Learners' own answers.

3 Word study

• Focus on the pictures and ask learners what they can see.
• Look at the words in the box and match them to the pictures. Ask learners first which pictures they can match, before telling them the correct answers.

> **Answers**
> **a** a blizzard
> **b** a flood
> **c** a drought
> **d** a hurricane
> **e** a tornado

 For further practice, see Activities 1 and 2 in the Activity Book.

4 Listen ㊱ [CD2 Track 9]

• There is lots of information in the recording. Before listening, discuss which strategies learners will need to help them answer the questions. Give examples. Talk in general about extreme weather and learners' experiences of it, if any.
• Learners listen to the recording and identify the weather conditions and where they are happening.

> **Audioscript:** Track 36
>
> **Weather forecaster:** We have just received a warning from the National Weather Service for the south-western coast of Western Australia. The severe thunderstorm has become much stronger and wind speeds are building up fast. The winds are starting to rotate and a possible tornado is taking shape just to the north-west of the coast. The storm is moving out to the east at about 40 mph. If you are in the area, you need to take cover. This is a very dangerous storm. If you are at home or in a building, find a room inside with no windows on the lowest floor, or take cover in a hallway and get under a big piece of furniture, like a table.
>
> If you are outside, you should take shelter in a safe and strong building. If you are in a car, do not try and drive away from the tornado. You should leave your car immediately.
>
> Reports are coming in to say that this storm is now turning into a tornado and lifting up into the clouds. It looks like it is going to be active for several hours and if it touches down on the ground, there is going to be a lot of damage, so please take cover. We'll keep you posted ...

> **Answers**
> There is a severe thunderstorm in Australia that is turning into a tornado.

5 Vocabulary

• Tell learners to look at the words and the definitions. In lower-level groups, check learners understand the definitions. Definitions **1**, **2** and **3** could be mimed.
• Match as many definitions as possible by asking the class which words they already know.
• Listen to the recording again and try and predict the meaning of the other words from the context.

> **Answers**
> **a** 4 **b** 6 **c** 7 **d** 1 **e** 2 **f** 3 **g** 5

6 ✎ Listen ㊱ [CD2 Track 9]

• Help learners make predictions about what they will hear. Ask questions like: *What should I do if there's a tornado? Where should I shelter? Should I drive?*
• Make sure learners understand that *should* is used for giving advice.
• Listen to the recording again (Track 36) and complete the safety advice.

> **Answers**
> windows
> lowest
> hallway
> furniture
> building
> drive
> leave

7 💬 Talk

- Write *last* and *ago* on the board and check learners understand the difference. Ask learners for different expressions they could use, for example: *two years ago, last week, during the last winter holiday.*
- Circulate and monitor while learners tell a partner about their experiences.

> **Answers**
> Learners' own answers.

8 💬 Talk

- Ask learners for suggestions and write examples on the board. Use the zero conditional which learners studied in **Unit 5**.
- Allow learners time to talk with their partners. Circulate and offer support, including help with new words.

> **Answers**
> Learners' own answers.

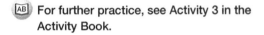 **For further practice, see Activity 3 in the Activity Book.**

📣 Wrap up

- **Critical thinking:** Learners give advice to the class about what to do in bad weather conditions.

Activity Book

1 Vocabulary

- Learners read the sentences about the weather and then rearrange the letters to make a weather word. Then they match the sentences to the pictures.

> **Answers**
> a hot/humid **2**   b rainy **4**   c hot/dry **6**   d sunny/mild **3**
> e thunder/lightening **1**   f snowy/cold **5**

2 📝 Read

- Learners read a weather report containing descriptions of extreme weather conditions and match each description to the name of the correct weather condition.

> **Answers**
> **1** a hurricane
> **2** a blizzard
> **3** a drought
> **4** a flood

3 📝 Read

- Direct learners' attention to the newspaper report. Learners read the text and decide whether the statements are true or false, correcting the false statements.

> **Answers**
> **1** false (25 people were hurt.)
> **2** false (He saw the green clouds before the storm.)
> **3** true
> **4** false (A tree fell on the family car.)
> **5** false (The storm will disappear in the next 24 hours.)

Differentiated instruction

Additional support and practice

- For extra practice using weather expressions, ask about today's weather in different parts of the world.
- Offer extra opportunities to practise weather expressions and revise the past simple/present perfect. For example, learners ask and answer questions like: *What has the weather been like today/ this week? What was the weather like yesterday? This week, it has been changeable; yesterday it rained …* Make sure they always use the past simple with a time expression referring to a finished time, e.g. *yesterday*, even if the question was *What has the weather been like this week?*

Extend and challenge

- Learners find and listen to a weather forecast in English about their country. They could hear one on satellite TV or on an English-speaking TV website or read one in an English-speaking (electronic) newspaper.
- Learners make their own weather forecasts for the next few days. They will need to use the future simple tense (*will* + base form) because they are making predictions.

Lesson 2: Australia

Learner's Book pages: 98–99
Activity Book pages: 78–79

Lesson objectives

Reading: Read an Australia fact file.

Speaking: Make comparisons between countries.

Critical thinking: Process important information represented by numbers and figures in a text.

Vocabulary: Geographical features: *desert, mountain range, coral reef, rock formation, coast, tropical rainforest;* numbers

Materials: Pictures of Australian landmarks, scenery and wildlife, for example: Uluru, Sydney Opera House, the Great Barrier Reef, kangaroos, koalas, wombats. There are plenty of books on Australia in libraries and pictures on the Internet.

Warm up

- Generate interest in this unique and fascinating country by showing pictures of Australian landmarks, scenery and wildlife. Try to include a desert, a mountain range, the Great Barrier Reef, a rock formation, a coast, and a tropical rainforest.
- If learners have visited Australia ask: *Did you see/visit …?* about the landmarks, scenery and wildlife. If not, change the question to: *Would you like/prefer to see/visit …?*

1 Talk about it

- Ask learners what they know about Australia. Look at the questions and discuss the answers, but wait for **Activity 3** to tell learners the correct answers.

Answers
Learners' own answers.

2 Word study

- Focus on the words and find the places on the map. If necessary, show the pictures from the **Warm up** again to check meaning.

Answers
Learners' own answers.

[AB] For further practice, see Activities 1 and 2 in the Activity Book.

Reading strategy

- Learners often panic when they see large numbers in reading texts, especially years, figures expressed as a percentage, fractions, etc. This is especially true when they are reading aloud as they may be unsure about the correct pronunciation. It is important that learners start to use numbers and figures as they often help us to understand important information in the text.
- Focus on the **Reading strategy** and discuss the kinds of information numbers and figures might represent.

3 Read

- Tell learners they are going to read a text to find out the answers to the questions in **Activity 1**. There is lots of additional information in the text, so make sure learners know which reading strategies to use to focus on the information they need. Learners will have a chance to focus on the figures and numbers later.

Answers
– Australia is a country *and* a continent.
– You might find snow on the mountain ranges along the east coast.
– Uluru is a huge sandstone rock in the centre of Australia.
– the Great Barrier Reef
– December to February

4 Read

- **Critical thinking:** Focus on the figures in the questions. Learners look for the figures in the fact file and answer the questions. See **Additional support and practice** to practise numbers and figures.

Answers
1 b   2 a   3 a   4 a
5 mountain ranges, tropical rainforests, Great Barrier Reef.

 For further practice, see Activities 3 and 4 in the Activity Book.

5 Talk

- Focus on the words in the **Word study (Activity 2)** and discuss ways of making comparisons. Learners are familiar with comparative adjectives (*long* and *short*) and words like *too, but, whereas*. Other useful words include *neither of them* and *neither X nor Y.*
- In lower-level classes, build up a list of examples on the board. In mixed-level classes, pair lower-level and higher-level learners together.
- Circulate and offer support while learners work in pairs to look for similarities and differences.

Answers
Learners' own answers.

Wrap up

- **Critical thinking:** To finish off, learners tell the class similarities or differences between Australia and their own country.

Note: Writing numbers and dates

- In some countries, a point is used to separate each three zeros in large numbers; in other countries, for example Britain, a comma is used. In these countries a point is used before decimals. Sometimes a space is used to separate the zeros.
- In some countries, the day comes before the month in dates. In other countries, the month comes before the day. This is important to consider as 5.6.2014 is *the fifth of June* in the UK, but *May sixth* in the USA.

Activity Book

1 Vocabulary

- Learners read the sentences about geographical features. They match the pictures to the descriptions and then write the words.

Answers
1 e   2 f   3 d   4 c   5 b   6 a

2 Word study

- Learners write sentences about their own country containing the words for geographical features.

Answers
Learners' own answers.

3 Read

- Learners read the dates and times and say why they are important.

> **Answers**
> Learners' own answers.

4 Challenge

- Learners choose five dates and times which are important in the history of their country. They draw a timeline and describe what happened at the times they have chosen.

> **Answers**
> Learners' own answers.

Differentiated instruction

Additional support and practice

- Offer extra opportunities to practise numbers and figures by playing *Bingo*. Write plenty of large numbers like 22 000 000 on the board and ask learners to practise saying them. Draw a bingo grid for six numbers for learners to copy. From the numbers on the board, learners choose and write six numbers in figures on the grid. Call out the numbers for learners to cross off. The first to cross off all the numbers is the winner and shouts *Bingo*.
- *Bingo* can be adapted for practice with fractions, years, ordinal numbers, etc.

Extend and challenge

- Learners compile an *Interesting facts and figures quiz*. They each find out five interesting dates or statistics, and they work with three other learners, giving a total of 20 facts. They turn the quiz into a multiple-choice activity by adding two false figures. They then ask the rest of the class, for example: *When was the French revolution? Was it **a** 1789, **b** 1879 or **c** 1989?*

Lesson 3: Animal matters

Learner's Book pages: 100–101
Activity Book pages: 80–81

Lesson objectives

Listening: Listen to a radio report.

Speaking: Describe endangered animals.

Pronunciation: Numbers.

Critical thinking: Give reasons why animals become extinct.

Language focus: Infinitive of purpose.

Vocabulary: (Wild) animals including animals from Australia and revision from other units: *kangaroo, crocodile, snake, spider, echidna, platypus, Tasmanian devil, koala, numbat, bilby, endangered species, rare, common*

Materials: Pictures of animals typically found in Australia, **Photocopiable activity 13**.

Learner's Book

☞ Warm up

- Have a competition to see which team can write the most animals in a minute. Give double points for Australian animals.
- The learners with the most points read out their list. Check the animals are correct before announcing the winners. Build up a list on the board.

1 ✎ Talk about it

- Check learners understand the meaning of *wild, rare* and *common* before discussing the answers.
- **Critical thinking:** Engage the learners in a class discussion based on these questions. Bring in as many visuals of endangered animals as possible.

> **Answers**
> Learners' own answers.

[AB] **For further practice, see Activity 1 in the Activity Book.**

Listening strategy

- To help learners predict the words they will hear in **Activity 2**, write words like *kangaroos/koalas* and *Australia/America* on the board. Ask learners for the words we can use when speaking about these when we want to avoid repetition, for example: *they, them, these* and *it, here (there)*. Make sure learners use this knowledge to help fill in the missing words in **Activity 2**.

2 ✎ Listen 37 [CD2 Track 10]

- Focus on the introduction. Learners listen for and complete the missing words. If you have a lower-level group, read the text first and discuss the kinds of words that could go in the spaces.

> **Audioscript:** Track 37
> See Learner's Book page 100.

> **Answers**
> **1** It **2** here **3** these **4** This

3 Listen 38 [CD2 Track 11]

- There is lots of information in the text, so it will be useful to revise strategies for overcoming the difficulties this will cause, especially in lower-level classes. Before listening, discuss ideas with learners to help them make predictions about what they will hear. See **Additional support** section.

- Learners listen to the recording and answer the questions. If necessary, listen twice and pause the recording for learners to write.
- After listening, there is an opportunity to have a more general discussion about endangered species and link this to a discussion about values.

Audioscript: Track 38

Unique Australian animals such as koalas, numbats, Tasmanian devils and bilbies are all examples of endangered species. So why do animals become endangered? Well, there are several reasons. Many species of animals lose their homes when towns are built on their habitats – places such as fields and forests where they live. In some parts of Australia, this has happened to the habitat of the koala. There are still large numbers of koalas in some parts of Australia, but in other parts, their numbers are dropping. Several hundred years ago, there were millions of koalas, now some experts think that there are fewer than 50 000 left in the wild.

The bilby is another unique Australian animal that is now rare in some parts of the country. Numbers of bilbies are getting smaller because human beings destroy their habitats to build houses and towns. Some animals become endangered because they are killed by other animals, such as cats and foxes. This has happened to large numbers of bilbies and another special Australian animal called the numbat. Native animals like bilbies, numbats and koalas have existed in Australia for many thousands of years. Animals like cats and foxes are quite new to Australia and were introduced by people who settled there a few hundred years ago.

Some animals become endangered because they catch diseases and become very ill. When one animal catches a disease, it is very easy for another to catch it too because they live close to each other and eat the same food. This has happened to the Tasmanian devil, a noisy and aggressive little animal that only lives in the state of Tasmania. There are still plenty of Tasmanian devils, but since the 1990s, many have died from a disease called DVTD. This disease is now present in 60% of the island of Tasmania. Australian scientists are doing research to find a cure for the disease and the Tasmanian devil has become a protected species.

Nowadays, the government of Australia works hard to protect its endangered animals. In some areas, there are rules to stop people building houses on the places where these animals live. Then they can live in peace and produce more young to make the population grow again.

Answers
1 because they have lost their homes when towns are built on their habitats
2 because they are killed by other animals
3 Many have died from a disease called DVTD.

4 📝 **Listen** 38 [CD2 Track 11]
- Learners copy the table into their notebooks, adding *Bilby, Numbat* and *Tasmanian devil.*
- **Critical thinking:** Play the recording again (Track 38). Learners listen for the information and complete the table. Make sure they only listen for the information requested. They will listen again to the last part of the recording later.

Answers

Endangered animal	Reasons
Koala	People destroy their habitats to build houses.
Bilby	People destroy their habitats to build houses. They are killed by other animals such as cats and foxes.
Numbat	They are killed by other animals such as cats and foxes.
Tasmanian devil	Many have died from a disease called DVTD.

Language detective

- Focus on the sentences from the listening activity. Ask concept-check questions to check learners have understood the meaning of *to build*. Tell them this structure is known as the *infinitive of purpose*.
- Work with the class to build up a list of sentences using the target structure. For example ask: *Where did you go yesterday? I went to the city centre. Why did you go there? To buy a t-shirt.* Write: *I went to the city centre to buy a t-shirt* on the board.

5 📝 **Listen** 39 [CD2 Track 12]
- Learners use the infinitive of purpose to complete the sentences. Read the sentences before listening and help lower-level groups to make predictions about the missing words.

Audioscript: Track 39

Some animals become endangered because they catch diseases and become very ill. When one animal catches a disease, it is very easy for another to catch it too because they live close to each other and eat the same food. This has happened to the Tasmanian devil, a noisy and aggressive little animal that only lives in the state of Tasmania. There are still plenty of Tasmanian devils, but since the 1990s, many have died from a disease called DVTD. This disease is now present in 60% of the island of Tasmania. Australian scientists are doing research to find a cure for the disease and the Tasmanian devil has become a protected species.

Nowadays, the government of Australia works hard to protect its endangered animals. In some areas, there are rules to stop people building houses on the places where these animals live. Then they can live in peace and produce more young to make the population grow again.

Answers
a to find
b to protect
c to stop
d to make

6 Pronunciation 40 [CD2 Track 13]
- Discuss which numbers learners have problems understanding before listening to the recording. Ask questions to check learners have understood the difference between *fifty* and *fifteen,* etc.

Audioscript: Track 40

1 fifty

2 sixty

3 fifteen

4 sixteen

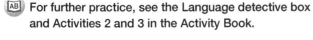 For further practice, see the Language detective box and Activities 2 and 3 in the Activity Book.

7 📝 💬 Talk

- On the board, talk through a list of animals which are/were common where learners live. In lower-level classes, you may need to discuss ideas for questions **1**, **2** and **3** before learners work together in pairs.
- **Critical thinking:** Allow time for learners to discuss in groups. Make sure you circulate and offer support.

Answers
Learners' own answers.

8 📝 💬 Over to you

- Learners use these ideas to make notes and prepare a short presentation to give the class. Encourage them to use as many props and visuals as possible.

Answers
Learners' own answers – Portfolio opportunity.

📤 Wrap up

- **Home–school link:** Learners produce a poster about animals living in their country. The poster can be taken home to share with parents or carers.

Activity Book

1 📝 🖼 Read

- Learners read about five types of animal, looking for information in the text to complete a table.

Answers

Animal	Type	Why it is special
Kangaroos, koalas, wombats	Mammal – marsupial	They have a pouch on their stomach to carry their babies.
Echidna	Mammal – monotreme	They give birth by laying eggs and carry their babies in a pouch.
Funnel-web spider	Arachnid – spider	It is one of the deadliest spiders in the world.
The Fierce Snake	Reptile	One of the most poisonous snakes in the world.
Emu	Bird	It can't fly but can run very fast.

2 Pronunciation 69 [CD2 Track 42]

- Learners listen to and repeat four numbers.

Audioscript: Track 69

1 Up to 60 kilograms

2 Up to 70 kilometres per hour

3 45 days

4 55 days

3 Listen 70 [CD2 Track 43]

- Learners hear the numbers again and, this time, identify the correct stress pattern.

Answers
1 b **2** a **3** a **4** a

Language detective

- Learners use the **Language detective** box to revise the use of the *infinitive of purpose.*

4 Word study

- Learners match six sentence halves giving reasons for actions.

Answers
1 b **2** f **3** d **4** e **5** a **6** c

Differentiated instruction

Additional support and practice

- Help learners overcome the difficulties caused by the length of the recording and high-level and topic-specific vocabulary in Learner's Book **Activity 3**. Before listening, ensure learners have a basic understanding of the topic by re-reading the second part of the introduction. Focus on the two general reasons about why species are endangered (large numbers are dying and fewer animals are producing babies). Discuss the possible causes of this. Introduce words like *habitats, wild, diseases, produce young* which learners will hear.
- Extra practice of the *infinitive of purpose:* write ten sentences, photocopy them and cut each sentence up into two halves, for example: (*first half*) I went to Australia... (*second half*) ... to see a kangaroo. Learners match the sentence halves. You could make *Infinitive of purpose dominoes* by following the procedure in **Photocopiable activity 8**.

Extend and challenge

- **Photocopiable activity 13:** *Talking about Australian animals.* Learners read mini fact files about three different animals found in Australia and use prompts to make questions about them.
- Using the mini fact files in **Photocopiable activity 13** as a model, learners choose another Australian animal, find out information about it and write their own mini fact file.

Lesson 4: Taking a trip

Learner's Book pages: 102–103

Activity Book pages: 82–83

Lesson objectives

Reading: Read a blog.

Writing: Make notes and write a blog.

Critical thinking: What to do and see in different places.

Language focus: Present perfect simple.

Vocabulary: Going on a trip to Australia: *tent, camping, campsite, the outback, go snorkelling;* wildlife: *endangered species, fish, turtles, snakes, spiders*

Materials: Pictures of interesting places to visit, **Photocopiable activity 14.**

Learner's Book

Warm up

- Learners come to the front and mime reasons for going on a holiday. Other learners guess the name of the activity. Write the activities on the board. Use the *infinitive of purpose* (the **Use of English** focus of the previous lesson), for example: *to swim in the sea, to go snorkelling, to relax, to sunbathe, to see a kangaroo.*

1 Talk about it

- Demonstrate the activity by asking learners their reasons for going away and how they keep in contact when they are away.
- Learners tell their partners their reasons for going away and how they keep in contact.

> **Answers**
> Learners' own answers.

2 Read

- Learners read the text to find out the purpose of the trip for Daniel and his mum. Remind learners of strategies for reading for specific information.

> **Answers**
> Learners' own answers.

3 Read

- Focus on the pictures and discuss what you can see. Ask learners which blue word goes with each picture.

> **Answers**
> 1 turtles 2 beach 3 rubbish

4 Read

- Focus on the three pieces of information learners need to look for in *Day 1*. For learners needing additional support, discuss which tense the information could be in, i.e. present continuous, past simple and *going to.*

- Learners re-read the text and look for the information.

> **Answers**
> He's sitting in his tent.
> They set off from Darwin.
> They're travelling to the beach.

5 Write

- Learners copy the headings into their notebooks to make notes on *Day 4* of Daniel's blog. Circulate and monitor as they make notes following the guidance from the **Writing tip**.

> **Answers**
> Learners' own answers.

Language detective

- Write a regular verb on the board and ask learners how to form the present perfect tense.
- Look at the **Language detective** box with the learners. Focus on the two examples of the present perfect tense with *for* and *since*. Ask concept-check questions to check learners understand this form is being used to connect the present and the past. (In the first example, it describes an ongoing state and in the second, it describes a series of actions from a specific point in the past up until the present time.)
- Practise using the present perfect to describe ongoing states. Ask learners questions like: *How long have you known your best friend? How long have you been in this class?*
- Practise using the present perfect to describe a series of actions from a specific point in the past up until the present time. For example, ask: *How much milk have you drunk this week? How many times have you spoken English since Monday?*
- See **Additional support and practice** and **Extend and challenge** for ideas about further practice and development.

6 Use of English

- Learners complete the blog using the present perfect tense. Lower-level learners may need help with the irregular past participle of *write.*

> **Answers**
> **a** have been   **b** has collected   **c** has written

 For further practice, see the Language detective box and Activities 1 and 2 in the Activity Book.

7 Write

- Step 1: Talk about places where learners would like to go for a trip. Discuss what they can do there.
- Learners choose a place and make notes about what they are going to do there.
- Step 2: Learners decide how long the trip will last and make notes on what they will do each day. Circulate and give extra support to lower-level learners.

- Step 3: Learners make notes under the three headings.
- Step 4: If necessary, list adjectives to describe the places and how people might feel when they visit them, before learners make notes on this information.
- Learners are now ready to write up the blog they have planned. See **Additional support and practice**. Circulate and offer help and support.
- Learners read their classmates' blogs and make notes following the procedure outlined in the **Writing tip**.

> **Answers**
> Learners' own answers – Portfolio opportunity.

 For further practice, see Activities 3 and 4 in the Activity Book.

Wrap up

- If you have Internet access in the classroom and it is permitted by your school, show learners other interesting blogs from learners of the same age. Otherwise, you could print some blogs out to show them.

Activity Book

Language detective

- Learners use the **Language detective** box to revise the form of present perfect with *for* and *since*.

1 Use of English

- Focus on the **Language detective** box and the verbs and complete Erin's blog with the correct form of the present perfect.

> **Answers**
> 2 haven't spoken
> 3 Has/forgotten
> 4 have had
> 5 've seen
> 6 hasn't written

2 Use of English

- Learners practise using the present perfect with *for* and *since* by completing a series of sentences.

> **Answers**
> 2 Since/'s written
> 3 've seen/since
> 4 haven't spoken/for
> 5 Since/'s visited
> 6 haven't done/for
> 7 haven't/sent/since

3 Make notes

- Learners match headings to Erin's notes about the saltwater crocodile.

> **Answers**
> **Population** c
> **Length** a
> **Description** e
> **Weight** b
> **Habitat** d

4  Challenge

- Learners write their own blog or journal entry about a place they've been to recently (Portfolio opportunity).

> ### Differentiated instruction
>
> **Additional support and practice**
>
> - Offer extra opportunities to practise the affirmative form of the present perfect. Write regular verbs on the board. Learners make sentences about themselves using these verbs with *for* and *since*.
> - In lower-level classes, before learners write up their blogs in Learner's Book **Activity 7**, focus on the verb tenses used in **Activity 6**. Circulate and ensure learners use the same tenses to talk about now, past and future time.
>
> **Extend and challenge**
>
> - **Photocopiable activity 14:** *What has the weather been like?* Learners use six cards as prompts to use the present perfect to talk about the weather (**Unit 7: Lesson 1**).
> - If learners enjoyed playing Bingo, pre-teach new past participles and play *Irregular past participles Bingo*. Choose about 12 past participles and write them on the board. Learners draw a bingo grid with six squares. They choose six verbs from the board and write the *base form* in the grid. Call out the past participle and learners tick off the verbs they have chosen when they hear them.

Note: For next lesson: ask learners to bring in examples of traditional stories they have at home.

Lesson 5: *Why emus can't fly*

Learner's Book pages: 104–107
Activity Book pages: 84–85

Lesson objectives

Speaking: Talk about traditional stories.

Critical thinking: Identify and understand traditional tales.

Vocabulary: *Synonyms* and describing movement

Values: What to do if you feel jealous.

Materials: Traditional stories, preferably in English from the learners' country. Learners could bring their own books if they have them.

Warm up

- Show the learners the story books. On the board, talk through a list of traditional stories. Practise using the present perfect from the last lesson by asking learners: *Have you read ... ?* Revise the *past simple* by asking: *Did you like it?*
- Ask: *Why?/Why not?* Build up a list of suitable adjectives on the board, for example: *boring, fantastic, exciting.*

1 Talk about it

- Allow a time limit for learners to think of as many traditional stories from their country as they can in pairs.
- **Critical thinking:** Write a list on the board (preferably in English). If they can't think of stories from their country, extend the activity to traditional stories in general. What is similar about them?
- Demonstrate the activity by asking higher-level learners the questions before allowing learners to work in pairs.

> **Answers**
> Learners' own answers.

2 Read and listen 41 [CD2 Track 14]

- Again, this is a long text with a lot of information for learners of this level. Learners will need to apply the reading strategies they have been developing. If necessary, before reading, discuss these strategies.
- Focus on the information learners need to look for in question 1, before reading and listening to the first part of the story.
- Repeat this procedure in order to answer the other questions related to the text.

> **Audioscript:** Track 41
> See Learner's Book pages 104–106.

> **Answers**
> 1 Dinewan the Emu and Goomblegubbon the Turkey.

> **Answers**
> 1 Learners' own answers.
> 2 It's a sign you are a special bird.
> 3 He walked home striding across the plain.
> 4 They took off their wings.
> 5 Brush Turkey
> 6 He was angry (and sad).
> 7 He laughed.
> 8 He had too many children to feed.
> 9 to send some of his children away
> 10 He sent his chicks to live with their aunts and uncles.
> 11 He laughed.

3 Talk

- Discuss which is the true reason, encouraging learners to justify their answers with ideas from the story. Your discussion can also include learners' general responses to the story. Lower-level learners may need more support for this.

> **Answers**
> Learners' own answers (2).

4 Talk

- Discuss what the message of the story could be and reasons for thinking this. Again, give lower-level learners more support.

> **Answers**
> Learners' own answers.

5 Word study

- Learners copy the words in the box into their notebooks. Check they know the meaning.
- Look at the first blue word *huge* and encourage learners to predict the meaning by looking at the whole sentence and the picture of the Emu, before looking for the synonym in the word box.
- Learners use these strategies to match the other blue words with their meaning from the word box. See **Additional support and practice**.

> **Answers**
> huge/very big   swiftly/quickly   tale/story   striking out/hitting
> tricked/silly   puzzled/confused   foolish/stupid

6 Word study

- Focus on the definitions and check learners understand them.
- Look at the first green word and encourage learners to predict the meaning from the context, before choosing the correct definition.
- Learners use this strategy to match the other green words with their definitions. See **Additional support and practice**.

> **Answers**
> 1 flapped
> 2 race
> 3 striding
> 4 sprinted
> 5 rushed at
> 6 landing

For further practice, see Activities 1, 2, 3 and 4 in the Activity Book.

7 Values

- Talk about situations where learners of this age might feel jealous.
- Learners discuss why the advice given is good or bad advice.

> **Answers**
> Learners' own answers.

☞ Wrap up

- Learners give advice about what to do in different situations when they feel jealous.

Activity Book

1 Read

- Learners re-read the story on pages 104–106 of the Learner's Book. They then correct the incorrect words in the sentences.

> **Answers**
> 2 flying/fly
> 3 walking
> 4 wife
> 5 take off
> 6 flies
> 7 wins

2 Read

- Learners read the sentences about the story and put them in order.

> **Answers**
> c e g a d b f

3 Vocabulary

- Learners complete sentences about the story. If necessary, they read the story again.

> **Answers**
> 2 swiftly
> 3 story
> 4 striking
> 5 tricked
> 6 puzzled
> 7 stupid

4 Vocabulary

- Direct learners' attention to the pictures. Learners match each picture to a verb of movement.

> **Answers**
> 1 sprint   2 stride   3 race   4 rush at   5 land   6 flap

Differentiated instruction

Additional support and practice

- Lower-level classes may find the matching activities in the Learner's Book (**Activities 5** and **6**) challenging. Offer some support by doing some examples together and by circulating and offering advice.
- Practise using the verbs for talking about movement from **Lessons 5–6**. Learners mime the verbs and the others guess.

Extend and challenge

- Learners write about a situation where they felt jealous, or someone felt jealous of them. Explain who felt jealous of whom, why and if/how they overcame these feelings.
- Encourage learners to read more short stories like this one, which have a message or a moral. Look for collections of *Aesop's Fables* on the Internet or in the library.

Lesson 6: Choose a project

Learner's Book pages: 108–109
Activity Book pages: 86–87

Lesson objectives

Writing: Project 1 Write a country fact file, or **Project 2** Write a report about an endangered animal.

Speaking: Present a fact file or report to the class.

Critical thinking: Describe a country or think about why an animal is endangered.

Language focus: Unit 7 Review

Materials: Interesting pictures of different countries and endangered animals, books with information about different countries. Learners could bring their geography books, or you could take them to the school library to find suitable books.

Learner's Book

☞ Warm up

- Generate interest in the first project by showing the pictures of different countries to the class.
- Learners think about their own country. Revise words and expressions from the unit that could go under the headings by having a competition in teams.
- Generate interest in the second project by showing the pictures of endangered animals.
- Choose an animal that learners have studied. See which team can remember the most facts about the

animal. Consider its habitat, what it looks like, what it eats and why it is endangered.

> **Answers**
> Learners' own answers.

Choose a project

- Learners work in pairs. Allow them time to choose one of the projects. Ask for a show of hands to indicate which project each pair has chosen and ask relevant questions about their choices.

1 Write a country fact file

- Take learners to the library or bring suitable reference books in to the class. Guide them to the most appropriate sources of information: books, encyclopaedias, magazines, the Internet (if school rules allow). Learners look for the information in Step 3 and create their fact files in Step 4.
- Circulate and offer help and suggestions while learners complete their posters.

2 Write a report about an endangered animal

- Take learners to the library or bring suitable reference books to the class. Guide them to the most appropriate sources of information: books, encyclopaedias, magazines, the Internet (if school rules allow).
- Step 1: Learners look for and choose two or three animals for their report.
- Step 2: Circulate and make sure learners include the information in their reports. Offer support where necessary.

☞ Wrap up

- Learners present their posters or reports to the class.
- **Portfolio opportunity:** If possible, leave the learners' projects on display for a while. Then consider dating and filing them, photos or scans of the work, in learners' portfolios.

Reflect on your learning

- Reintroduce the Big question from **Lesson 1**: *What can we learn about one country?* Discuss learners' responses to the question now and compare them with their comments at the beginning of the unit. Has much changed?
- Divide the class into two teams (or more if your class is very large).
- Choose two team members from each team to come to the front for each question. Learners take turns to give an example of extreme weather.
- Give each team a point for each correct answer.

- Continue the competition with other learners using the other tasks.
- The winning team is the one with more points at the end of the competition.

> **Answers**
> Learners' own answers.

Look what I can do!

- **Aim:** To check learners can do all the things from **Unit 7**.
- Whichever approach you choose for these revision activities (asking for volunteers to show the class evidence that they can do one of the things on the list, making them into a competition, etc.) remember to give support to lower-level learners and use the activities as an opportunity to assess what learners have learned. As always, use this information to customise your teaching as you go on to **Unit 8**.

> **Answers**
> Learners' own answers.

Activity Book

Unit 7 Revision

- Direct learners' attention to the multiple-choice revision activity. Learners complete sentences by choosing the correct word.

> **Answers**
> 1 c   2 a   3 b   4 c   5 b   6 a
> 7 c   8 a   9 c   10 c   11 b   12 c.

My global progress

- Learners think about what they have studied in the unit and answer the questions.

> **Answers**
> Learners' own answers.

> ### Differentiated instruction
> #### Suggestions for further reading
> There are lots of fairy tales, short stories, etc. that learners might be interested in. It is worth a trip to the library to encourage them to choose something which they find interesting.

8 The human race

Unit overview

In this unit learners will:

- talk about physical appearance
- learn about traditional dances
- read about a crime
- write about a crime
- role play an interview
- read about a famous crime
- identify homophones.

Learners will learn how to describe people before listening to descriptions and matching them with photos. They will develop an awareness of different dances around the world and learn how to describe dances using verbs of movement.

Learners will apply their new knowledge from **Lessons 3 and 4** by reading about theft and listening to the description of a thief. They will learn expressions for speaking about crimes while developing their reading and listening skills. Learners will use the new vocabulary to describe a crime, including a description of the suspect and how the crime was resolved.

At the end of the unit, learners will apply and personalise what they have learned and practise reading strategies by reading a crime story. They will develop writing skills by learning how to plan and write a newspaper article or create a piece of writing about a modern dance.

Language focus

Adjectives to describe movement, verbs of movement, quantative pronouns, phrasal verbs.

Vocabulary topics: describing people, dancing, crime.

Self-assessment

- I can talk about facial characteristics.
- I can describe a traditional dance.
- I can understand the sequence of events of a crime.
- I can write about a crime.
- I can interview someone.
- I can identify homophones.
- I can understand an account of a famous crime.

Teaching tip

While learners are doing speaking activities using newly acquired expressions of grammar, remember to monitor how effective they are in applying their new knowledge. You can do this by circulating as learners are participating in the activity, but try to do so without interfering with their confidence. Make sure learners feel they have freedom to express ideas and remember that making mistakes is an important part of the learning process.

Lesson 1: The human race

Learner's Book pages: 110–111

Activity Book pages: 88–89

Lesson objectives

Listening: Listen to descriptions and instructions.

Speaking: Describe people.

Vocabulary: Describing people: *face, eyes, nose, lips, skin, hair, long, straight, wavy, fine, blonde, dark, fair, pale, round*

Materials: Pictures of children and adults to show to the class to demonstrate long/short hair, dark/fair hair, etc.

Learner's Book

Warm up

- Introduce the Big question: *What makes people different? What makes them the same?* Discuss this with the learners. Write down their ideas and save them for the end of the unit.
- This unit explores the different ways people look. Please stress that differences in looks do not have good or bad values – everyone is equally worthy. This is simply a way of describing people.
- Play a game. Show the class a picture of a child with *dark hair*. Ask the class to put up their hands if they've got dark hair. Repeat for *blonde hair, long/short/straight/wavy hair, blue/brown eyes, pale/fair/dark skin,* etc.
- Build up a list of useful vocabulary on the board.
- Ask questions with superlative adjectives, for example: *Who is the tallest? Who has the longest hair?*

1 🗨 Talk about it

- Learners describe the people in the photos. Encourage the use of the vocabulary on the board.
- Encourage the use of comparative and superlative adjectives, for example: *The girl in picture **a** has the longest hair, boy **b** has shorter fairer hair than boy **d**.*

> **Answers**
> Learners' own answers.

2 📝 Listen 42 [CD2 Track 15]

- Learners listen to the recording and match the people to the pictures. As they have practised describing the people in the pictures, learners shouldn't have any problems with this task.

> **Answers**
> **a** 3 **b** 2 **c** 1 **d** 4

> **Audioscript:** Track 42
> 1 She's got short, straight, dark hair and little eyes. She's got a small round face and a small nose.
> 2 He's got fine, blond hair and blue eyes. He's got a straight nose.
> 3 She's got long, black, straight hair. She's got small brown eyes.
> 4 He's got black hair and big brown eyes.

3 📝 Listen 42 [CD2 Track 15]

- Play the recording again, so learners can complete the sentences. In lower-level classes, pause the recording to give learners time to write.

> **Answers**
> 1 straight, dark
> 2 fine, blond
> 3 black, straight
> 4 black, brown

4 Word study

- Learners copy the table into their notebooks. Demonstrate the activity by looking at the first two words together and discussing where they could go. (Sometimes there is more than one possibility.) In lower-level classes, give learners more support by discussing more examples together.
- Allow learners time to complete the activity in pairs, before checking the answers.

> **Answers**
>
> | face | hair | eyes |
> | --- | --- | --- |
> | thin | dark | dark |
> | wide | fair | shiny |
> | round | thick | round |
> | square | fine | little |
> | oval | shiny | |
> | pointed | spiky | |
> | little | thin | |

[AB] For further practice, see Activities 1, 2 and 3 in the Activity Book.

5 Talk

- Demonstrate by asking a learner to describe a famous person for the class to guess who it is.
- Learners work in pairs. Circulate and offer help and assistance especially to lower-level learners.

> **Answers**
> Learners' own answers.

6 🗨 Talk

- Look at the first character as a class. Ask learners to say one thing each about the character. If learners have difficulties, ask questions to help them, for example: *What about his/her hair? Is it dark?*

> **Answers**
> Learners' own answers.

7 📝 Listen 43 [CD2 Track 16]

- Ask a learner or learners who like drawing to come to the front. Give them a board pen to draw the cartoon face on the board.
- Play the recording. Learners try and draw the cartoon face on the board following the instructions in the recording.

> **Audioscript:** Track 43
>
> First of all, you draw the round nose.
>
> Then you add the eyes which are very big. Over the top of the eyes, draw two small eyebrows.
>
> Next, draw the shape of the face, from the nose around the face to the other side. Draw an ear.
>
> After that, draw a big smiling mouth.
>
> Finally, draw the spiky hair.

8 🗨 Talk

- The class votes for the face which is the closest to the description. See **Additional support and practice**.

> **Answers**
> Learners' own answers.

9 📝🗨 Over to you

- Allow learners time to draw their own cartoon faces, encouraging them to be as creative as possible and make sure their partners can't see.
- Demonstrate by asking a learner to describe a face, while another learner draws it on the board. Ensure the learner uses the new vocabulary. In lower-level classes, more examples may be necessary.
- Allow time for learners to describe their face for their partners to draw. Circulate and offer support and assistance especially to lower-level learners.
- Learners compare their cartoons.

> **Answers**
> Learners' own answers – Portfolio opportunity.

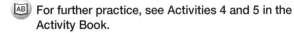 For further practice, see Activities 4 and 5 in the Activity Book.

☞ Wrap up

- Put the cartoon drawings on the wall. Learners describe one of them without saying which it is. The class guesses which picture is being described.

Activity Book

1 Vocabulary

- Direct learners' attention to the pictures of children. Match the pictures with the words.

> **Answers**
> **A** straight hair, shiny hair
> **B** curly hair, a little nose
> **C** spiky hair, big eyes

2 Vocabulary

- Learners look at the pictures and say whether the sentences are true or false.

> **Answers**
> **1** True
> **2** True
> **3** False (spiky hair)
> **4** False (curly, dark hair)
> **5** True
> **6** True

3 📝 Write

- Learners write more sentences describing the children.

> **Answers**
> Learners' own answers.

4 Listen 71 [CD2 Track 44]

- Learners listen to the recording and complete the notes about the cartoon faces.
- Then they draw the cartoon face, following the notes.

> **Audioscript:** Track 71
>
> First draw a big, square face.
>
> Then draw the eyes which are small and round.
>
> Above the eyes draw two thick eyebrows. One is higher than the other.
>
> Next draw a long, pointed nose and two small ears.
>
> After that, draw a big, wide, smiling mouth.
>
> Finally draw lots of short, curly hair on top of his head.

> **Answers**
> **2** round **3** thick **4** pointed **5** small **6** wide **7** short

5 Challenge

- Learners write instructions for drawing a cartoon face.

> **Answers**
> Learners' own answers.

Differentiated instruction

Additional support and practice

- If learners enjoyed drawing on the board, give instructions to draw more cartoon faces. Other learners come to the front and try and draw a cartoon face while their classmates say if they have drawn the face correctly according to the instructions.
- Play *Guess who!* Choose a learner to think of a classmate without saying who it is. The class take turns to ask about what the classmate looks like, in order to guess who the classmate is. Make sure only complimentary things are said. Remember to start: *Is it a boy or a girl?* and then guess: *Is it Petra, etc.?*

Extend and challenge

- Learners look for pictures of celebrities who have changed their look. They can look in magazines or websites for learners of their own age. Revise and practise structures like the past simple, present perfect and/or comparative adjectives to compare the pictures, for example: *She has changed her hair. It was darker before. She had shorter hair before.*

Lesson 2: Traditional dances

Learner's Book pages: 112–113
Activity Book pages: 90–91

Lesson objectives

Reading: Read about traditional dances.

Speaking: Talk about traditional dances.

Critical thinking: Awareness of different types of dances around the world.

Language focus: Verbs of movement.

Vocabulary: Dancing: *stamp your feet, slap your arms, pull faces, clap your hands*

Materials: Photocopiable activity 15.

Learner's Book

Warm up

- Ask learners if they know the names of any dances. Ask about dances they did at nursery school as well as famous dances from their country and other countries. Build up a list on the board.
- Mime *stamp your feet, slap your arms, pull faces, clap your hands* and write the new words on the board.

- Ask learners to mime a dance they know. Write the words for the different movements on the board.

1 🗩 Talk about it

- Focus on the pictures. If learners don't know where the dances are from, write *might, may, could* and *must* on the board and encourage them to speculate. This will help them make predictions about what they will read.

> **Answers**
> Learners' own answers.

2 Read

- Learners read the texts quickly to see if they were right. There is lots of other information in the texts. Make sure learners know that, for now, they only need to find this information. Discuss reading strategies if necessary.

> **Answers**
> The Haka dance is from New Zealand.
> Flamenco is from Spain.

3 📝 Read

- Focus on the statements. Help learners make predictions by discussing whether they think the sentences are true or false.
- Learners re-read the text and check their predictions.

> **Answers**
> 1 false (It is famous all over the world.)
> 2 true
> 3 false (In ancient times, it was performed to intimidate and threaten opponents before a war.)
> 4 false (It is performed by men and women.)
> 5 true

Reading strategy

> Focus on the **Reading strategy** and discuss ways of guessing the meaning of new words. Discuss why it is useful to do this.

4 📝 🗩 Read

- Focus on the first blue word in the text, i.e. *ancient*. Discuss what part of speech the word is. Look at the clues in the text to help learners guess the meaning, for example: it gives more information about *times*. The dance *was performed before a war*. Note the use of the simple past tense.
- If learners can't guess, look at the definitions to see which one could fit. Eliminate descriptions that are the wrong part of speech or have a meaning that doesn't fit the context.
- Learners work in pairs and match the definitions with the blue words. In lower-level classes, more examples and support may be necessary.

Answers
1 several
2 passionate
3 ancient
4 intimidate
5 opponents

 For further practice, see Activities 1 and 2 in the Activity Book.

Language detective

- Focus on the verbs of movement in the **Language detective** box. Read the text again and look for them. Demonstrate what they mean by miming them. See **Additional support and practice**.

5 Use of English

- Focus on the body parts. Learners match the verbs of movement with the relevant body parts.

Answers
bend – arms, knees
lift – arms, hands, feet
pull – arms, face
stamp – feet
slap – face, knees, arms
clap – hands
curve – arms, hands

 For further practice, see Activities 3, 4 and 5 in the Activity Book.

6 💬 Talk

- Write the names of some dances from the learners' country or countries on the board.
- **Critical thinking:** Ask learners to describe how to perform the dance before allowing time for learners to talk about it with a partner. If learners have difficulties, offer support by asking questions like: *Do you bend your arms?*
- While learners work in pairs, circulate and offer help and support.

Answers
Learners' own answers – Portfolio opportunity.

👉 Wrap up

- Learners tell the class how to perform the dance. The class listens and tries to perform the dance. Portfolio opportunity – take photos of this.

Activity Book

1 Read

- Direct learners' attention to the text and the pictures, paying particular attention to the underlined sentences. Learners read the text and match the pictures with the underlined sentences.

Answers
A 2 **B** 3 **C** 1

2 Word study

- Learners use the advice from the **Reading strategy** and **Activity 4** in the Learner's Book to help them match the bold words to the correct definition.

Answers
1 a 2 b 3 b 4 a 5 a

3 Use of English

- Focus on the verbs of movement and the pictures. Learners match the verbs to the correct pictures.

Answers
1 bend 2 stamp 3 twist 4 lift 5 clap 6 curve

4 Use of English

Learners complete the description for each picture by adding a verb and the correct part of the body. If necessary, revise the present continuous tense.

Answers
1 He is bending his knees.
2 She is stamping her feet.
3 They are twisting their waists.
4 He is lifting his arms.
5 She is clapping her hands.
6 They are curving their bodies.

5 Write

- Learners write sentences describing a dance they know about.

Answers
Learners' own answers.

Differentiated instruction

Additional support and practice

- Practise using the verbs of movement in the **Language detective** box by playing *Simon Says.* Give instructions for the class to follow using the verbs of movement, for example: *Simon says bend your arms.*

- 💬 **Photocopiable activity 15:** *Let's invent a new dance.* Learners create their own new dance using the vocabulary from the lesson. They write their answer to the first question, fold back the paper so it can't be read and then pass it on to the next pair to fill in the second part, and so on.

- **Home–school link:** They perform the dance for their families.

Extend and challenge

- Learners find out and make notes about other dances. They can look on the Internet or in the library. Learners tell the class about the dance, using their notes. The class votes for the most interesting dance.

Lesson 3: *The Golden Falcon*

Learner's Book pages: 114–115

Activity Book pages: 92–93

Lesson objectives

Reading: Read about a famous theft.

Listening: Listen to a description of a thief.

Pronunciation: Homophones.

Critical thinking: Analysing activities in reading.

Language focus: Quantative pronouns: *somewhere, everywhere, nowhere, anywhere, someone, somebody, no-one, nobody, anybody, everybody, something, nothing, everything, anything.*

Vocabulary: A theft: *valuable exhibits, stolen, the alarm began to sound, security guards, an eyewitness, a thief*

Learner's Book

Warm up

- Revise the dance vocabulary from the previous lesson. Learners mime a dance move and the class uses the new vocabulary to describe the dance move.

1 Talk about it

- Learners think of famous objects that have been stolen. If you have Internet access in the classroom, show learners examples of one of the many websites dedicated to the subject.

2 Read

- Learners read for specific information to answer the questions.

> **Answers**
> 1 An exhibit has been stolen from the Sachy Museum.
> 2 It happened during the early hours of Sunday morning.
> 3 It happened at the Sachy Museum.

[AB] **For further practice, see Activity 1 in the Activity Book.**

Language detective

- Focus on the words in the **Language detective** box. Tell learners to re-read the text and look for examples of the quantative pronouns. Write examples on the board and underline the quantative pronouns.
  - *Security guards did not see <u>anybody</u> entering or leaving the museum*
  - *An eyewitness confirms seeing <u>somebody</u> ...*
  - *Investigators have looked <u>everywhere</u> ...*
  - *... they are <u>nowhere</u> to be found.*
  - *<u>Nothing</u> else was stolen from the museum.*
- Elicit the rule from the learners by asking concept-check questions about each pronoun to help learners understand why it used, for example: *Does it refer to a person/a place/an object? Is it a question/a negative/an affirmation?*

3 Listen 44 [CD2 Track 17]

- Learners use the quantative pronouns to complete the activity before listening to the recording and checking their answers.

> **Audioscript:** Track 44
>
> Good evening. As you all know by now the Golden Falcon has been stolen by someone. Police teams are looking everywhere in the museum for fingerprints and other evidence which will help them find the thief, but so far nothing has been found. Nobody has reported seeing the thief enter the building, but the guards did hear something strange around eight o'clock, so they did a security check, but didn't find anything. We also have an eyewitness who saw somebody running out of the building and that is all the information we have for now.

> **Answers**
> 1 someone
> 2 everywhere
> 3 nothing
> 4 Nobody
> 5 something
> 6 somebody

[AB] **For further practice, see Activities 2, 3 and 4 in the Activity Book.**

4 Listen 45 [CD2 Track 18]

- **Critical thinking:** Help learners predict the kind of information they will hear by focusing on the four suspects and asking them to describe what they look like.
- Play the recording and ask learners to analyse the information to decide which man is the thief.

> **Audioscript:** Track 45
>
> **Policeman:** OK, could you describe what you saw last night, please?
>
> **Eyewitness:** Well I was doing the washing up and looking out of the window as I always do. It was about eight o'clock when I heard a door bang shut. Our dog started barking. I looked out of the window and there was a man running away from the museum. I saw part of his face and hair. He had dark, straight hair. I think he had brown eyes, but I'm not sure. Oh and, I nearly forgot, he had a very long, pointed nose.

> **Answers**
> Suspect 3

5 Pronunciation 46 [CD2 Track 19]

- Focus on the five pairs of words. Learners may be surprised to hear that each pair have the same pronunciation.
- Discuss the difference in meaning before listening to the recording and judging from the context which is the correct word.

Audioscript: Track 46

1   Well, I was doing the washing up.

2   It was about eight o'clock when I heard a door bang shut.

3   Our dog started barking.

4   I looked out of the window and there was a man running away from the museum.

5   Oh, and I nearly forgot he had a very long, pointed nose.

Answers
1 I   2 eight   3 our   4 there   5 nose

6   Pronunciation

• Focus on the sentences. Learners use clues from the context to find the mistakes and correct them.

Answers
1 No one **knows** who the thief is.
2 The guard **ate** a snack.
3 **Our** dog started to bark.
4 **There** was a man running out of the door.
5 He had a very long, pointed **nose**.

 For further practice, see Activity 5 in the Activity Book.

☞ Wrap up

• Learners work in pairs and write sentences containing homophones. Circulate and offer support.
• Learners read their sentences to the class, who use the context to say which is the correct word.

Activity Book

1 Read

• Focus on the quantative pronouns in the story. Learners read the story and choose which quantative pronouns are correct and circle them.

Answers
1 somebody   2 Nobody   3 nobody   4 everything
5 anywhere   6 somewhere

2 Read

• Learners read the story again and put the pictures in order.

Answers
b   d   e   a   f   c

3 Use of English

• Learners use one of the quantative pronouns to complete each of the sentences.

Answers
1 nowhere
2 anybody
3 nothing
4 something
5 Nobody

4 Quantifiers

• Learners match quantative pronouns to the words they represent in sentences.

Answers
1 e   2 a   3 d   4 c   5 b

5 Pronunciation 72 [CD2 Track 45]

• Focus on the homophones. Learners match the words that sound the same, before listening and checking their answers.

Audioscript: Track 72

1 ate	c eight
2 our	a hour
3 there	e their
4 knows	b nose
5 eye	d I

Answers
1 c   2 a   3 e   4 b   5 d

Differentiated instruction

Additional support and practice

• Offer extra opportunities to practise the quantative pronouns and questions with *happen*. Find out about a famous crime and tell learners to ask you questions, for example: *When did it happen? Did the thief steal anything valuable? Did anyone see the thief? Did the police arrest anyone?*

Extend and challenge

• 🗨 Play the *Alibi Game*. Choose four learners to come to front of the class. Tell the class the four are suspected of stealing the Golden Falcon. Each 'suspect' tells the class what they were doing on Saturday evening and Saturday night. The other learners ask *who/why/what* questions to check the suspects' alibis, for example: *Who were you with? Why did you go there? What time did you...? Did you see anyone?*

• Learners look for information about a famous object that was stolen. They could look on the Internet, in the library, or ask people for information. Find out: *Where was the object stolen from? When did it happen? Was the object ever found?* Use this information to write paragraphs about the theft. Include quantative pronouns.

Lesson 4: *The Golden Falcon flies home*

Learner's Book pages: 116–117

Activity Book pages: 94–95

Lesson objectives

Reading: Read a newspaper article.

Writing: Plan and write a newspaper article, punctuation, speech.

Vocabulary: Descriptions of people (revision from **Lesson 1**); crime (revision from **Lesson 3**): *passport control officers, prison*

Language Focus: speech marks.

Materials: Photocopiable activity 16.

Learner's Book

Warm up

- Have a competition in pairs. Allow a time limit to see who can recall the most facts from the story about the theft from the previous lesson.
- Learners with the most facts read them out to the class. Note the main points on the board.

1 🗨 Talk about it

- Write *might, may, must* and *can't* on the board. Focus on the headline. Use the modals to help speculate about what might have happened.

> **Answers**
> Learners' own answers.

2 Read

- **Critical thinking:** Learners read the article in order to assess how close it comes to their predictions.
- Discuss their reaction to the outcome – how many had predicted that?

> **Answers**
> The person who stole the Golden Falcon has been caught and the Golden Falcon has been flown back to the Sachy Museum.

3 📝 Read

- Focus on the five statements about the article. Ask learners questions to check they understand the statements before allowing them time to read the article again and see if they are true or false.

> **Answers**
> 1 false (He was getting on a plane.)
> 2 true
> 3 true
> 4 false (He had dark, straight hair.)
> 5 true

4 Punctuation

- Learners read the text again and find examples of where speech marks are used.
- Write examples on the board and ask questions to check learners understand why speech marks are used in the article. See **Additional support and practice**.

> **Answers**
> 1 when we write exactly what a person says.
> 2 inside

5 Write

- Learners use their new knowledge to punctuate the sentences. Demonstrate the activity with an example. Remind learners about where to use question marks and exclamation marks.

> **Answers**
> 1 'Someone has stolen the Golden Falcon,' cried the museum curator.
> 2 'Look! The thief is running away!' shouted the eyewitness.
> 3 'What were you doing?' asked the police officer.
> 4 'What did you see?' asked the reporter.
> 5 'What did he look like?' asked the police officer.

🔲 **For further practice, see Activities 1, 2 and 3 in the Activity Book.**

6 📝 Write

- Focus on the four pictures about a theft. Ask learners what they can see in the first picture. If necessary, ask questions like: *Where is the picture? Who is the woman? What is she doing?*
- Build up notes about the picture on the board, for example: *10 a.m., in a jeweller's shop, sales assistant waiting for customers.* Unless you have a high-level class, repeat for the other pictures.
- Learners use the pictures and the notes to make full sentences about each picture, for example: *At 10 a.m., the sales assistant was waiting for a customer in the jeweller's shop in the main street.*
- Circulate and offer support. Check learners are using the correct verb tenses, for example: past simple and continuous.

> **Answers**
> Learners' own answers.

7 📝 Write

- Step 1: Discuss ideas for the newspaper headline, before telling learners to write their own.
- Step 2: Look back at the language used in the introductions to the articles in **Lessons 3** and **4**. Learners use similar language (present perfect or present simple) to write an introduction for their articles.

- Steps 3 and 4: Learners write a paragraph to answer the questions.
- Step 5: If necessary, look back at **Lesson 1** and think about ideas for describing people, before learners write their own descriptions.
- Step 6: Lastly, learners write a short paragraph about how the crime was resolved.

Answers
Learners' own answers – Portfolio opportunity.

 For further practice, see Activity 4 in the Activity Book.

Wrap up

- Learners present their newspaper articles to the class.

Activity Book

1 Read

- Focus on the sentences. These are statements from the characters in the story. Learners match the sentences with the gaps in the text.

Answers
1 I was standing at my post when I heard a noise.
2 They hit me with a wooden stick and I fell to the ground,
3 No, I couldn't see well.
4 Guards, guards, over here!

2 Punctuation

- Learners practise using speech marks by inserting them in the correct place in the statements.

Answers
1 'I was standing at my post when I heard a noise,'
2 'They hit me with a wooden stick and I fell to the ground,'
3 'No, I couldn't see well.'
4 'Guards, guards, over here!'

3 Write

- Learners write phrases **a** – **e** in the correct column of the table.

Answers
Headline – c
Where did it happen? – a
What was stolen? – e
What did the thief look like? – b
How was the crime resolved? – d

4 Challenge

- Learners write a newspaper story about the robbery. Follow the instructions and if necessary, refer to the steps in the Learner's Book about how to write a newspaper article.

Answers
Learners' own answers.

Differentiated instruction

Additional support and practice

- Offer extra opportunities to practise punctuating sentences. Make up sentences and write them on the board without punctuation. Learners come to the board and punctuate them.
- After the writing exercises, learners cover up the story and try to recall it from memory. Ask *Who/ What/ Why?* questions to help if they get stuck.

Extend and challenge

- **Photocopiable activity 16:** *An interview with the thief who stole the Mona Lisa*. Learners read a short newspaper article with some missing information. They ask questions to find out this information.
- Learners bring a simple newspaper article in English that interests them to the class for other learners to read. They could look on the websites or special publications for learners of their age.

Lesson 5: The Mona Lisa

Learner's Book pages: 118–121
Activity Book pages: 96–97

Lesson objectives

Reading: Read a crime story.

Critical thinking: Understanding the features of a crime text.

Vocabulary: Phrasal verbs, crime

Materials: Pictures of the Louvre. If you have Internet in the classroom, show pictures of the Louvre and its exhibits, using the museum's website: www.louvre.fr

Learner's Book

Warm up

- Ask learners to write the names of as many famous museums as they can think of in one minute.
- Ask learners the name of the museum they have written. Practise the present perfect by asking: *Have you been there?* In the case of a positive answer, practise the past simple by asking: *What did you see there?*
- Show pictures of the Louvre and ask learners if they have been there and if so, what they saw. If they haven't been there, ask learners if they know anything about it.

1 Talk about it

- Focus on the picture and discuss the questions with the learners.

Answers
Learners' own answers.

2 Read

- Learners read the first part of the fact file and check if their answers were correct.

> **Answers**
> The Mona Lisa, painted by Leonardo da Vinci. It is a painting of Lisa Gherardini Giocondo.

3 Read and listen 47 [CD2 Track 20]

- **Critical thinking:** Learners will be getting used to looking for specific information in texts like this one which contains a lot of extra information. They should be developing the reading strategies needed to deal with the difficulties this causes. If necessary, before doing the activity, discuss reading strategies like making predictions and scanning a text for specific words.
- Learners read and listen for the answers to the questions 1–5 in the first part of the crime story on pages 118–119.
- Next focus on questions 6–10 which relate to the second half of the story on page 120. Learners read and listen to the end of the crime story.

> **Audioscript:** Track 47
> **See Learner's Book pages 118–120.**

> **Answers**
> 1 the following day
> 2 five years
> 3 Tuesday, August 22nd
> 4 a whole week
> 5 stared at the empty space on the wall
> 6 two years later
> 7 Alfredo Geri, a well-known antique dealer
> 8 half a million lire
> 9 hidden in a wooden trunk
> 10 he recognised the Louvre stamp on the back of the painting

4 Read

- Focus on the events 1–10. Ask questions to check learners understand words and expressions like *make contact, antique dealer, shortly after, at the bottom, wooden trunk, arrested, interviewed, recognised*.
- Demonstrate the activity by asking learners to look for the first two events in the text. In lower-level groups, more examples may be necessary.
- Allow time for learners to read the story again and put the events in order. Circulate and offer support.
- Discuss the text to ensure comprehension.

> **Answers**
> 3, 5, 1, 8, 2, 4, 9, 6, 10, 7

5 Read

- Learners scan the text, looking for the time expressions in green and match them with the sentence halves.

> **Answers**
> 1 f 2 c 3 a 4 b 5 e 6 d

6 Word study

- Focus on the first phrasal verb in the text – *look into*. Discuss ways learners know to help them predict the meaning of new words.
- Look at the words around *look into* and ask: *Who are 'investigators'? What do they do about crimes?* Look at the definitions and choose the one that matches best. In lower-level groups, more examples may be necessary.
- Allow learners time to do the activity, while you circulate and offer help where necessary.

> **Answers**
> 1 get away with
> 2 look into
> 3 broken into
> 4 made off with
> 5 locked up
> 6 ran off with

7 Talk

- Learners work in pairs. Tell them to cover up the story and see how much they can remember. Circulate and if learners get stuck, ask questions to help them remember.

> **Answers**
> Learners' own answers.

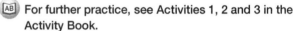 **For further practice, see Activities 1, 2 and 3 in the Activity Book.**

Wrap up

- Ask learners to retell the story to the class.

Activity Book

1 Read

- Learners read the story again on pages 118–120 of the Learner's Book. They choose the correct answer in the multiple-choice activity.

> **Answers**
> 1 a 2 a 3 b 4 b 5 b 6 b 7 b 8 a 9 b 10 b

2 Write

- Learners use the information from the story on pages 118–120 of the Learner's Book to complete the Police Report.

> **Answers**
> Learners' own answers.

3 Vocabulary

- Learners practise phrasal verbs for talking about crime by replacing the underlined words in the text with a phrasal verb from the selection.

Differentiated instruction

Additional support and practice

* Offer extra opportunities to practise phrasal verbs. Learners cut a piece of A4 paper into eight squares. Tell them to write a phrasal verb from the activity on one side of each square and, on the other, its definition. They will need to think of two extra phrasal verbs and their definitions. Spread the squares out with the phrasal verb facing up. Learners take turns to point to one and say the definition. Turn over the square and check.

* Learners make up sentences with the phrasal verbs in and write them on a class poster. Leave plenty of space and whenever you come across a new phrasal verb, add it to the list with an example sentence.

Extend and challenge

* Find out more information about the Louvre museum. Use this information to write a fact file. Include information about when the Louvre opens, where it is and how to get there. Focus on one of its exhibits and give information about the artist, when it was painted and what it shows.

* **Home–school link:** Learners find out about a museum they can visit in their own country. Tell them to look for a museum on a subject that interests them, for example, space, air travel, history, dinosaurs. Make a poster about what you can see there and other useful information for visitors, for example: when the museum opens, where it is and how to get there. Learners take this poster home to share with parents or carers.

Lesson 6: Choose a project

Learner's Book pages: 122–123

Activity Book pages: 98–99

Lesson objectives

Writing: Write a description of a modern dance (**Project 1**) or a newspaper article about a theft (**Project 2**).

Language focus: Unit 8 Review

Learner's Book

☞ Warm up

* Have competitions in teams to revise vocabulary from the unit: talking about different dance moves from **Lesson 2**, descriptions from **Lesson 1** and crime from **Lessons 3–5**.

* Learners from each team come to the front and answer questions about the language focus of each lesson of **Unit 8**, for example: for dance moves, mime and ask the name of the move. Award points for each correct answer.

Choose a project

* After the competition, tell learners they are going to choose one of the projects: *Describe a modern dance* or *Write a newspaper article about a theft*.

1 Describe a modern dance

* Work together to compile a list of modern dances on the board.
* Point to the names of the dances and ask questions, for example: *Where is this dance from? Can you describe this dance? How is it performed?* Ask the names of different movements.
* Elicit the sequencing words that learners know.
* Remember to give more support in lower-level classes, before focusing on the dance steps in the Learner's Book. Make sure learners follow these steps to create their own piece of writing.

2 Write a newspaper article about a theft

* Think up some ideas about *what* could have been stolen, and *where* and *when* it could have happened.
* Discuss ways of entering a building, making sure learners know the correct phrasal verbs and prepositions of movement.
* Focus on the steps in the Learner's Book and make sure learners follow these to create their own piece of writing.
* Circulate and give help and advice, especially about paragraph structure and sequencing words.

☞ Wrap up

* Learners present their projects to the class.
* **Portfolio opportunity:** If possible, leave the learners' projects on display for a while. Then consider dating and filing the projects, photos or scans of the work, in learners' portfolios.

Reflect on your learning

* Reintroduce the Big question from **Lesson 1**: *What makes people different? What makes them the same?* Discuss learners' responses to the question now and compare them with their comments at the beginning of the unit. Has much changed?
* Higher-level learners can work in pairs to do the activities. Circulate and assess their progress.
* Some learners will need more support.
* In **Activity 2**, learners can mime as well as saying how to perform the dance.

Answers
Learners' own answers.

Look what I can do!

- **Aim:** To check learners can do all the things from **Unit 8**.
- Whichever approach you choose for these revision activities, remember to give support to lower-level learners and use the activities as an opportunity to assess what learners have learned. As always, use this information to customise your teaching as you go on to **Unit 9**.

Answers
Learners' own answers.

Activity Book

Unit 8 Revision

1 Use of English

- Learners practise using the verbs of movement from **Lesson 2** by matching them to body parts.

Answers
1 c 2 a 3 e 4 b 5 d

2 Use of English

- Learners revise quantative pronouns from **Lesson 3** by using them to complete sentences.

Answers
1 everywhere
2 anybody
3 everything
4 Someone
5 something

3 Vocabulary

- Learners revise phrasal verbs about crime from **Lesson 5** by writing sentences containing them.

Answers
Learners' own answers.

4 Write

- Learners revise describing people from **Lesson 1** by writing descriptions about themselves and their families.

Answers
Learners' own answers.

My global progress

- Learners answer the questions to help them develop their critical thinking skills. They assess which topics and activities they enjoyed, think about any help they might need and what they would like to know more about.

Answers
Learners' own answers.

Differentiated instruction

Suggestions for further reading

Learners could look for further information about Leonardo da Vinci and his art.

Review 4

1 Listen 48 [CD2 Track 21]

- Think of strategies for listening for specific information, for example: listening for specific words, making predictions and using pictures to help. This is especially important for lower-level groups.
- Focus on the statements and encourage learners to make predictions. Ask learners what they can see in the picture.
- Play the recording to see if the statements are true or false. If necessary, play the recording again, pausing for learners to hear the relevant information.

```
Answers
1 false (There has been a tornado today.)
2 false (He's talking to a woman.)
3 true
4 false (The tornado destroyed her car.)
5 false (He was in his truck chasing the tornado.)
6 false (She doesn't think he's funny.)
```

Audioscript: Track 48

Reporter: There has been a terrible tornado in Littletown today. Winds are still high but people are starting to come back to their houses – or in some cases what's left of their houses. Here is one home owner. Hello, Mrs Robinson – what has happened to your house?

Mrs Robinson: What house?! Everything has gone. I've got nothing left. It's terrible.

Reporter: You seem very upset – you look pale and exhausted.

Mrs Robinson: Yes, well, my house has just blown away. It's not a normal day, is it?

Reporter: What about your car?

Mrs Robinson: Well … you're standing on what's left of my car. Everything else has disappeared.

Reporter: What about your family. Where are they?

Mrs Robinson: Well that's a strange thing. You see my husband has got an unusual hobby. He's a tornado chaser. He loves tornadoes. So he's out in his truck chasing the tornado that's completely destroyed my house.

Reporter: Isn't that funny!

Mrs Robinson: No, it's not funny. It's ridiculous.

2 Talk

- Demonstrate the activity with an example. Choose one of the weather words at random and describe it to see who can guess what the weather is.
- Circulate and offer help and support while learners continue the activity in groups.

3 Vocabulary

- Learners revise the homophones they met on page 115. They look at the words, choose a homophone and say the meaning of both words.

- If learners have difficulties remembering the homophones, make a card game to help them practise in class or at home. Each learner cuts an A4 sheet of paper into nine pieces. On each piece, learners write a word. On the back, they write the homophone in a different colour. Learners play the game by guessing the homophone and turning the card over to check.

```
Answers
1 ate
2 you're
3 knows
4 which
5 flower
6 wood
7 site
8 new
9 tail
```

4 Use of English

- Learners read the text about the Tasmanian devil and choose the correct option.
- This activity revises the present perfect (including time expressions), large numbers and quantitative pronouns. Use the activity to asses whether revision is necessary before going on to **Unit 9**.

```
Answers
1 someone
2 Since
3 two hundred
4 have lived
5 for
6 three thousand
7 Anyone
8 Nobody
```

5 Read

- Learners work in pairs to list as many facts they can about the Tasmanian devil from **Activity 4**.
- Check the information is correct by asking the pairs with the longest list to read them out to the class.

6 Write

- Make a list of the kinds of expressions learners have learned for describing people, before telling them to write a description of the thief using the prompts.
- For an extra challenge, higher-level learners write a dialogue about the thief returning the Tasmanian devil to the zookeeper. Before allowing learners to work alone or in pairs, ask the class for suggestions about the kind of things they might say to each other.

7 Talk

- Learners discuss **Units 7** and **8**. They discuss which country they would like to visit.
- Learners then contrast the units, saying which they liked better and which unit taught them more new things.

9 Looking backwards and forwards

Big question Why are some activities enjoyable?

Unit overview

In this unit learners will:
- talk about school holidays
- listen to an interview
- read advertisements for holidays
- do a class survey
- write an email
- read and practise a play.

Learners will look back over the year and carry out a class survey to find out which activities were most enjoyable and which were the most difficult. They will practise their listening skills by hearing what learners around the world do on holiday and revise free-time activities. Learners develop communication skills by talking about what they like and dislike about the long holidays. They will read advertisements about activity holidays and plan a holiday trip together.

Learners will further develop their literature skills by reading a short play about going back to school. The value focus of the unit is *being sympathetic.* Finally, the first project of the unit is a *Challenge plan poster* with fun challenges to encourage learners to apply their new knowledge of English and their new cultural knowledge during the holidays. The second project is *Creating a short play* which practises being sympathetic.

Language focus
Future simple for predictions

Making plans with *going to; we'll have to ...; we'll need ...*

Making suggestions

Most of us, some of us, a few of us

Vocabulary topics: holiday activities and equipment, agreeing and disagreeing, expressing numbers.

Self-assessment
- I can talk about school holiday activities.
- I can understand advertisements about holiday trips.
- I can make predictions about things to take on a holiday trip.
- I can carry out a class survey about study habits.
- I can write an email explaining plans for a celebration.
- I can understand a short play.
- I can read lines from the play using expression in my voice.

Teaching tip

This is a useful opportunity to find out what learners of this age enjoy and find difficult. The information can be used in the future to help you adapt your teaching strategies to the strengths and weaknesses of learners and to concentrate on activities they find interesting and stimulating.

However, remember that every class is unique and learners of every age have different interests and may enjoy different types of activities. What learners find easy or difficult will also depend on their culture and first language.

Lesson 1: Looking backwards and forwards

Learner's Book pages: 126–127

Activity Book pages: 100–101

Lesson objectives

Listening: Listen to a radio interview.

Speaking: Talk about school holidays.

Critical thinking: Forming opinions – agreeing and disagreeing.

Vocabulary: Holiday activities, agreeing and disagreeing

Learner's Book

Warm up

- With the learners, build up a list of things learners can do in the school holidays. Practise using structures that learners have studied throughout the year. Ask and answer questions like: *Do you go swimming in the summer holidays? How often? Who with? Have you ever been to a summer camp? Did you go last year? Are you going on holiday this year?*

> **Answers**
> Learners' own answers.

1 Talk about it

- Learners tell their partners about the kinds of activities they do in the summer holidays.
- Introduce and discuss the Big question: *Why are some activities enjoyable?* Discuss what it is about these activities that they like/don't like. Discuss and note their ideas.
- Ask learners the other questions about school holidays.

> **Answers**
> Learners' own answers.

2 Listen 49 [CD2 Track 22]

- Focus on the pictures of the children and the activities in the table. Make predictions about what the children do in the school holidays. Play the audio and check the predictions.

> **Audioscript:** Track 49
>
> **Reporter:** What do you all do in your school holiday? We've invited some of you into the studio to find out what you all have in common ... and what's different about the way you spend your school holidays ...
>
> So let's go first to Ana, from Brazil. Hi Ana!
>
> **Ana:** Hi!
>
> **Reporter:** Tell us something about how you spend your long school holidays ...
>
> **Ana:** Well, I spend a lot of time with my grandparents because my mum and dad are at work during the day.
>
> **Reporter:** OK, and what do you get up to?

> **Ana:** Well, Grandma lets me bake cookies and we all go to the park with the dog. We go shopping too and sometimes go on a day trip to the seaside. Last year my sister and I did jobs around the house to earn extra pocket money.
>
> **Reporter:** Thanks, Ana. And what about you, Luis?
>
> **Luis:** We always go camping near the sea during our summer holidays.
>
> **Reporter:** Really? What do you like about that?
>
> **Luis:** I love being outside and eating food that we've cooked on the camp fire. Last year it was very windy and we nearly set fire to the tent! It's really good fun though – we play football on the beach, go fishing and go swimming as well ...
>
> **Reporter:** That's great. Now let's hear from someone else. Jassim, from Jordan. Tell us about your school holidays ...
>
> **Jassim:** Well, for most of my holidays, I help in my mum and dad's shop.
>
> **Reporter:** Ah, yes ... and how do you help out?
>
> **Jassim:** I serve customers and tidy the shelves, go with my dad to the warehouse, that sort of thing ... It's great because I earn extra pocket money and it stops me getting bored at home!
>
> **Reporter:** Ha ha! And do you work there every day of the holidays?
>
> **Jassim:** No, not every day. When I'm not there, I go to my cousin's house and we play football or go out on our bikes.
>
> **Reporter:** Thanks, Jassim ... Now over to Carly ...
>
> **Carly:** I love going to sports camp. I've been every year for the last three years.
>
> **Reporter:** And what do you like about it?
>
> **Carly:** It's really great – you get to do sports like football, basketball and swimming every day and you make lots of new friends. There is something to do all day every day and you never get bored.
>
> **Reporter:** OK, thanks guys ... Now let's move on to ...

> **Answers**
> **Ana:** spend time with grandparents, go to the park
> **Luis:** go camping, play football
> **Jassim:** help in a shop, play football
> **Carly:** go to a sports camp, play football

3 Talk

- Discuss what learners have in common with the children from the recording by asking which activities the children mentioned from the list you made in **Activity 1**.

> **Answers**
> Learners' own answers.

4 Listen 49 [CD2 Track 22]

- Focus on the statements. Ask questions to check learners have understood words like *pocket money, set fire to, spend time* and *the same place,* for example: *Who gets pocket money: children or adults? What do they use it for? Do they have to work to get it?*

- Listen to the recording again (Track 49) and decide if the statements are true or false. Correct the false statements.

> **Answers**
> 1 false (Jassim helps in his mum and dad's shop.)
> 2 false (They nearly set fire to a tent.)
> 3 true
> 4 false (She has been for the last three years.)

5 Word study

- Write the headings *Indoors* and *Outdoors* on the board. Ask learners for suggestions about where they do certain activities in their country. Ask if they think people in other countries do things differently. Build up the list.
- Look at the activities in the box and discuss if learners do them indoors, outdoors or both.

6 Listen 50 [CD2 Track 23]

- Quickly revise the disadvantages of long school holidays that learners discussed in **Activity 1**.
- Learners listen to the recording and complete the second part of the interview. Make sure they listen only for the specific information.
- When correcting the activity, ask learners questions like: *Do you agree?*

> **Audioscript:** Track 50
>
> **Reporter:** ... Now let's move onto another aspect of the school holidays ... I'd like to know if there's anything you don't like about the long holidays ... Who'd like to start? OK, Carly, off you go ...
>
> **Carly:** Well ... I often get bored when I'm at home and sometimes I think that the holidays are just too long!
>
> **Jassim:** Me too – when I'm at home, sometimes I run out of things to do ...
>
> **Reporter:** That's interesting and quite unexpected! What do the rest of you think?
>
> **Luis:** I see what you mean but I don't really agree! I love the holidays so much that I don't want them to end. The only thing I don't like are holiday traffic jams. We always get stuck in traffic on the way to the campsite – there are loads of cars on the roads because it's the summer holidays.
>
> **Reporter:** Thanks, Luis. Ana – would you like to have the last word?
>
> **Ana:** I agree with Jassim and Carly. I love school holidays but sometimes I wish they were a bit shorter – then it wouldn't be so hard to go back to school afterwards!

> **Answers**
> **Carly:** too long
> **Jassim:** run out of things to do
> **Luis:** don't like ... traffic jams
> **Ana:** shorter ... hard ... go back

7 Word study

- Learners read and listen again to the second part of the interview (Track 50) and look for the words used for agreeing and disagreeing. Make sure they listen

carefully to the correct intonation. See **Additional support and practice**.

> **Answers**
> **Agree:** Me too, I agree
> **Disagree:** I don't really agree!

8 Talk

- Discuss the good and bad things about the long school holidays.
- **Critical thinking:** Learners work in pairs and write down three things that they like and one that they don't like about them.
- Demonstrate the activity with an example. Ask a learner to tell the class one of their examples and ask the class for their reactions, using: *Me too, I agree. I see what you mean, but I don't really agree.* In higher-level classes, ask learners for a reason.

> **Answers**
> Learners' own answers.

[AB] For further practice, see Activities 1 to 5 in the Activity Book.

Wrap up

- Learners make sentences to tell the class about themselves and their partners, for example: *I think the school holidays are too long, but Ahmed doesn't agree. We agree that we get too much homework.*

> **Answers**
> Learners' own answers.

Activity Book

1 Vocabulary

- Focus on **Activity 1** on page 100. Learners choose the correct prepositions to go with the holiday activities.

> **Answers**
> 1 around 2 on 3 to 4 in 5 with 6 on 7 to 8 on

2 Vocabulary

- Learners tick the activities that they do during the school holidays.

> **Answers**
> Learners' own answers.

3 Vocabulary

- This activity is an extension of **Activity 1**. Learners write the name of the activities they can see in the pictures.

> **Answers**
> Learners' own answers.

4 Use of English

- Learners practise the new expressions for agreeing and disagreeing from the lesson by completing the dialogues.

Answers
1 I agree with you
2 Me too
3 I see your point, but I don't really agree
4 Me too
5 I don't agree

5 Challenge

- This activity provides further practice of the new expressions for agreeing and disagreeing. Learners write their own responses to the statements in **Activity 4**.

Answers
Learners' own answers.

Differentiated instruction

Additional support and practice

- For extra practice in talking about the school holidays, ask learners to bring some pictures of themselves taken during the holidays. Learners describe their pictures and ask and answer questions about what their partners are doing in the pictures.
- Offer extra opportunities to practise the expressions: *Me too, I agree. I see what you mean/ see your point, but I don't really agree.* Make up sentences and say them to learners to elicit one of the reactions, for example: *Learners should stay at school until 8 p.m.*

Extend and challenge

- Learners find out about something interesting they can do in the long school holidays. They make notes and tell the class about what they have found out. For example, they could look for language courses or an adventure holiday suitable for their age group. Information can be found in brochures, on websites, etc.

Lesson 2: Holiday fun

Learner's Book pages: 128–129
Activity Book pages: 102–103

Lesson objectives

Reading: Read some holiday advertisements.
Listening: Listen to people talking about holidays.
Speaking: Talk about holiday issues.
Critical thinking: Problem solving.

Language focus: *Will* for future predictions.
Vocabulary: Holidays

Materials: Pictures of 8–10-year-olds on holidays.

Learner's Book

☞ Warm up

- Compile a list together of different types of holiday and what you can do on them. Revise *indoor* and *outdoor* from **Lesson 1** and expressions from **Unit 1** for talking about sports activities.
- Practise using structures that learners have studied throughout the year. Ask and answer questions like: *Do you go on adventure/camping/activity holidays? How often? Who with? Have you ever been on a camping holiday? Did you go last year? Are you going on holiday/to the seaside/mountains this year?*

Answers
Learners' own answers.

1 ✎ Talk about it

- Discuss which kinds of holidays and activities could be considered relaxing, before discussing the kinds of holidays learners enjoy.

Answers
Learners' own answers.

2 Read

- Talk generally about holiday camps. Find out if learners have been on a holiday camp and what they were like.
- Focus on the three advertisements. Help learners predict the kinds of things they will read about, by asking if they would like to try one of the holiday activity camps and *why*.
- Learners read the advertisements and answer the two questions.

Answers
Sports camps are the longest.
Camping and sports camps are suitable for older children.

3 Read

- Focus on the information about the four children. Discuss the kinds of things they could do on holiday or the kinds of holiday they might enjoy. Decide which holiday camp would be best for each child. In lower-level groups, re-read the text.

Answers
1 camping 2 art course 3 camping 4 sports camp

4 Listen 51 [CD2 Track 24]

- Help learners predict what they might hear by asking them to say what they can see in the pictures in the adverts. Make a note of any new words.

Audioscript: Track 51

Girl 1: It says here that tents and cooking equipment are provided – I think we'll have to take everything else ourselves.

Girl 2: What do you think we'll need? What about clothes for a start?

Girl 1: Well, definitely a waterproof jacket and jeans …

Girl 2: No, not jeans! They're too hot to walk in and take ages to dry if they get wet. Tracksuit bottoms are better because they're light and made of cotton. And shorts too …

Girl 1: Yes, you're right. OK, what about at night?

Girl 2: We'll definitely need sleeping bags to keep us warm in the tent – and a torch, because there'll be no electric light …

Girl 1: Do you think we'll need things for eating? Plastic utensils like knives, forks, spoons, bowls, plates …

Girl 2: I don't think so. Cooking equipment is provided, so I think the organisers will supply everything for us to eat with too …

Girl 1: We're only allowed to take one backpack, so we can't take many things. What else are you going to take? What couldn't you live without for the week?

Girl 2: My MP3 definitely! What about you?

Girl 1: I'm going to put some photos in my journal – so if I get homesick, I can look at pictures of my dog!

Answer
camping

Language detective

* Listen to the recording again and ask learners for examples of the *future simple* used to make predictions. Write examples on the board.
* Ask learners to make predictions about their own holidays: *I think we'll need … I think the weather will be* … See **Additional support and practice**.

5 📝 💬 **Word study** 51 [CD2 Track 24]

* Check learners understand the meaning of the items in the box. Ask questions, for example: *Do you know any examples of plastic utensils? What can you use them for? What do you use a backpack for? How do you carry it?*
* Listen to the recording again (Track 51) and tick the items the girls are going to take.

Answers
backpacks, a torch, a journal with photos, waterproof jackets, an MP3 player, sleeping bags

6 📝 **Listen** 51 [CD2 Track 24]

* Discuss which sentence halves could go together. If lower-level learners have problems, ask questions to help them understand why some sentences can't go together, for example: *Is there a main verb in the sentence?*
* Play the recording again and check.
* Practise the structure by encouraging learners to think of other ways to finish the sentences.

Answers
1 c   2 d   3 b   4 a

 For further practice, see the Language detective box and Activities 1 and 2 in the Activity Book.

7 Listen 52 [CD2 Track 25]

* In lower-level groups, discuss key words that the boys might use to talk about each advertisement before listening to the recording. This will help learners make predictions and listen only for specific information without worrying about difficult words.
* Learners listen to the recording to find out what the problem is.

Audioscript: Track 52

Boy 1: Come on, what's the matter? Why don't you want to go? Mum's already paid for us to go …

Boy 2: I know but I'm rubbish at sport! I'm not very good at football, or basketball, or hockey …

Boy 1: That's OK. How about trying a new sport? … Something you haven't done before …

Boy 2: But what if I'm not very good … ?

Boy 1: You don't know until you try. It says here that you can try a new sport. That means that there will be beginners' classes for all the sports. So everyone else in those classes will be beginners too.

Boy 2: So does that mean that no-one in the classes has done the sport before?

Boy 1: Yes, so everyone has to start at the beginning. No-one is better than everyone else because everyone is a beginner! Let's join a class together. I'd like to learn something new too.

Boy 2: OK, that would be good. Why don't we do one of the martial arts classes … like judo or karate? Let's try something different, something that's not a ball game!

Answers
They are talking about a sports camp. One of the boys is not very good at football or basketball or hockey.

8 Listen 52 [CD2 Track 25]

* Ask learners if they know any expressions for making suggestions. Write examples on the board that show the verb form. *How about playing football? Let's play a game. Why don't we have an ice cream?*
* Ask learners for more suggestions before listening to the recording again and noting one of the boy's suggestions.
* See **Additional Support and practice 2**.

Answers
a How about trying a new sport?
b Why don't we do one of the martial arts classes …
c Let's join a class together; let's try something different

9 💬 **Talk**

* Discuss problems that learners might have about going on one of the trips. Make a list on the board. Invite learners to make suggestions using the expressions from **Activity 8** and the correct verb forms.

- Learners practise making suggestions in pairs, before agreeing on a holiday course.

> **Answers**
> Learners' own answers.

 For further practice, see Activities 3 and 4 in the Activity Book.

☞ Wrap up

- To finish off, pairs of learners perform mini dialogues using problems and suggestions, for example:

Learner A:	*Let's go on the art course.*
Learner B:	*No, I'm not very good at drawing!*
Learner A:	*If you're not very good at drawing, why don't you try learning a new drawing skill?*
Learner B:	*OK, good idea. Let's go on the art course!*

Activity Book

Language detective

- Learners use the **Language detective** box to revise the rule about using *will* for future predictions.

1 Use of English

- Open the Activity Book at page 102. Focus on **Activity 1.** This provides controlled practice using *will* + base form for making future predictions.

> **Answers**
> **2** 'll have to   **3** will/be   **4** won't need   **5** will/spend
> **6** 'll be

2 Vocabulary

- Learners match the bold words in the text with the definitions.

> **Answers**
> **2** sleeping bag
> **3** waterproof jacket
> **4** journal
> **5** tent
> **6** backpack

3 Vocabulary

- Learners revise how to make suggestions using expressions from Learner's Book **Activity 8**.

> **Answers**
> **1** going   **2** do   **3** Why don't we

4 Challenge

- Learners practise these new expressions to make suggestions about what to take on trips.

> **Answers**
> Learners' own answers.

Differentiated instruction

Additional support and practice

- For extra practice of using *will* + verb to make predictions about the future choose a subject, for example: the weather at the weekend. Encourage predictions, for example: *I think it will be sunny.* Practise the language form: *Me too, I agree. I see what you mean, but I don't really agree* which was the vocabulary focus of the last lesson.
- Offer extra opportunities to practise: *How about ...? Let's ... Why don't we ...?* Write a dialogue containing these structures, but leave the verbs blank. Photocopy the dialogue and distribute a copy to each learner. Learners fill in the blanks and then practise it with a partner. Learners write their own dialogue on a different subject.

Extend and challenge

- 💬 Learners work in groups and plan their own summer holiday camp. They create a poster advertising the holiday camp including information about the dates, what they can do, how long it is and a timetable.

Lesson 3: Looking back

Learner's Book pages: 130–131
Activity Book pages: 104–105

Lesson objectives

Reading: Read survey results.

Speaking: Conduct a survey.

Writing: Express survey results.

Critical thinking: Analyse what the class have found interesting and difficult about this year of English.

Vocabulary: Expressing numbers

Materials: Photocopiable activity 17.

Learner's Book

☞ Warm up

- Compile a list of activities that learners have done in English this year. Build up a list on the board.
- In lower-level classes, look through the Learner's Book and learners' notebooks at this year's activities and pick out which ones were interesting or difficult.
- Ask learners questions about the activities: *Did you enjoy it? Did you prefer ...? Was it difficult?*

> **Answers**
> Learners' own answers.

1 Talk about it

- Learners tell the class which activity has been their favourite and which has been the most difficult.

Answers
Learners' own answers.

Reading strategy

- Before focusing on the **Reading strategy**, discuss with the class why it is useful to read the questions about a text before reading the text itself.

2 Read

- Read the questions and encourage learners to predict what kind of answers they might read.
- Tell learners they are going to read children's comments about their year of English and look for answers to the questions. Make sure they understand they won't find answers to all the questions.
- In lower-level classes, break the task down into three smaller tasks. Learners read the first text and decide which question it answers. Repeat for the other two texts. In higher-level groups learners read all three together.

Answers
2 b 4 c 5 a

3 Talk

- Learners ask and answer the questions 1–6 in pairs from **Activity 2**. Circulate and make sure learners write their partners' answers. Offer extra support to lower-level learners.
- Learners report back to the class about what their partners told them.

Answers
Learners' own answers.

4 Pronunciation 53 [CD2 Track 26]

- Learners listen and repeat using the correct intonation and pronunciation of unstressed words, for example: *have, the, do you*. See **Additional support and practice**.

Audioscript: Track 53
– Which have you enjoyed the most?
– Which do you find easier?

5 Word study

- In lower-level groups, discuss the differences between the expressions before putting them in order.

Answers
2 most of us
3 some of my friends
5 hardly any of us

 For further practice, see Activities 1 and 2 in the Activity Book.

6 Talk and write

- Learners choose three questions they want to ask from **Activity 2**. They stand up and circulate and ask ten classmates, making sure they make a note of their answers.
- Allow learners time to write a paragraph about their findings.

Answers
Learners' own answers.

7 Over to you

- **Critical thinking:** Focus on the bar chart on page 131. Check learners understand the concept by discussing how to interpret it.
- Allow learners time to draw their own bar chart, giving extra support where necessary.

Answers
Learners' own answers – Portfolio opportunity.

8 Talk

- Learners read their paragraph and show their bar chart to the class. The other learners take notes.

Answers
Learners' own answers.

For further practice, see Activities 3, 4 and 5 in the Activity Book.

Wrap up

- **Home–school link:** Learners use the information from their survey and the notes they made in **Activity 8** to produce a poster showing the answers to the questions in **Activity 2**. The poster can be taken home and shared with parents/carers.

Answers
Learners' own answers.

Activity Book

1 Word study

- Open the Activity Book at page 104. Focus on **Activity 1**. Learners choose a quantity expression from the box to replace the numbers in the report.

Answers
1 All 2 a few 3 Most 4 most 5 Some 6 hardly any

2 Word study

- Learners find three more phrases in the text that describe numbers of people.

---

3 Word study

- Learners use the information from the report in **Activity 1** to label the bar chart.

Answers
A 1
B 3 and 4
C 2
D 5
E 6

4 Pronunciation 73 [CD2 Track 46]

- Learners listen to the recording and repeat the questions. Listen carefully to the pronunciation of unstressed *have* and *do*.

Audioscript: Track 73
- Which cartoons have you seen in English?
- Which do you like best?
- Do you like listening to music in English?
- Have you ever read an English book?

5 Challenge

- Focus on the information about the school trip. Learners use the information to write a summary based on these notes and a bar chart for one of the questions. Lower-level learners may need extra support and guidance.

Answers
Learners' own answers.

Differentiated instruction

Additional support and practice

- Offer extra opportunities to practise the intonation and pronunciation of unstressed sounds in questions. Write questions on the board using structures like the present simple, past simple, present perfect and drill the correct pronunciation.
- If your class enjoyed the class survey, choose another subject, for example *favourite free-time activities, favourite subject* for another class survey. The information can be presented in a bar chart or in another type of chart or graph.

Extend and challenge

- Look for information about what learners of English from around the world find interesting or difficult. If learners have penfriends, they can write and ask for the information; otherwise try looking on blogs.
- **Photocopiable activity 17: *Design an advert for a summer camp*.** Learners design a web advert for a summer holiday activity. Higher-level learners extend the activity by writing a radio or TV advert for the camp and performing it.

Lesson 4: Party planning

Learner's Book pages: 132–133
Activity Book pages: 106–107

Lesson objectives

Reading: Read emails.
Speaking: Talk about celebrations.
Writing: Write an email invitation and reply.
Critical thinking: Make plans for a party.

Language focus: *Going to* for plans.

Materials: Photocopiable activity 18.

Learner's Book

☞ Warm up

- Talk about different things you can do to celebrate your birthday. Build up a list on the board.
- Practise the present perfect by asking learners *Have you ever ...?* about the different activities.

Answers
Learners' own answers.

1 Talk about it

- Look at the ways of sending invitations. Learners discuss the advantages and disadvantages of each one.
- Learners tell the class what they did to celebrate their last birthday, if they invited any friends and how they invited them.

Answers
Learners' own answers.

2 Read

- Before reading, ensure learners understand they only need to find out the purpose of Man Yi's email.

Answers
She is writing to invite Lauren to her birthday party. The purpose of Lauren's reply is to accept the invitation.

3 Read

- Focus on the paragraph topics. Help learners make predictions about what kind of information they might find in the paragraphs.
- Learners read Man Yi's email again and match the paragraphs with the topics.

Answers
1 e   2 a   3 b   4 d   5 c

Language detective

- Ask learners which different ways they know for talking about the future. Write examples of sentences with *will* and *going to* on the board.
- Learners look for examples of the two forms in the emails. Write: *We're going to have lunch … It'll be really great.* Discuss the difference in meaning. In lower-level classes, ask: *Which form expresses a plan? Which expresses a prediction?*

4 Use of English

- Focus on the **Language detective** box and tell learners they are going to complete Man Yi's reply by saying what the plans for the party are.
- Allow learners time to complete the letter.
- **Note:** There are cases where *will* would also be correct as Man Yi is referring to future facts.

> **Answers**
> 1 are going to meet
> 2 is going to be
> 3 Is/going to come?
> 4 isn't going to email

 For further practice, see the Language detective box and Activities 1 and 2 in the Activity Book.

Writing tip

- Focus on the **Writing tip** and discuss the words that have been left out. Make sure learners know they can only do this in informal situations.

5 Read

- Read the emails again and complete the sentences.

> **Answers**
> 1 I   2 I'll   3 I'm   4 I'll

6 Write

- Discuss what type of plans learners might have for a birthday party or an end-of-term celebration.
- Remind learners of the paragraph structure Man Yi used in her first email. Then allow them time to write their own email inviting a friend and explaining the plans for the event. Make sure learners write on a loose piece of paper. Circulate and offer help and support.
- Learners read their partners' email and say whether they can come and why not if they can't.

> **Answers**
> Learners' own answers – Portfolio opportunity.

 For further practice, see Activities 3, 4 and 5 in the Activity Book.

☞ Wrap up

- Mix up the emails and read them out. Learners guess who wrote them.

Activity Book

Language detective

- Learner's use the **Language detective** box to revise the use of *going to* for talking about plans for the future.

1 Use of English

- Focus on **Activity 1** on page 106. Learners practise talking about future plans using *going to* + verb to complete sentences. They choose the verbs from the words in the box.

> **Answers**
> 2 Are/going to try
> 3 isn't going to do
> 4 is going to earn
> 5 are going to make
> 6 are going to stay
> 7 is going to learn

2 Plans

- Learners use *going to* + verb to make sentences about the holiday plans of the children in the pictures.

> **Answers**
> Learners' own answers.

3 Read

- Focus on the sentences from the email. Learners put the sentences in order. If learners have difficulty, ask them questions about the purpose of each sentence and refer back to Man Yi's email.

> **Answers**
> d, c, b, e, a.

4 Read

- Learners match the sentences from the email with the headings.

> **Answers**
> 1 e   2 d   3 b   4 a   5 c

5 Write

- Look back at the headings in **Activity 4**. Learners use these to plan and write an email to a friend inviting them to take part in one of the activities in **Activity 2**.

> **Answers**
> Learners' own answers.

Differentiated instruction

Additional support and practice

- Offer extra opportunities to practise using *going to* to talk about plans. Each learner tells the class about three plans they have for the summer holidays.
- Learners answer their partners' invitations. If they can't come, make sure they explain what they will be doing instead. If they can come, they should ask for more information about the party – *Where is it exactly? How do I get there? Who else is coming?*

Extend and challenge

- Look for information about how children from around the world celebrate their birthdays. If learners have penfriends, they can write and ask for the information; otherwise try looking on blogs.
- **Photocopiable activity 18:** *Planning and writing a story about a summer holiday*.

Lesson 5: *Back to school*

Learner's Book pages: 134–137
Activity Book pages: 108–109

Lesson objectives

Reading: Read about going back to school.

Listening: Listen to a play.

Speaking: Act out a play, help a friend with a problem talk about feelings.

Values: Being sympathetic.

Critical thinking: How to be sympathetic in different situations.

Learner's Book

👉 Warm up

- Compile a list of preparations that learners make before their first day back at school. Make a list on the board and ask learners questions like: *Do you buy new books/a new uniform? Does someone make your lunch for you? Do you bring a snack? Do you wear special clothes?*

> Answers
> Learners' own answers.

1 💬 Talk about it

- Learners take turns to tell the class how they feel about going back to school after a long holiday and the preparations they make for the first day back.

> Answers
> Learners' own answers.

2 Listen and read 54 [CD2 Track 27]

- Focus on the picture and help learners make predictions about what they might hear. Discuss how the children are feeling and why.
- Listen to **Parts 1** and **2** of the play and find out what the children are talking about.

> **Audioscript:** Track 54
> **See Learner's Book pages 134–135.**

> Answers
> They are talking about going back to school.

3 Listen 55 [CD2 Track 28]

- Focus on the questions on page 135. Learners listen to the first part of the text again and answer the questions.

> Answers
> 1 They feel sad because they don't want to go back to school.
> 2 He doesn't want to start a new class with a new teacher.
> 3 He's going to tell his mum and dad he's not going back to school.

4 Listen 56 [CD2 Track 29]

- Focus on the questions about the second part of the play. Check learners understand the meaning.
- Play the recording again so learners can look for the answers. In lower-level classes extra guidance may be necessary, for example: pausing the recording after the information needed for each question and checking learners have the right answer.

> Answers
> 1 Yes.
> 2 Because no-one admits it.
> 3 She says even adults feel the same way.
> 4 She says her dad gets nervous when he thinks about the pile of work waiting for him when he gets back from a holiday.
> 5 She tells them to think about all the good things about going back to school

 For further practice, see Activities 1 and 2 in the Activity Book.

5 📝 Word study

- Focus on the first sentence. Look at the first word in blue and discuss whether the meaning of the sentence fits the context. Do the same with the other blue words.
- Allow learners time to follow the example and match the sentences to the remaining blue words.

> Answers
> 1 Me neither – I really don't want to start school again tomorrow.
> 2 Me neither – The holidays have been great and I don't want them to end!
> 3 Me too! – I've got a horrible feeling in my stomach.
> 4 Me too! – I liked our old class. I want to go back there!
> 5 Me too! – I always feel like this …
> 6 Really? – I'm feeling a bit like that too …

6 Talk

- Learners think about their own feelings. Demonstrate the activity by reading statements and asking learners to respond using: *Me neither! Me too! Really?*
- Learners work in pairs. They read the statements and respond to them.

Answers
Learners' own answers.

7 Punctuation 57 [CD2 Track 30]

- Ask learners the name of the punctuation mark at the end of the expressions. Discuss why the writer uses an exclamation mark and how its use changes the meaning.
- Play the recording. Learners repeat using the correct intonation.

Audioscript: Track 57

a ... and he's forty-two!

b I feel a bit sick!

c Nothing! Nothing at all!

d Of course!

8 Listen 57 [CD2 Track 30]

- Check learners understand words like *upset, hide, emphasise* and *surprising* in the questions. Play the recording again and ask learners the questions.

Answers
1 upset – speaker b
2 hide something – speaker c
3 emphasise something is right – speaker d
4 emphasise surprise – speaker a

9 Talk

- Divide the class into groups of four. Tell each learner to choose a part and ask for a show of hands to see who is acting out each role.
- Check learners understand the directions. Learners practise reading out the play in their groups. Circulate and check pronunciation, especially intonation.
- Give feedback, particularly in lower-level groups, about typical mistakes with pronunciation.
- Ask a confident group to read the play out to the class.

Answers
Learners' own answers.

10 Values

- Write the word *sympathetic* on the board and ask if anyone knows the meaning. Demonstrate the meaning by reading out examples of things that Sara said that were sympathetic.
- Ask learners for examples of people (parents, carers, teachers, friends, etc.) being sympathetic to them.

- **Critical thinking:** Focus on the situations. Discuss ways of being sympathetic, before allowing learners time to create a role-play in pairs. Check learners use the correct intonation.

Answers
Learners' own answers.

[AB] **For further practice, see Activities 3, 4, 5 and 6 in the Activity Book.**

Wrap up

- To finish off, learners perform their role-plays in front of the class.

Answers
Learners' own answers.

Activity Book

1 Read

- Open the Activity Book at page 108. Learners read the play on pages 134–135 in the Learner's Book and decide whether the questions in the Activity Book are true or false.

Answers
2 true
3 false
4 false
5 true
6 false
7 false
8 false
9 true
10 false

2 Write

- **Critical thinking:** Learners complete the summary of the play. Lower-level learners may need additional support.

Answers
Learners' own answers.

3 Use of English

- Learners read the dialogue and circle the correct ways of responding to the statements.

Answers
1 Me neither
2 Me too
3 Me too
4 Me too
5 Me too
6 Me too

4 Punctuation

- Learners use what they have learned about punctuation in **Activity 7** in the Learner's Book to change some full stops into exclamation marks.

> **Answers**
> Learners' own answers.

5 Values

- This aim of this activity is to check learners understand the concept of *being sympathetic*.

> **Answers**
> are listening/care

6 Values

- Learners write ways that they have been sympathetic to people they know in the last week.

> **Answers**
> Learners' own answers.

Differentiated instruction

Additional support and practice

- Offer learners extra opportunities to practise reacting using *Me neither! Me too! Really?* Write some statements that you think will elicit a reaction from your class. Photocopy the statements and distribute one copy to each pair. Tell learners to take turns reading the statements and react using the expressions.
- To give learners more practice being sympathetic, think of other situations that might make learners feel nervous, worried or upset, for example, the day before an exam, a visit to the dentist, or an important competition.

Extend and challenge

- Learners work in groups of four. Choose one of these situations (or another similar situation) and write a play about it.
- Learners look for short plays that are suitable for their age to read. Look for graded readers for their age and level, on the Internet, etc.

Lesson 6: Choose a project

Learner's Book pages: 138–139
Activity Book pages: 110–111

Lesson objectives

Writing: Create a *Challenge plan poster* or write a short play about one of the problems listed.

Language focus: Unit 9 Review

☞ Warm up

- Have a competition in teams to see which team can recall the topics of each unit of the Learner's Book.
- Look at the problems in **Project 2**. Talk about the issues that these problems might cause. Build up a list on the board.

> **Answers**
> Learners' own answers.

Choose a project

- Tell learners they are going to work in groups of four and choose one of the projects: create a *Challenge plan poster* or *Create a short play*.

1 Challenge plan poster

- Talk about the kind of challenges that learners could carry out for **Unit 1**.
- Remember to give more support in lower-level classes, before focusing on the steps in the Learner's Book, for example, look at other units and discuss challenges that learners could carry out.
- Circulate and make sure learners follow the steps on page 138 to create their own piece of writing.

2 Create a short play

- Look at the three problems and tell learners to choose one or think of their own.
- Focus on the steps in the Learner's Book and make sure learners follow these to create their own piece of writing. For example, ask groups their title and which characters they have chosen.
- If necessary, revise ways of being sympathetic and how to use exclamation marks.
- Circulate and offer learners support.

☞ Wrap up

- Learners present their project to the class.
- **Portfolio opportunity:** If possible, leave the learners' projects on display for a while. Then consider dating and filing the projects, photos or scans of the work, in learners' portfolios.

Reflect on your learning

- Reintroduce the Big question from **Lesson 1:** *Why are some activities enjoyable?* Discuss learners' responses to the question now and compare them with their comments at the beginning of the unit. Has much changed?
- More able learners do the activities in pairs. Remember some learners may need more support.
- Use the information from **Activity 3** to help tailor your lessons in the future.

> **Answers**
> Learners' own answers.

Look what I can do!

- **Aim:** To check learners can do all the things from **Unit 9**.
- Whichever approach you choose for these revision exercises, remember to give support to lower-level learners and use the activities as an opportunity to assess what learners have learned. Use this information to see if any revision is necessary before next year.

> **Answers**
> Learners' own answers.

Activity Book

Unit 9 Revision

- Open the Activity Book at page 110. Learners revise information from each lesson of the unit by solving the crossword puzzle.

> **Answers**
> **Across: 3** few **7** going **9** most **10** around **11** to **12** waterproof.
> **Down: 1** spend **2** torch **4** will **5** don't **6** too **8** neither **10** about

My global progress

- Learners answer the questions about the unit. This provides useful feedback for the teacher.

> **Answers**
> Learners' own answers.

> ### Differentiated instruction
> **Suggestions for further reading**
>
> If you are expected to give holiday homework, choose a graded reader text that has grammar activities based on the structures learners have studied during this year of English.

Review 5

Learner's Book pages: 140–141

Photocopiable activity 19.
- Learners have a competition in teams to see which team can get the most points by following the instructions for each of the ten activities.

Suggestions
- For **Activity 1**, a learner from each team has a turn at the front of the class to act out the holiday activities while the other team members guess.
- Check the lists in **Activity 2** by asking team members to read out the words and say how each word is spelt.
- After **Activities 3** and **4**, ask teams their reasons and award points accordingly.
- In **Activity 5**, award extra points to teams with learners who can discuss why one activity is better than another/others, and especially for the correct use of comparatives and superlatives.
- For **Activity 6**, choose a member of each team to tell the class what they wrote and ask the class to guess where the place is. Award points to teams for good forecasts and sensible guesses.
- For **Activity 7**, choose a member of each team to tell the class what the team wrote. Award extra points to teams with learners who can discuss why one activity is better than another/others, and especially for the correct use of comparatives and superlatives.
- For **Activity 8**, award a point for each type of food and two points if the spelling is correct.
- For **Activity 9**, award 20 points for the best advert, 15 for the second best, etc.
- Add up the points and announce the winning team.

Make up a certificate for each learner using
Photocopiable activity 19.
Don't forget to celebrate their achievements!

Photocopiable activity 1

Sports snakes and ladders: *Do you like/enjoy/prefer/hope/want/learn?* (*-ing* vs infinitive)

Aim: Learners play a *Snakes and Ladders* style board game in groups of four. They ask group members questions using the prompts on the square on which they land.

Preparation time: 5 minutes.

Language focus: Asking and answering *present simple* questions: *Do you like/enjoy/prefer* + verb + *-ing? Do you hope/learn/want* + infinitive?

Vocabulary: *play/do/go* + the sports vocabulary on page 10 of the Learner's Book.

Materials: For each group of learners: One copy of **Photocopiable activity 1:** *Sports snakes and ladders* and one coin with a head/tails side, small objects (e.g. pencil sharpener, etc.) to represent each learner on the board game.

Procedure

- Build up a list of words learners will need for the game. Point to pictures of different sports on page 10 in the Learner's Book. Ask the class the name of the sports and write under the heading '*Play, do, go*'.
- Build up a list of questions learners will need for the game. Write question prompts in two columns on the board. Elicit the full questions and short answers, e.g.

1 *Do you like ... ?*	**2** *Do you hope ... ?*	*Yes, I do.*
Do you enjoy ... ?	*Do you learn ... ?*	*No, I don't.*
Do you prefer ... ?	*Do you want ... ?*	*It's OK.*
*... play**ing** football?*	*... **to play** football?*	

- Higher-level learners can use the more natural sounding: *Are you learning ... ? Yes, I am./No, I'm not.*
- Distribute one copy of **Photocopiable activity 1:** *Sports snakes and ladders* and coin to each group of learners. Make sure every learner has a small object to mark their place on the board game.
- Make sure learners understand the game is called *Sports Snakes and Ladders* because if you land on the head of a snake you go down to the bottom. If you land on the bottom of a ladder, you go up to the top of it.
- Choose a group and demonstrate the game. Player 1 tosses the coin: if it lands on the 'heads' side, move forward one space; if it lands on the 'tails' side, move forward four spaces. The player asks a question using the prompts on the square he/she is on (e.g. square 1): *Do you like/enjoy/prefer playing football?*
- To check learners understand the questions they will ask, point to random squares, and ask for the question and short answer. (Refer to the examples on the board if necessary.)
- Allow time to play the game while you circulate, giving assistance and noting common errors with form and pronunciation. The game ends when one player reaches the finish.
- Give class feedback on common errors.

Photocopiable activity 1: Sports snakes and ladders

Do you like/enjoy/prefer/hope/want/learn? (-ing vs infinitive)

Photocopiable activity 2

Re-order a story: *How the Moon was kind to her mother*

Aim: Learners test their understanding of the story on pages 14–17 of the Learner's Book by putting the six parts of the summary in order.

Preparation time: 10 minutes.

Language focus: Past simple questions. Note that learners will not have to form the questions themselves, but they will be expected to understand that *did* is the past of *do* and *does* in the question form.

Vocabulary: Family members from **Lesson 1** and words from the story in **Lesson 5**: *greedy, unpleasant, beautiful, unkind, silver gown, hot and blazing, blowing*

Materials: For each pair of learners: one copy of the **Photocopiable activity 2:** *How the Moon was kind to her mother*, cut up as indicated.

Procedure

- Distribute one copy of the **Photocopiable activity 2:** *How the Moon was kind to her mother*, cut up as indicated, to each pair of learners.
- Skim through the extracts together as a class and identify the beginning of the story, for example: the card beginning *'Once upon a time ...'*
- Focus attention on the clue question at the bottom of each part, for example: *Who were Thunder and Lightning?* Use the clue to elicit which is the next part of the story, for example: the card beginning '*... their aunt and uncle.*'
- Ask a learner to read the 'story so far' to the class to check it fits together before allowing time to re-order the rest of the story.
- Circulate and check learners are following the procedure outlined.
- Learners draw a picture of each part of the story onto each card in the space provided.

Wrap up

- Learners tell the story again without looking at the text. Start with higher-level learners. That way they will have more of a challenge and lower-level learners will have more support.

Photocopiable activity 2: *How the Moon was kind to her mother*

Once upon a time, a beautiful shining Star lived with her three daughters – the Sun, the Wind and the Moon. Thunder and Lightning were ...

Who were Thunder and Lightning?

... their uncle and aunt. One evening, Thunder and Lightning decided to have a wonderful dinner party. They invited ...

Who did Thunder and Lightning invite to their dinner party?

... the Sun, the Wind and the Moon to the dinner party. The three sisters went to the party looking very beautiful. The Sun wore a golden dress and the Moon wore ...

What did the Moon wear?

... a lovely silver gown. There was a lot of food at the dinner party and the three sisters enjoyed themselves very much. The Sun and the Wind ate ...

What did the Sun and the Wind eat?

... everything. Only the Moon thought of her mother. She was the only daughter to take some of her food back home. When the three sisters got home, the Moon gave her mother ...

What did the Moon give her mother?

... some of her dinner.

Because the Moon was thoughtful, her mother made her cool, calm and beautiful.

The Sun and the Wind were greedy and unkind. Their mother made the Sun hot and blazing and the Wind blowing in hot weather, which is very unpleasant.

Photocopiable activity 3

Relative clauses quiz cards

Aim: Learners use the quiz cards as a basis for practising sentences containing the relative pronouns *that, where* and *who*.

Preparation time: 5 minutes.

Language focus: Practice of relative pronouns, *that, where* and *who*.

Vocabulary: Vocabulary from **Unit 2, Lesson 2** of the Learner's Book: *fire-fighter, trophy, tournament, valley, beasts;* words connected with reading topic: *library;* other common words suitable for this level: *doctor, medicine, ill, lemonade, snack bar, food, school*

Materials: For each group of three learners: one set of *Relative clauses quiz cards* cut up as indicated. If desired, when photocopying, the handout can be expanded to A3 size.

Procedure

- Tell learners they are going to work in pairs and do a quiz.
- Distribute one set of *Relative clauses quiz cards* to each group and tell learners to look for the card headed *A meal is ...*
- Demonstrate the activity by asking a learner to read out the information and invite the class to guess the answer. Ask for a show of hands for each possibility, before checking the answer, which is written on the card.

- Tell learners to put the cards in a pile, face down. Learners take turns to take a card from the top of the pile and read out the information on each card. The other group members guess the answer.
- In lower-level groups, check learners have understood by asking groups to pick up cards and perform the activity until you are satisfied learners have understood how it works.
- Allow time for them to complete the activity while you circulate and monitor.
- Higher-level learners could make some more cards of their own and continue the activity. Make a list of objects, people and places and allow learners time to write one correct and two false definitions. Offer help and guidance and make sure they use the relative pronouns.

Wrap up

- Learners report back to the class on what they have learnt.

Photocopiable activity 3: Relative clauses quiz cards

A *meal* is ...

a ... a thing that you eat.
b ... a place where you sleep.
c ... a person who works in a restaurant

Answer: a

Medicine is ...

a ... a thing that you take if you're ill.
b ... a place where you go if you're ill.
c ... a person who you see if you're ill.

Answer: a

A *library* is ...

a ... a thing that you read.
b ... a place where you find books.
c ... a person who writes books.

Answer: b

Lemonade is ...

a ... a thing that you drink.
b ... a place where you buy drinks.
c ... a person who serves drinks.

Answer: a

A *doctor* is ...

a ... a thing that you take if you're ill.
b ... a place where you go if you're ill.
c ... a person who helps if you're ill.

Answer: c

A *snack bar* is ...

a ... a thing that you eat.
b ... a place where you buy food.
c ... a person who serves food.

Answer: b

A *fire-fighter* is ...

a ... a thing that you use to stop fires.
b ... a place where fires start.
c ... a person who helps if a house is on fire.

Answer: c

A *school* is ...

a ... a thing that you learn.
b ... a place where you go to learn.
c ... a person who learns.

Answer: b

A *trophy* is ...

a ... a thing that you get if you win a tournament.
b ... a place where you can do a tournament.
c ... a person who wins a tournament.

Answer: a

An *experiment* is ...

a ... a thing that you do to learn or discover if something works.
b ... a place you go to do things.
c ... a person who tried to do something.

Answer: a

Photocopiable activity 4

Past simple prompt cards

Aim: Learners use prompt cards and ask and answer questions using the past simple tense. They then report back affirmative sentences to the class.

Preparation time: 5 minutes.

Completion time: 30 minutes.

Language focus: Past simple tense; asking questions, short answers and affirmative statements; time expressions to ask about specific times: *yesterday, last week/weekend/month*; regular verbs: *cheer, help, learn, participate, try*

Vocabulary: Reading vocabulary from **Unit 2** of the Learner's Book, Sports vocabulary from **Units 1 and 2** of the Learner's Book, Family vocabulary from **Unit 1** of the Learner's Book.

Materials: For each learner: one set of *Past simple prompt cards* cut up as indicated.

Note

- To give higher-level learners a challenge and extend their knowledge of the past simple forms, the following irregular verbs are used in the exercise:
  Cards 1–2 *buy → bought, find → found, read → read*
  Cards 3–4 *do → did, have → had, see → saw, win → won.*
- With lower-level groups, use only **Cards 1–2**, so you can give learners more support.

Procedure

- Write the base forms of verbs from the activity on the board. Ask for the past simple forms and write them next to the base forms.
- On the board, build up examples of past simple questions learners need for the activity, for example: *Did you read/watch/win?*
- Distribute one set of prompt cards to each learner and focus attention on **Card 1**. Tell learners they will ask several partners questions to try to find someone who answers *yes*.
- Check learners understand what questions to ask. If necessary, refer to examples on the board.
- Ask higher-level learners to demonstrate the activity. When you are satisfied learners have understood how it works, allow them time to ask and answer the questions with different partners, while you circulate and offer help.
- Give feedback on common errors before repeating the procedure with the other prompt cards.

Wrap up

- Learners report back to the class, for example: *Judith bought a good comic. Bader read an exciting story ...*

Photocopiable activity 4: Past simple prompt cards

Card 1
Reading: Fiction

Find someone who ...

... read a funny cartoon last month.

Did you read a funny cartoon last month?

... bought a good comic yesterday.

... read an exciting action story last week.

... read an exciting adventure last week.

... learned about a character with special powers last weekend.

... read about a fearless superhero yesterday.

... read about a wicked enemy last week.

Card 2
Reading: Non-fiction

Find someone who ...

... used a website last week.

Did you use a website last week?

... read a boring magazine last month.

... found something interesting in an encyclopaedia last week.

... learned something new about Science yesterday.

... read a factual book last month.

... read a boring newspaper yesterday.

... read an interesting factual book last month.

Card 3
Sport

Find someone who ...

... watched a football match last week.

Did you watch a football match last week?

... won a sport competition last year.

... won a trophy last year.

... cheered for their favourite team yesterday.

... participated in a swimming competition last week.

... did judo last weekend.

... tried trampolining last year.

Card 4
Family

Find someone who ...

... saw their cousin last week.

Did you see your cousin last week?

... helped their parents around the house yesterday.

... had breakfast with their family this morning.

... had dinner with their grandparents last Sunday.

... wrote a letter to a relative last week.

... did something kind for their parents yesterday.

Photocopiable activity 5

Expressing time: *in, at, on, last*

Aim: Learners use prompt cards to ask and answer questions about whether people do certain things at certain moments using time expressions: *in, at on* and *last.*

Preparation time: 5–10 minutes.

Language focus: Practising the different ways of expressing time – see **Unit 3, Lesson 1** of the Learner's Book: *in* (times of day), *at* (specific times), *on* (days of the week; further practice of asking and answering questions about daily routines.

Materials: One set of *Prompt cards: expressing time: in, at, on, last,* cut up as indicated, per pair of learners.

Procedure

- Distribute one set of the *Expressing time: in, at, on, last* prompt cards to each pair of learners. Tell them they are going to practise asking and answering questions about whether they do certain activities at certain times.
- Tell learners to look for **Card 1**. Ask them which preposition they need to use with the days of the week. Make sure learners know which preposition of time to use for the remaining cards. If your class is low level, tell learners to write the prepositions on the cards.

- Elicit a model dialogue similar to the following for **Card 1** and write it on the board for future reference.

  Learner A: *Do you go to school on Friday?*
  Learner B: *Yes, I do./No, I don't.*
  Learner A: *Do you go to school on Saturday?*
  Learner B: *Yes, I do./No, I don't.*
  Learner A: *Do you go to school on Sunday?*
  Learner B: *Yes, I do./No, I don't.*

- Learners practise the dialogues in pairs.
- Pairs of learners show they have understood the activity by performing their dialogues.
- Allow the class 10 minutes to practise the dialogues while you circulate, giving assistance and noting common errors with form and pronunciation.
- Give class feedback.

Photocopiable activity 5: Expressing time – *in, at, on, last*

1 Do you usually ... ?

.... go to school ...

... stay up late ...

_____ Friday?

_____ Saturday?

_____ Sunday?

2 Do you usually ... ?

... go hiking ...

... go swimming ...

_____ the morning?

_____ the afternoon?

_____ the evening?

3 Do you usually ... ?

... study English ...

... feel tired ...

_____ Tuesday?

_____ Wednesday?

_____ Thursday?

4 Do you usually ... ?

... meet your friends ...

... play basketball ...

_____ night?

_____ midday?

_____ midnight?

_____ weekends?

5 Do you usually ... ?

... get up ...

... visit your grandparents ...

_____ 5.00 am?

_____ 10.00 am?

_____ 11.30 pm?

6 Do you usually ... ?

... watch TV ...

... listen to music ...

_____ midnight?

_____ midday?

_____weekends?

Photocopiable activity 6

Comparatives quiz cards

Aim: Learners use quiz cards to ask and answer questions using comparative adjectives. The activity should give the learners ideas and support for the writing activity on page 39 of the Learner's Book.

Preparation time: 5 minutes.

Language focus: Practice asking questions with comparative adjectives to compare features of landscape, climate and size.

Vocabulary: Comparative adjectives: *longer, shorter, higher, bigger, smaller, wider, older, drier, wetter, hotter*

Materials: One set of *Comparatives quiz cards*, cut up as indicated, per pair or small group of learners.

Procedure

- Tell the learners that they are going to receive a quiz in the form of 12 cards to do with their partners.
- Distribute one set of the *Comparatives quiz cards* to each pair of learners. If your class is lower ability, you could use only the first six cards. In a mixed class, pair lower- and higher-level learners together.
- To demonstrate the activity, ask learners the question from **Card 1**: *Which is older – Rome or London?* Cover up the answer.
- Nominate learners and ask their opinions before telling them to look for **Card 1** and find the answer.
- Explain that they are going to continue asking and answering questions like this one with their partner.
- Allow time to continue the activity in pairs, while you circulate, giving assistance to lower-level learners.
- Higher-level learners could make some more cards of their own and continue the activity. They could use their knowledge from other subjects, or they could research facts for the quiz for homework.

Wrap up

- Give higher-level learners an extra challenge by having a competition to remember the most facts within a set time. Lower-level learners will benefit from hearing repetition of the target structure.

Photocopiable activity 6: Comparatives quiz cards

1 Which is **older** ... ... Rome or London? **Answer:** Rome	**2** Which is **higher** ... ... Mount Everest or Mount Snowdon? **Answer:** Mount Everest	**3** Which is **wider** ... ... the River Nile or the River Amazon? **Answer:** River Amazon
4 Which is **bigger** ... ... London or Sydney? **Answer:** London	**5** Which is **bigger** ... ... France or Germany? **Answer:** France	**6** Which is **drier** ... ... the Sahara Desert or London? **Answer:** Sahara Desert
7 Which is **smaller** ... ... New York or Edinburgh? **Answer:** Edinburgh	**8** Which is **smaller** ... ... New Zealand or Australia? **Answer:** New Zealand	**9** Which is **hotter** ... ... Glasgow or Bangkok? **Answer:** Bangkok
10 Which is **smaller** ... ... South America or Asia? **Answer:** South America	**11** Which is **longer** ... ... the Rio Grande or the River Thames? **Answer:** Rio Grande	**12** Which is **wetter** ... ... Cherrapunji (India) or Taipei (Taiwan)? **Answer:** Cherrapunji

Photocopiable activity 7

Questions about people's homes

Aim: Learners ask and answer questions about three people's homes. To help them do this, they read short texts and use prompts to make questions about them.
Preparation time: 5 minutes.

Language focus: Asking and answering present simple questions.
Vocabulary: Homes and building materials

Materials: For each pair of learners – one set of *Question and answer cards: people's homes* cut up as indicated.

Procedure

- Distribute one set of *Question and answer cards: people's homes* to each pair of learners.
- Learners read the first card about Giuliana and use the information to draw a picture of her house in the space. Repeat for the other cards.
- Lower-level groups focus on the question prompts on the Giuliana card. Ask learners the full questions and write them on the board for learners to copy. Learners write the full questions on all three **question cards**. Higher-level groups proceed directly to the next stage.
- Pairs of learners practise asking the questions on the **question cards** and answering using corresponding **answer cards**. Allow time to ask and answer in pairs.
- Circulate and give assistance with form and pronunciation.
- Give class feedback on common errors.

Wrap up

- In a higher-level class, learners work in pairs to make comparisons about the three homes. They use comparative and superlative adjectives and words like *whereas, but, too, the same,* for example. If your group is mixed ability, encourage higher-level learners to make the comparisons for the class.

Answers

Questions

Giuliana: *Does she live in a bungalow? Does she live in a detached house? How many bedrooms has it got? Has it got a garden? Why does she like it?*
Vladimir: *Does he live in an eco-house? Has it got large windows? Has it got a wood burner? Has it got solar panels? Has it got a roof garden?*
Razheen: *Does she live in a high-rise flat? Has it got spectacular views? Does she live near her friends? Does she live near her school? Does she like her house?*

Photocopiable activity 7: Question and answer cards – people's homes

Q Giuliana	A Giuliana
... live in a bungalow? *Does she live in a bungalow?* ... live in a detached house? _____ How many bedrooms has ...? _____ Has ... got a garden? _____ Why ... she like it? _____	My house isn't a bungalow, it has two floors. It's a semi-detached house which has a big garden. There's a living room, a kitchen, three bedrooms and a bathroom. The best thing about my house is that I have my own bedroom with all my toys and games. **My picture**
Q **Vladimir**	**A** **Vladimir**
... an eco-house? *Does he live in an eco-house?* Has ... large windows? _____ Has ... a wood burner? _____ Has ... solar panels? _____ Has ... a roof garden? _____	My house is an eco-house. It's very energy efficient. On the roof, there are solar panels for energy for heating water. I use a wood-burner to heat the house. The house is built of wood and stone and it has large windows for letting light in. In the summer, I grow my own vegetables in the roof garden. **My picture**
Q **Razheen**	**A** **Razheen**
... live in a high-rise flat? *Does she ... live in a high-rise flat?* _____ Has ... spectacular views? _____ ... live near her friends? _____ ... live near her school? _____ ... like her house? _____	I live in a flat, but it's not a high-rise flat. The views of the city are spectacular because we live on a hill. Some of my friends live in the same building as me so we sometimes play together. I like my flat very much because it's near the city. It's also near to my school. **My picture**

Photocopiable activity 8

Modal dominoes

Aim: Learners practise modals of *probability* from page 53 of the Learner's Book by matching sentence halves.

Preparation time: 5 minutes.

Completion time: 30 minutes + extension activity for higher-level learners only.

Language focus: *It must be ... , it might be ... , it could be ... , It can't be ...* for making deductions.

Materials: One set of *Modal dominoes*, cut up as indicated, per pair of learners.

Procedure

- Distribute one set of *Modal dominoes* to each pair of learners and tell them that they are going to practise making deductions by playing a game of dominoes by matching sentence halves.
- Learners study the sentences on the photocopy, before cutting the dominoes out as indicated.
- Pick up random dominoes and elicit whether they can go together.
- Choose a higher-level pair to demonstrate the game. Learners mix up their dominoes and take six each. Player 1 plays a domino and Player 2 puts down a domino which completes a logical sentence. Players take turns to play a suitable domino. A player, who doesn't have a suitable domino, misses a turn. The first player to put down all their dominoes is the winner.
- Allow time to play the game while you circulate, giving assistance.
- To give higher-level learners an extra challenge and possibilities for extension, photocopy one set of the *Blank modal dominoes* grid and ask them to fill them in with their own sentences. Cut the dominoes up and play as the main activity.

Photocopiable activity 8 (i): Modal dominoes – *It must ..., It might ...,*
It could ..., It can't ...

... they might live in a high-rise flat.	... it must be in the country.
This house has solar panels so ...	His house isn't near a city, so ...
... it must be energy efficient.	... it might be near a farm.
There are lots of fields near his house so ...	Her house has five bedrooms, so ...
... it must be very big.	... it might be a theatre.
Their flat only has one bedroom, so ...	It's a large modern building so ...
... it can't be very big.	... it could be a shopping centre.
The building is in the city centre so ...	There are lots of desks and computers, so ...
... it must be an office.	... it might be a bank.
Children always play outside this building so ...	They go up and down stairs a lot, so ...
... it must be a school.	... they can't live in a bungalow.
There's a queue outside the building, so ...	They have spectacular views, so ...

Photocopiable activity 8 (ii): Blank modal dominoes

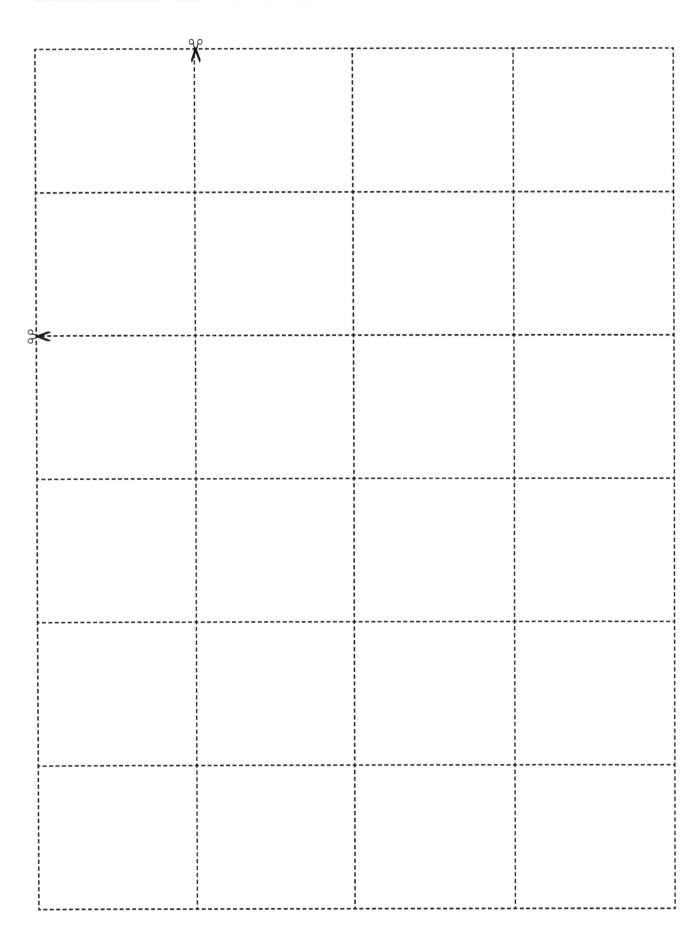

Photocopiable activity 9

Board game: *Did you ... ?*

Aim: Learners play a board game in pairs or groups of three. They travel around the board, picking up *question prompt cards* and using them to ask questions.

Preparation time: 10–15 minutes.

Language focus: Asking and answering using *Did you ... ?* for past actions seen in previous units of the Learner's Book.

Vocabulary: Methods of transport and safety

Materials: For each pair/small group of learners: **Board game: *Did you ... ?*** and one set of ***Did you ... ?*** **Question prompt cards** photocopied and cut up as indicated. One coin with a head/tails side and one small object (e.g. a pencil sharpener) to represent each learner on the board game.

Procedure

- Tell learners they are going to play a game to practise asking partners about holidays and transport using the past simple. Elicit the question: *Did you* + verb? that learners will need for the game.
- Practise with verbs from the game, (*travel, use, walk, visit, hike*). Check learners know they should answer *Yes, I did. /No, I didn't.*
- Distribute one **Board game** and one set of **Question prompt cards** and a coin with a head/tails side to each pair/group. Make sure every student has a small object to mark their places on the board game.

- Learners sort the **Question prompt cards** into two piles – one pile of the cards about *getting home from school yesterday* and the other about *your last holiday.*
- Learners toss the coin and move one space if it lands on the 'head' side and two spaces for 'tails'. They pick up a card and ask questions using *Did you ... ?* Point to random squares to check learners know which card to pick up and how to ask for the question (and short answer). Tell them if they land on the **?** square, they should invent a question with: *Did you ... ?*
- Nominate a group of learners to show they have understood how the game works by demonstrating.
- Allow 15 minutes to play the game, while you circulate and give assistance and note common errors.
- Give class feedback on common errors.

Differentiated instructions

Using the game with different levels

- This game uses a lot of new vocabulary from **Unit 5**, as well as some from **Unit 4.** If it is too much for a lower-level group, consider not using all of the cards.
- In a mixed class, put lower- and higher-level learners together.
- For higher-level classes, consider deleting *Did you ... ?* from the centre of the board. Brainstorm different structures and expressions that learners know and encourage them to use all these to ask questions, for example: *How often?/When? + present simple, Have you ever ... ?, Would you like to ... ?*

Photocopiable activity 9 (i): Board game – *Did you ... ?*

6 getting home from school yesterday	**7** your last holiday	**8** getting home from school yesterday	**9** your last holiday	**10** ?
5 ?				**11** getting home from school yesterday
4 your last holiday				**12** your last holiday
3 getting home from school yesterday		**Did you ...?** Place cards here		**13** getting home from school yesterday
2 your last holiday				**14** your last holiday
1 getting home from school yesterday				**15** ?
Start	**Finish**	**18** ?	**17** on your next holiday	**16** getting home from school yesterday

Photocopiable activity 9 (ii): Question prompt cards – *Did you ... ?*

getting home from school yesterday	getting home from school yesterday	getting home from school yesterday	getting home from school yesterday	getting home from school yesterday
... travel home ... ... by tuk tuk? ... by jeepney?	... travel home ... ... by tram? ... car?	... travel home ... ... on a motorbike? ... a crowded train?	... travel home ... ... by rickshaw? ... by motorbike? ... by lorry?	... travel home ... ... on a crowded underground train? ... on a bus?
getting home from school yesterday	getting home from school yesterday	getting home from school yesterday	getting home from school yesterday	getting home from school yesterday
... travel home ... ... by helicopter? ... boat?	... travel home ... ... alone? ... with a relative?	... walk home? ... cycle home?	... travel home at high speeds? ... ride home over the treetops?	... travel home down a main road? ... wander home along a sandy trail?
getting home from school yesterday	getting home from school yesterday	getting home from school yesterday	getting home from school yesterday	getting home from school yesterday
... wear a helmet? ... a seat belt?	... use a pedestrian crossing? ... cross busy roads?	... see a snake on your way home? ... see a rabbit on your way home?	... see a fox on your way home? ... see a crocodile on your way home?	... be careful on your way home? ... wear reflective armbands?
your last holiday	your last holiday	your last holiday	your last holiday	your last holiday
... make a journey? ... stay at home?	... travel by land? ... travel by air? ... travel by water?	... travel to New York? ... travel to Sydney?	... travel to London? ... travel to San Francisco?	... stay in a hotel? ... stay in a tent?
your last holiday	your last holiday	your last holiday	your last holiday	your last holiday
... stay with a friend? ... stay in a caravan?	... travel alone? ... travel with a relative?	... travel to the Moon? ... travel by ferry?	... travel by plane? ... travel by spaceship?	... hike through the jungle?
your last holiday	your last holiday	your last holiday	your last holiday	your last holiday
... trek in the mountains? ... trek in a lush forest?	... travel by skytrain? ... travel at high speeds?	... travel to the seaside? ... travel to the mountains?	... visit a museum? ... visit a landmark?	... wait in lots of traffic jams? ... wait in a queue?

Photocopiable activity 10

Matching halves of sentences: *zero conditional*

Aim: Learners play a card game in which they match sentence halves.

Preparation time: 10 minutes.

Language focus: Using the *zero conditional: If/When* + present simple + present simple for things that are always true.

Vocabulary: Methods of transport and road safety

Materials: For each pair of students, one copy of the **Matching halves of sentences: *Zero conditional* cards**, cut up as indicated.

Procedure

- Focus on two examples of the target structure from the unit, for example:

    When I ride my bike, I always **wear** a helmet.
    If I can't find a pedestrian crossing, I **find** a quiet place to cross the road.

- Write another *if* and another *when* clause, on the board. Ask learners for suggestions for the second half of the sentence. Ensure learners know the *if* and *when* clause could come after the 'second half'.

- Distribute one copy of the **Matching halves of sentences: *Zero conditional* cards**, cut up as indicated, to each pair of learners.

- Explain the game by choosing a pair of learners to demonstrate. Each takes seven cards. Put the rest of the cards face down in a pile for learners to pick up from. The first learner puts down a card at random, for example: *If I cross the road,*. The second looks for a card which could logically follow, for example: *I look for a quiet place with no traffic, I don't cross at corners* or *I'm always careful.* For each card, there are at least two possibilities, but if the player can't go, he/she picks up a card from the pile. After each turn, learners pick up a card from the pile. The winner is the first to put down all their cards.

- Read out some sentences that would be 'wrong', and check learners know why.

- Allow learners time to play the game in pairs while you circulate and check they are playing correctly and answer any queries.

Wrap up

- Learners tell the class about what they do to stay safe on the roads.

When I walk alone,	I don't talk to strangers.	**When I travel by car,**	I always wear a seatbelt.	**If I take my seatbelt off,**	my father makes me put it on again.
If I walk alone,	I look carefully before I cross the main road.	**When I ride my bike,**	I use the cycle track.	**When I take my seatbelt off,**	my mother stops the car.
If I can't find a pedestrian crossing,	I look for a quiet place with no traffic.	**If I ride my bike,**	I always wear a helmet.	**If I walk at night,**	it's difficult for drivers to see me.
If I cross the road,	I don't cross at corners.	**When my older brother isn't with me,**	I don't cross the main road.	**When it gets dark,**	I wear reflective armbands.
When I cross the road,	I'm always careful.	**If my older brother isn't with me,**	I stay on the main road.	**If I travel by plane,**	I always sit near the window.

Photocopiable activity 11

Flashcards: *What's it made of?*

Aim: Learners match typical products with the main materials they are made of. They then ask questions using *What is/are … made of?*

Preparation time: 5 minutes.

Language focus: Asking and answering the question: *What is/are … made of?*

Vocabulary: Everyday objects and names of materials

Materials: For each pair of learners, one set of *What's it made of?* flashcards, cut up as indicated.

Procedure

- Distribute one set of *What's it made of?* flashcards to each pair of learners. Learners sort the cards into two piles 'objects' and 'materials'.
- Take an 'object' card (e.g. *paper*) and ask learners to look for the corresponding 'materials' card.
- With lower-level groups, ask learners to demonstrate they have understood by picking more 'object' cards and finding the corresponding 'materials' cards.
- Allow learners time to match the rest of the cards while you circulate. Give assistance (if necessary) and check learners have matched the cards correctly.

- Pick two cards at random (one singular and one plural) and ask the questions: *What is/are … made of?* to elicit the appropriate response. With lower-level groups, more examples may be necessary.
- Learners ask and answer the questions: *What is/are … made of?* in pairs.
- Higher-level learners work in groups and use the blank cards to make more: *What's it made of?* flashcards. To do this, they write the name of an object on one card and the material(s) it is made from on another.

Wrap up

- Pairs of learners compete to see how many questions they can ask and answer in a given time limit.

Photocopiable activity 11: Flashcards – *What's it made of?*

paper	trees (and other things)		
bread	flour, yeast, water		
pasta	flour, and water (and sometimes egg)		
pancakes	milk, egg and flour		
ketchup	tomatoes, sugar and vinegar (and other things)		
shoes and boots	leather (and other things)		
jeans and t-shirts	cotton		
warm jumpers	wool		
keys	metal		
houses	wood, bricks, stone, concrete and metal (and other things)		

Photocopiable activity 12

Shopping dialogues

Aim: Practice of shopping dialogues.

Preparation time: 5 minutes.

Completion time: 20–30 minutes.

Language focus: Shopping expressions: *Would you like … ? I'll have … Can I have … ?*

Vocabulary: quantity expressions: *any, a bottle, a can, a carton, a cup, a few , a little, a loaf, many, much, a packet, a slice* (new!)*, some, a tub*

Materials:

One copy of the *Shopping dialogues* handout per learner.

Note: In the UK, the word *crisps* usually refers to thinly-sliced flavoured potatoes sold in packets and eaten cold. In other parts or the world, these are known as *chips.* In the UK, the word *chips* (from *chipped potatoes*) usually refers to long, thin pieces of potato eaten hot, often with salt and vinegar and sometimes tomato ketchup.

Suggestion for lower-/higher-level learners

The handout has been designed to give opportunities for revision. It provides the chance to give lower-level learners necessary support and practice to reinforce the language of **Unit 6 Lesson 3**. See **Procedure** for suggestions for higher-level learners.

Procedure

- Distribute one copy of the *Shopping dialogues* handout to each learner.
- Skim through the dialogues as a class and identify where they take place.
- With lower-level learners, look at the dialogues together and discuss the possibilities for the gap fill activity, before drilling pronunciation and allowing time for learners to practise the dialogues in pairs.
- In a higher-level class, learners read dialogues directly with correct quantity expressions before using the handout as a basis for creating their own dialogues.

Wrap up

- Learners perform their dialogues for the class.

Photocopiable activity 12: Shopping dialogues

1 Match the dialogue with a place.

Choose from: *In a grocer's shop,* or *In a sandwich bar.*

2 Complete each dialogue with the quantity expressions below.

1

any	can	many	packet	some

Customer:	Can I have a _____ of crisps, please?
Assistant:	Here you are. Is that everything?
Customer:	No, I'd like a _____ of cola. Have you got _____ sandwiches?
Assistant:	Yes, but there aren't _____ left – only cheese.
Customer:	I'll have _____ cheese ones then please.

2

any	any	bottle	little	slice	much

Assistant:	Yes, please?
Customer:	A _____ of mushroom pizza please.
Assistant:	Here you are, _____thing else?
Customer:	Yes, a small _____ of water please. Have you got _____ chocolate ice cream?
Assistant:	Yes, but only a _____.
Customer:	Sorry?
Assistant:	Yes, but there isn't _____ left.

3

any	carton	few	loaf	much	some

Customer:	_____ orange juice please.
Assistant:	How _____ would you like?
Customer:	One _____ please. Could I have a _____ of white bread?
Assistant:	Here you are, _____thing else?
Customer:	Yes, could I have _____ apples please?
Assistant:	Yes, is four OK?
Customer:	Yes, thank you.

4

any	little	much	some	tub

Customer:	A _____ of ice cream please.
Assistant:	What kind?
Customer:	Coffee please.
Assistant:	Sorry, there isn't _____ left.
Customer:	OK, strawberry then, please. Can I also have _____ cheese?
Assistant:	Yes, is that much OK?
Customer:	That isn't very _____. A _____ more please.

Photocopiable activity 13

Talking about Australian animals

Aim: Learners read mini fact files about three different animals found in Australia and use prompts to make questions about them.

Preparation time: 5 minutes.

Language focus: Asking and answering *present simple* questions.

Vocabulary: Australian animals

Materials: For each pair of learners one set of *Australian animals mini fact file cards*. If possible, bring in pictures of the three animals: the bilby, the Tasmanian devil and the saltwater crocodile.

Procedure

- Generate interest in the subject by showing pictures of the three animals.
- Distribute one set of *Australian animals mini fact file cards* to each pair of learners.
- Learners draw a picture of the animals (optional).

- Lower-level groups: focus on the question prompts on the bilby question card. Ask learners the full questions and write them on the board for learners to copy. Learners write the full questions on all three question cards. Higher-level groups proceed directly to the next stage.
- Pairs of learners practise asking the questions on the question card and answering using corresponding mini fact file cards. Allow learners time to ask and answer the questions in pairs.
- Circulate and give assistance with form and pronunciation.
- Give class feedback on common errors.

Wrap up

- In a higher-level class, learners could create more fact files of their own and work in pairs to make comparisons about the animals. Make sure they use comparative and superlative adjectives and words like *whereas, but, too, the same,* etc. If your group is mixed ability, encourage higher-level learners to make the comparisons for the class.

Photocopiable activity 13: Australian animals mini fact file cards

The bilby (Questions)

1 How big? How big is the bilby?

2 ... a nocturnal animal?

3 What/the bilby look like?

4 Where/live?

5 ... endangered?

6 What/eat?

My picture of a bilby

Mini fact file: The bilby

The bilby is a nocturnal animal which is endangered. It eats at night and rests during the day.

It looks like a rabbit – it is the same size and has rabbit-like ears and a tail. The male is bigger than the female and weighs about 2.5 kg.

The bilby lives in Alice Springs, parts of Western Australia and Queensland. It eats insects, seeds, fruit and fungi.

The Tasmanian devil (Questions)

1 How big? How big is the Tasmanian devil?

2 ... a nocturnal animal?

3 What/the Tasmanian devil look like?

4 Where/live?

5 ... endangered?

6 What/eat?

My picture of a Tasmanian devil

Mini fact file: The Tasmanian devil

The Tasmanian devil is a nocturnal animal that lives alone and only in the state of Tasmania.

It is black and has a long tail. It is the size of a small dog but is heavy – a male is about 9 kg. Females are lighter.

The preferred food of the Tasmanian devil is dead meat. Tasmanian devils can be very noisy and fight about their food.

The saltwater crocodile (Questions)

1 How big? How big is the saltwater crocodile?

2 ... a nocturnal animal?

3 What/look like?

4 Where/live?

5 ... endangered?

6 What/eat?

My picture of a saltwater crocodile

Mini fact file: The saltwater crocodile

The saltwater crocodile or 'salty' is the biggest reptile in the world. It is about 4 m long and greyish brown.

The 'salty' is a protected species found along Australia's north coast. They live in the sea, where some rivers meet the sea and in swamps up to 200 km from the sea.

An adult 'salty' can attack and eat large animals and fish, including people and cows. They also eat dead animals.

Photocopiable activity 14

What has the weather been like?

Aims: Learners use six cards as prompts to talk about the weather.

Preparation time: 5 minutes.

Language focus: the present perfect.

Vocabulary: the weather

Materials: For each pair of students, one set of *Weather cards*, cut up as indicated, a world map and weather reports for the places on the cards. If you can't get hold of a report, learners can invent the weather.

Procedure

- Create a list of words connected with weather from **Unit 7, Lesson 1**. Have a separate column for extreme weather. Write the words in a sentence, for example:

Weather	Extreme weather
There are thunderstorms.	There are severe/ dangerous (thunder) storms.
The storms are lifting.	It's stormy with thunder and lightning.
It's windy.	There are tornadoes/ hurricanes.
It's cold and rainy.	There's a flood/flooding.
It's snowy and frosty.	There's a blizzard.
It's hot and dry.	There's a drought.
It's sunny and mild/ cloudy/humid.	

- Distribute one set of *Weather cards* to each pair and tell learners they are going to fill in information about the weather for the six different places.
- Focus attention on the Los Angeles card. Show Los Angeles on the world map. If you have a weather report, read it or if you have Internet access in the classroom, do a quick search for recent weather.
- Fill in the Los Angeles card – underline a word to describe the temperature and wind speed, write the temperature and weather (e.g. *hot and humid*). Learners can invent the weather if a weather report is unavailable.
- Repeat the procedure for the other cards.
- Use the information on the card to build up a model dialogue like the following on the board:

  Learner A: *What has the temperature been like today in … ?*

  Learner B: *It's been hot/cold/freezing – ___°C.*

  Learner A: *What has the wind speed been?*

  Learner B: *It's been low/normal/high.*

  Learner A: *And what has the weather been like?*

  Learner B: *It's been hot and humid.*

- Check the class has understood by asking pairs to perform their dialogues.
- Circulate and check learners are following the procedure outlined.

Wrap up

- Nominate learners to report back to the class about what the weather has been like.
- To give higher-level learners more of a challenge, when they have finished the activity with the present perfect, ask them to make forecasts about tomorrow using *will* and *going to*.

Photocopiable activity 14: Weather cards

Los Angeles, USA

Temperature:
(very) hot/cold/freezing _____ °C

Wind speed:
low/normal/high/tornado

Weather:
_____

Dallas, USA

Temperature:
(very) hot/cold/freezing _____ °C

Wind speed:
low/normal/high/tornado

Weather:
_____

Melbourne, Australia

Temperature:
(very) hot/cold/freezing _____ °C

Wind speed:
low/normal/high/tornado

Weather:
_____

London, UK

Temperature:
(very) hot/cold/freezing _____ °C

Wind speed:
low/normal/high/tornado

Weather:
_____

Cape Town, S. Africa

Temperature:
(very) hot/cold/freezing _____ °C

Wind speed:
low/normal/high/tornado

Weather:
_____

Beijing, China

Temperature:
(very) hot/cold/freezing _____ °C

Wind speed:
low/normal/high/tornado

Weather:
_____

Photocopiable activity 15

Let's invent a new dance!

Aim: Learners create their own new dance using the vocabulary from Unit 8 **Lesson 2**.

Preparation time: 5 minutes.

Completion time: 20–30 minutes.

Language focus: verbs of movement.

Vocabulary: Speaking about traditional dances

Materials: One *Let's invent a new dance!* handout for each pair of learners.

Procedure

- Revise the verbs of movement. Ask learners what they can do with their arms, hands, legs, knees, feet – for example: *bend*, *lift*, *clap*, *point*, *stamp*, *swirl*. Try to demonstrate this.
- Ask learners the five questions from the main activity about the dances they like doing.
- Tell learners they are going to invent a new dance and distribute a handout to each pair of learners.
- Learners write the answer to the first question on the handout. Encourage them to be as creative and funny as possible.
- Learners fold back the section of the page so it can't be read, before passing the handout on to the next pair to fill in question 2 and so on to question 5.
- Unfold the handouts and ask learners to read them to the class.

Wrap up

- Choose some interesting dances and try and perform them.

Photocopiable activity 15: Let's invent a new dance!

Create a new dance by answering the question, folding back the page along the dotted line and passing it along to a friend.

When is the dance performed?

_____

- -

What do the dancers do with their arms and hands?

_____

- -

What do the dancers do with their legs (including knees)?

_____

- -

Do the dancers sing or shout?

_____

- -

What do the male dancers wear?

_____

- -

What do the female dancers wear?

_____

- -

Photocopiable activity 16

An interview with the thief who stole the Mona Lisa

Aim: Learners write an interview with Vincenzo Peruggia, the thief who stole the Mona Lisa.

Preparation time: 10 minutes.

Language focus: Revision of present perfect and past simple questions and answers.

Vocabulary: Crime

Materials: One copy of **Photocopiable activity 8b** per learners.

Procedure

- Tell learners they are going to work in pairs. One person will play the part of a journalist and the other, the art thief, Vincenzo Peruggia.
- To revise the past simple and present perfect interrogative forms, ask learners the kind of questions they would like to ask Vincenzo Peruggia. Write some examples on the board.
- Distribute one copy of the worksheet to each learner. Remember to detach the answer slip from the bottom if the learners are working at a high level.
- Demonstrate how to complete the questions by focusing on the first question and eliciting the correct question form.
- Circulate and offer support and assistance while learners write the questions. With a very high-level group, miss out this stage and move directly to the next step.

- In lower-level groups, tell learners to select the correct answer from the answer slip at the bottom.
- Learners can write the answers to the questions using information from the story on pages 118–20 of the Learner's Book.
- Learners practise the dialogue in pairs.

Wrap up

- Lower-level learners perform the dialogues for the class.
- Higher-level learners write a report for a television channel. Confident learners come to the front of the class and play the role of the TV presenter and report to the class.

Differentiated instructions

Vincenzo Peruggia's answers (not in the correct order) can be found at the bottom of the handout. These are intended to be used only to give guidance to lower-level learners. If you have a higher-level class, detach and discard.

Photocopiable activity 16: An interview with the thief who stole the Mona Lisa

Imagine you are a journalist and you are going to interview the famous art thief Vincenzo Peruggia.

A Complete the questions you could ask him. Use the verb in brackets.

B Use the story in the Learner's Book (pages 118–120) to help you write Mr Peruggia's answers.

Journalist:	1 Where *(be)* <u>were</u> you born Mr Peruggia?
Vincenzo Peruggia:	<u>I was born in Italy.</u>_____
Journalist:	2 *(work)*_____ you ever _____ at the Louvre museum?
Vincenzo Peruggia:	_____
Journalist:	3 When *(steal)*_____ you _____ the painting?
Vincenzo Peruggia:	_____
Journalist:	4 Where exactly *(steal)* _____ you _____ it from?
Vincenzo Peruggia:	_____
Journalist:	5 How *(hide)* _____ you _____ it?
Vincenzo Peruggia:	_____
Journalist:	6 *(break into)* _____ you _____ _____the museum when it was closed?
Vincenzo Peruggia:	_____
Journalist:	7 *(see)* _____ anyone _____ you?
Vincenzo Peruggia:	_____
Journalist:	8 How long after the crime *(arrest)*_____ the police _____ you?
Vincenzo Peruggia:	_____
Journalist:	9 Who *(try)*_____ you _____ to sell the painting to?
Vincenzo Peruggia:	_____
Journalist:	10 How much money *(ask)* _____ you _____ for?
Vincenzo Peruggia:	_____
Journalist:	11 Who *(call)* _____ the antique dealer _____?
Vincenzo Peruggia:	_____
Journalist:	12 How *(know)*_____ the antique dealer _____the painting was the real Mona Lisa?

✂

Match the answers:

a I took it out of the frame and hid it under my smock.

b The painting had the Louvre stamp on the back.

c From the Salon Carré in the Louvre Museum in Paris.

d I wanted half a million lire. That's Italian money.

e An antique dealer called Alfredo Geri.

f No, I didn't. I was just passing through when I saw the room was empty.

g Yes, I have.

h Two years later.

i He called the police.

j On August 21st 1911.

k No, they didn't.

l In Italy.

Photocopiable activity 17

Design an advert for a summer camp

Aim: Learners design a web advert for a summer holiday activity.

Preparation time: 5 minutes.

Vocabulary: *plastic utensils, a backpack, a torch, jeans, tracksuit, shorts, cooking equipment, a journal, a tent, a waterproof jacket, an MP3 player, a sleeping bag, riding, rafting, canoeing, camping, climbing, trekking, windsurfing, sitting by a camp fire, mountains, lakes, the seaside*

Materials: For each group of about four learners: one *Design an advert for a summer camp* handout. Bring some brochures and adverts for children's activity camps to the class. If you have Internet access, it would be useful to show websites. Many have promotional videos showing children participating in exciting activities. If learners have their own brochures or even photos of them participating in activities, they could bring these along and use the pictures for their adverts.

Procedure

- Generate interest in the activity and give learners ideas for their adverts by showing brochures, pictures and/or promotional videos of young people having fun participating in activities at summer camps. If you have a magazine advert to show the class, it will give an idea of what is expected later.

- Build up lists of useful vocabulary on the board by asking learners questions about what they see. Talk about the kind of places that could host the activity camps and what the landscape is like. Ask learners who they can see at the activity camps – their age, nationality, etc. Make a list of the activities they see, what kind of equipment they can see and other equipment people would need to take.

- Ask learners about the kinds of places where the children could sleep: *tents, dormitories*, etc.

- To each group of about four learners, distribute one *Design an advert for a summer camp* handout. Tell groups they are going to invent their own activity camp and write a magazine advert for it.

- Allow time for learners to discuss and make notes under the headings. This activity is designed to help them plan their activity camp and advert.

- Distribute one A3 sheet to each group to write up their advert. Circulate and offer support to learners while they convert their notes into their adverts. Make sure learners leave room for drawings or pictures of children participating in the activities.

Wrap up

- Learners present their adverts to the class.

- Higher-level learners use their advert for the basis of a radio or TV advert for the activity camp and perform it to the class.

Photocopiable activity 17: *Design an advert for a summer camp*

How to plan your advert

a Answer the questions to help you plan your summer camp.

b Look for pictures of children participating in the activities. If you don't have any pictures, draw your own!

c Use the information to help you make an advert for your summer camp on the piece of paper that your teacher gives you.

1 **Where is your summer activity camp? What's the landscape like?**

_____

_____

2 **How can you get to the summer camp?**

_____

_____

3 **Who is the summer activity camp for?**

_____

_____

4 **What do the participants need to bring? What equipment is provided at the camp?**

_____

_____

5 **What activities are there at the camp? Make a timetable.**

Monday	Tuesday	Wednesday	Thursday	Friday	Saturday
am	am	am	am	am	am
pm	pm	pm	pm	pm	pm

6 **Where do participants stay?**

_____

_____

7 **Where can people who are interested get more information?** _____

Photocopiable activity 18

Planning and writing a story about a summer holiday

Aim: Learners plan and write a story.

Preparation time: 5 minutes.

Language focus: The past simple tense, in particular the irregular forms *did, got there, went, going to* for intentions.

Vocabulary: holidays

Materials: For each learner, one *Planning and writing a story about a summer holiday* handout.

Procedure

- Ask learners where they went for their last summer holiday and build up a list on the board.
- Ask more questions like: *Who did you go with? How long did you stay? What did you do? Are you going again this year?*
- Distribute one copy of the handout to each learner.
- Tell learners they are going to write a short story on a separate sheet and ask them to read the sentences and choose one to begin their story. They also decide if the story is about themselves or a friend.
- Focus on the questions and tell learners to make notes. If your class is working at a very low level, give feedback and extra help and support after each question.
- Circulate and offer support while learners write their short stories and draw a picture.

Wrap up

- Mix the stories up and read them out. Learners guess who wrote which story.
- Higher-level learners could give a PowerPoint presentation using photos about their story.

Unit 9

Photocopiable activity 18: Planning and writing a story about a summer holiday

You are going to write a short story about something that happened to you or a friend in the summer holidays.

1 Read the different ways of beginning the story.

a Last year I / my friend _____ went on a summer activity camp. It was brilliant!

b In the summer holidays I / my friend _____ had a really good time on our holiday in ...

c I / my friend _____ went to an English language summer school in ...

d In the summer holidays I / my friend _____ went camping in ...

2 Choose one way to start your story and make notes.

a How did you (or your friend) get there?

_____

b Who did you (or your friend) go with?

_____

c What did you (or your friend) do?

_____

d How long did you (or your friend) stay?

_____

e Did you (or your friend) learn anything new?

_____

f Are you (or is your friend) going to do it again this year?

_____

3 Write your story here.

_____

_____

_____

_____

_____

_____

_____

_____

_____

_____

_____

_____

Photocopiable activity 19: Congratulations certificate for completing Stage 4 of *Cambridge Global English*

Congratulations!

You have completed Stage 4 of *Cambridge Global English.*

Name: _____

Class: _____

Teacher: _____

Word lists

advice	beautiful	behave	brought	burn
busy	engineer	especially	feed	fetch
fitness	gardening	grandparents	gymnastics	healthy
hobbies	kind	medal	night	outdoor
relationship	routine	share	shining	special
thoughtful	training	trekking	whereas	without

action	adventure	athletic	beginning	brilliant
building	cartoons	character	dangerous	difficult
encyclopaedia	exclaimed	expression	factual	fearless
fictional	guideline	instructions	intelligent	journey
keen	magic	participate	science	special
stones	sword	trophy	whispered	wild

Unit 3

basketball	creature	dangerous	daylight	desert
difficult	drier	high	hike	hour
humid	landscape	middle	midnight	nocturnal
north	orbit	outside	paws	planet
rainforest	refuse	rhyme	savannah	scales
sharp	sneaker	solar system	tired	usually

Unit 4

building	bungalow	climb	computer	concert
detached	discover	eco-home	energy-efficient	entertainment
floors	hole	landmark	library	might
mountain	museum	musician	neighbour	natural
provide	rich	rides	river	route
theatre	upstairs	vegetable	windows	woodland

Unit 5

across	achievement	astronaut	avoid	balloon
bottom	bushes	dangerous	directions	famous
ferry	follow	hours	hungry	journey
keep	neigbourhood	normal	pedestrian	quickly
reflective	responsibility	safely	sky	through
towards	transport	underground	wear	village

Unit 6

bottle	carton	chocolate	churn	dessert
everybody	factory	generous	gift	ground
handle	harvest	materials	meal	mixture
objects	packet	plastic	plenty	products
recycle	right	river	sculpture	selfish
spray	sweet	typical	usually	waterfall

Unit 7

already	amazing	animal	area	coast
damage	desert	destroy	drought	endangered
extreme	feathers	features	fly	frosty
habitat	jealous	laugh	lightning	peace
rare	scared	sorry	species	stormy
tomorrow	tornado	weather	wildlife	wings

Unit 8

agree	around	describe	false	feeling
guards	hair	human	identity	important
interview	knees	million	noticed	nowhere
painting	performed	photograph	police	prison
shout	simpler	skin	stare	steal
straight	strange	theft	thief	wear

actually	advertisements	again	arrangements	birthday
celebrate	definitely	earn	equipment	everywhere
exactly	feeling	fire	holiday	homework
improve	information	invite	neither	nervous
night	nothing	people	preparations	season
sometimes	suggest	supply	tomorrow	upset